THE FOUR SEASONS BOOK OF COCKTAILS

THE FOUR SEASONS BOOK OF COCKTAILS

Tips, Techniques, and More Than 1,000 Recipes
from New York's Landmark Restaurant

FRED DuBOSE
with bartenders
GREG CONNOLLY,
CHARLES CORPION,
and JOHN VARRIANO

STERLING INNOVATION
An imprint of Sterling Publishing Co., Inc.

New York / London
www.sterlingpublishing.com

STERLING, the Sterling logo, STERLING INNOVATION, and the Sterling Innovation logo are registered trademarks of Sterling Publishing Co., Inc.

Library of Congress Cataloging-in-Publication Data

DuBose, Fred.
  The Four Seasons book of cocktails : tips, techniques, and more than 1,000 recipes from New York's landmark restaurant / Fred DuBose with Greg Connolly ... [et al.].
    p. cm.
  Includes index.
  ISBN 978-1-4027-7096-8
  1. Cocktails. 2. Four Seasons (Restaurant) I. Title.
  TX951.D765 2010
  641.8'74--dc22

                 2010004860

10 9 8 7 6 5 4 3 2 1

Published by Sterling Publishing Co., Inc.
387 Park Avenue South, New York, NY 10016
© 2010 by Fred DuBose and The Four Seasons
Distributed in Canada by Sterling Publishing
c/o Canadian Manda Group, 165 Dufferin Street
Toronto, Ontario, Canada M6K 3H6
Distributed in the United Kingdom by GMC Distribution Services
Castle Place, 166 High Street, Lewes, East Sussex, England BN7 1XU
Distributed in Australia by Capricorn Link (Australia) Pty. Ltd.
P.O. Box 704, Windsor, NSW 2756, Australia

All photographs by Gilbert King, except those on pages 12–14, which are ©shutterstock.com, and pages 18, 44, 54, 65, 106, 144, 174, 185, 198, 204–05, and 218, which are by Jennifer Calais Smith.

Printed in China
All rights reserved

Design by Lisa Force

Sterling ISBN 978-1-4027-7096-8

For information about custom editions, special sales, premium and corporate purchases, please contact Sterling Special Sales Department at 800-805-5489 or specialsales@sterlingpublishing.com.

CONTENTS

WELCOME   9

YOUR HOME BAR   11

THE PERFECT DRINK   21

SCOTCH   35

BOURBON   45

WHISKEY COCKTAILS   55

GIN   67

VODKA   83

RUM   107

TEQUILA   129

BRANDY   145

LIQUEURS   159

APERITIFS & DIGESTIVES   175

CHAMPAGNE & WINE   187

PUNCHES   199

FROZEN DRINKS   209

HOT DRINKS   219

NO-ALCOHOL DRINKS   227

BAR BITES   235

INDEX   248

ABOUT THE AUTHOR & ACKNOWLEDGMENTS   255

ABOUT THE FOUR SEASONS   256

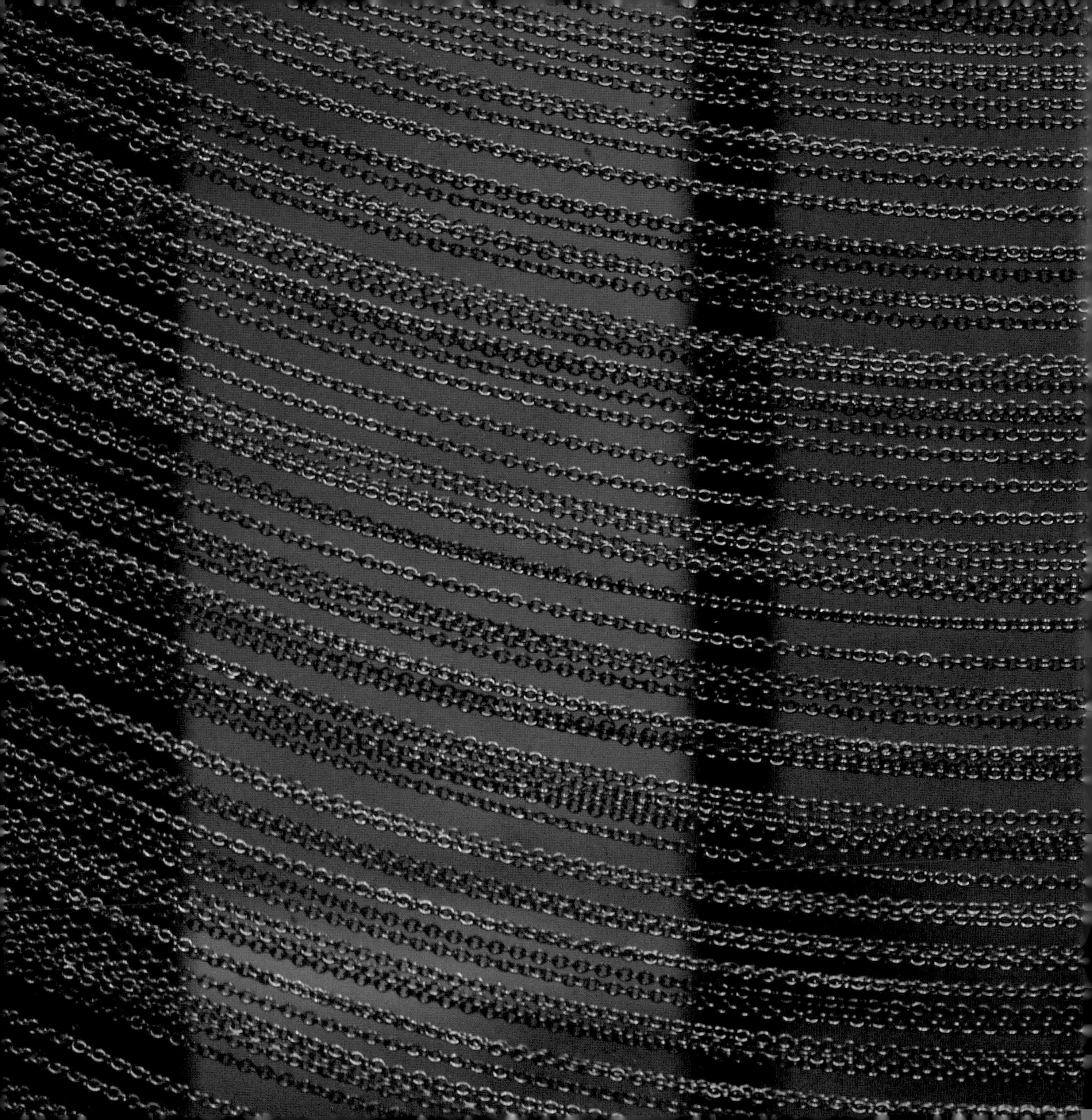

THE FOUR SEASONS

WELCOME

If you would like to infuse the drinks you mix at home with a certain panache, who better to guide you than the bartenders at New York's most famous restaurant? With *The Four Seasons Book of Cocktails*, virtuosos Greg Connolly, Charles Corpion, and John Varriano invite you to try your hand at duplicating their creations. They also encourage you to drop by Park Avenue at 52nd Street for a taste of the unique Four Seasons experience. If you're unable to visit in person, this book is the next best thing.

The Four Seasons first opened its doors in 1959, and to instant acclaim. The restaurant is housed in the Seagram Building, the vision of world-renowned architect Mies van der Rohe and an essential stop on any tour of Manhattan architectural treasures. Like the building itself, the restaurant's interior—the work of architect Philip Johnson—enjoys landmark status. When granting the designation in October 1989, the chairman of the New York City Landmarks Preservation Commission described the restaurant, with its soaring but spare expanses of French walnut and Italian marble, as "one of the most elegantly refined and beautifully proportioned and richly created spaces in the modern movement." Sprinkled among the thousand-plus recipes in this book are glimpses of the beauty and history of the quarters where Greg, Charles, and John work their magic—how the Seagram Building and The Four Seasons came to be (page 43); theories on why the 25-foot-high beaded curtains in the Grill and Pool Rooms mysteriously began to ripple as soon as they were installed (page 105); how a 22-by-18-foot tapestry by Pablo Picasso found a home in the restaurant (pages 158–59); and more.

Over the past three decades, The Four Seasons has flourished under the guidance of Managing Partners Alex von Bidder and Julian Niccolini, whose restaurant is known as much for its top-flight cuisine as its ambience. A first-time customer might be surprised to learn that a dining establishment so amiable and serene was the birthplace of the power lunch. It was also the site of President John F. Kennedy's dinner for his forty-fifth birthday before setting off for Madison Square Garden, where Marilyn Monroe (also no stranger to the restaurant) serenaded him with her now-legendary "Happy Birthday, Mr. President." Famous names notwithstanding, The Four Seasons Grill Room bar is a place where people from all walks of life join in the conviviality and feel right at home.

FOUR SEASONS MIXOLOGY

This book—a new incarnation of *The Ultimate Bartender's Guide: 1000 Fabulous Cocktails from The Four Seasons Restaurant*—adds scores of new drink recipes to the mix. And the qualities that made the original a best seller remain intact: the unique twist given to cocktails, be they classic or brand-new; bits of expert advice; and notes on the origins of spirits and liqueurs. The "Your Home Bar" and "The Perfect Drink" chapters help you get off on the right foot, with instructions for everything from stocking a home bar to shaking a drink to garnishing it. At book's end are "Bar Bites" from The Four Seasons kitchens—seasonal hors d'oeuvre to serve at parties or special dinners.

At the heart of the book are the wondrous creations of the bartenders, native New Yorkers all. Charles Corpion (far left) followed in the footsteps of his father, who tended bar at New York's Copacabana in the 1950s. Head bartender Greg Connolly (right) was enshrined in the Bartender's Hall of Fame but modestly says he's "a husband and father first." John Varriano (center) is a successful painter who became a bartender back in his "starving artist" days—and has a love of opera to boot. (Some of his artwork is featured in this book.) Together, the men have more than half a century of bartending experience, the fruits of which they now invite you to enjoy.

YOUR HOME BAR

Your success as a home bartender doesn't depend on having a wealth of bar equipment (required for Scotch and Soda: glass, ice, and hand for pouring), much less every kind of liquor known to man—but there are still a few essentials you'll want to stock up on.

EQUIPMENT

Cocktail Shaker

That gleaming martini shaker familiar from so many 1940s movies may be synonymous with glamour, but it has a rather ordinary name: the standard, or regular, shaker. The other choice is the Boston shaker, preferred by most professional bartenders because it's so easy to use.

Standard shaker

This all-in-one shaker generally has three pieces: the shaker cup; a built-in strainer; and a cap. It comes in stainless steel and aluminum, though stainless steel is preferred because it keeps the drink colder. Standard shakers made of heavy glass are sometimes found in specialty shops.

Boston shaker

The two halves of this shaker—a mixing glass and a slightly larger stainless steel container—fit together in a jiffy with overlapping rims. You'll need a separate strainer when using this model.

Mixing Glass

In this guide, "mixing glass" simply refers to the container used for mixing a cocktail's ingredients. In the case of **shaken drinks**, that means the glass container of a Boston shaker or the metal cup of a standard shaker. **Stirred drinks** meant for martini-size glasses (or smaller) can be prepared in a mixing glass or pitcher with a lip for pouring—or, for that matter, an iced-tea tumbler or any other large glass from your cabinet. (For stirring drinks directly in the drinking glass, see page 22.)

Barspoon

For stirring (page 22), try a barspoon or use any other long-handled spoon. An alternative is a glass **stirring rod**, which often comes with a lipped mixing glass or pitcher but is also sold separately.

Strainer

If you don't own a standard shaker (the one with a built-in strainer), buy a handheld Hawthorne strainer—a flat, round tool with a spring coil around the head. It fits inside the top of a Boston shaker mixing glass and strains the drink as you pour.

Ice Scoop

Using a bartender's ice scoop to put ice in a mixing glass/shaker is less a matter of hygiene than of presentation—something to consider when you're mixing drinks for guests. The scoop can also serve as a measuring tool: In general, one heaping scoop of ice is the amount to use when shaking or stirring a cocktail.

Ice Bucket and Tongs

An ice bucket is useful when you're preparing several drinks. You may also want to use tongs or an ice scoop to transfer the ice to a shaker or glass.

Jigger

The double form of this metal measuring tool has a small cup on one side (usually 1 ounce or 1½ ounces) and a larger cup on the other (usually 2 ounces). Single and double jiggers also come in other sizes but top out at 3 ounces. Some jiggers are fitted with long handles.

Measuring Spoons

Jiggers rarely have a ½-ounce marking, so you'll need a set of measuring spoons (½ ounce equals 1 tablespoon). Measuring spoons also come in handy when a drink recipe calls for spices in ⅛- or ¼-teaspoon amounts.

Muddler

A wooden bar muddler is used to crush ingredients such as cherries and mint leaves, often right in the bottom of the cocktail glass. The broad "muddling" end is either rounded or flat. If you're thinking a long-handled spoon could muddle ingredients, it can—but less effectively than the tool designed for the job.

Juicer

Handheld wooden or metal citrus reamers come in handy when you need to juice only a lemon or two. But the most common citrus juicer is the manual two-piece type, with a reamer plate (right) sitting atop a juice collection bowl; this old standby now comes in a number of styles.

Electric juicers are available in several models, and are able to liquefy virtually any kind of fruit or vegetable. Just be sure to seed a fruit first; whether semi-pureed or merely bruised, seeds (citrus, in particular) will add a bitter note to your drink.

Pitcher

Whenever you prepare a mixed drink meant for three or more people, you might want to transfer it to a pitcher for serving. A medium-size, straight-sided glass pitcher also makes a good mixing glass for stir-and-pour iced drinks.

ODDS AND ENDS

A well-stocked home bar also makes room for the following appliances and tools.

Blender

For making margaritas, daiquiris, and other frozen drinks

Bottle opener

To pop the top off bottled soft drinks

Can opener

The punch type, for opening cans of cream of coconut and such

Champagne stopper

Keeps Champagne and other sparkling wines bubbly as you mix drinks whose recipes call for them

Citrus stripper

A tool used to cut ¼-inch strips from citrus rinds

Coasters

To protect wooden tabletops

Corkscrew

Choose from several styles. Many bartenders prefer the compact jackknife-style corkscrew.

Cutting board

For when you slice citrus fruits and other garnishes

Dropper

Use a clean dropper to add a drop (or more, depending on the drink recipe) to a cocktail. One drop amounts to about $\frac{1}{96}$ of a teaspoon.

Ice crusher

Whether manual or electric, this appliance isn't as costly as you might think.

Knife

Use a small paring knife to slice garnishes—and the sharper, the better.

Napkins

Use as coasters or to insulate an ice-filled glass

Straws

For certain iced or frozen drinks

Swizzle sticks

For stirring drinks in the drinking glass

Toothpicks, cocktail

Long, often decorative, plastic picks for spearing olives, berries, and other small garnishes

Vegetable peeler

For peeling garnishes or stripping citrus rinds

GLASSWARE

Because glass volumes are anything but standardized, these notes give you the size range for each glass. Also indicated is the Four Seasons glass size, to which we've more or less tailored the cocktails in this book. Truth be told, "more or less" is the name of the game when matching cocktails and glasses, and the major player is simple common sense.

Note: A silhouette of one of the fourteen kinds of glasses shown on these two pages appears beside each of the book's cocktail recipes.

Rocks/Old-Fashioned
The glass with two names holds from 5 to 10 ounces. Four Seasons size: 8 ounces.

Highball/Collins
Technically, the highball glass is the larger of these two tall glasses, but the size for both can range from 8 to 16 ounces. Four Seasons size: 12 ounces.

Martini
Also called a cocktail glass. Nowadays the size ranges from 4 to 14 ounces— an example of some manufacturers' notion that "bigger is better." We prefer "small is beautiful." Four Seasons size: 5 ounces.

White Wine
While these are sold in sizes ranging from 5 to 10 ounces, the most practical size is 8 ounces. Four Seasons size: 8 ounces.

Red Wine
The wider mouth of the red wine glass allows the wine to breathe. And who knows? Maybe even a red wine-based cocktail could use a little aeration. Sizes range from 8 to 14 ounces. Four Seasons size: 10 ounces.

Flute
The tall, narrow shape of this glass helps Champagne stay bubbly—unlike the classic coupe glass of old movies, which has made a comeback with aficionados of retro items. Four Seasons size: 6 ounces.

Tulip

Named for its shape, this glass typically holds 6 to 8 ounces. Four Seasons size: 7 ounces.

Snifter

This glass, which comes in several sizes, is the traditional vessel for brandy served neat; the snifter's large bowl is cupped in the hand to warm the contents. Snifters are occasionally used for cocktails as well. Four Seasons size: 16 ounces.

Sour

Either tulip-shaped or straight-sided with a rounded bottom, this glass usually holds 4 to 6 ounces. Four Seasons size: 6 ounces.

Margarita

The bowl of most margarita glasses has a narrow neck above the stem, but some glasses are balloon-shaped and neckless. Capacity ranges from 12 to 16 ounces. Four Seasons size: 14 ounces.

Liqueur/Sherry

In this book, liqueur and sherry glasses are considered interchangeable. Both range in size from 3 to 6 ounces and come in different shapes. Four Seasons size: 4 ounces.

Irish Coffee

Hot drinks call for this clear glass with a handle; it generally tops out at 10 ounces. Four Seasons size: 8 ounces.

Cup/Mug

Cups and mugs used for hot coffee- and tea-based cocktails are interchangeable, though the mug is slightly larger than the cup. Four Seasons sizes 6 to 8 ounces.

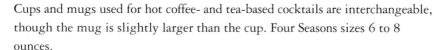

THE WELL-STOCKED BAR

The list of spirits below lays out what you might need at one time or another. For the sake of thriftiness, buy large bottles of whichever spirit you use the most. At the same time, remember that the higher the quality of the spirit, the better your finished product—so buy the best you can afford. In the interest of moderation, we also suggest that you check the proof (see box).

Also listed are the mixers and flavorings that home bartenders might choose to use, many of which are detailed in Mixers Et Cetera (page 25).

Note: The cocktail recipes in this book occasionally specify certain brands of spirits, but only to remind (or inform) you of what's available—particularly when the product may be hard to find (e.g., blueberry liqueur, amaro, white peach aperitif). Almost any brand will do just fine in your cocktail, of course, though it's a good idea to avoid pairing a high-end brand of a spirit with a low-end one.

Spirits
Aperitifs and digestives of choice
Bourbon
Brandy (including Cognac)
Gin
Liqueurs of choice
Rum (light, gold, dark)
Scotch (blended, single-malt)
Tequila (silver, gold)
Vermouth (dry, sweet)
Vodka (plain, flavored)
Whiskey (blended, Tennessee, rye)
Wine (Champagne, white, red)

Mixers
Bottled water (still, sparkling)
Club soda
Coconut water
Cream (light, heavy)
Cream of coconut
Fruit juices
Fruit purees
Soft drinks
Tomato juice
Tonic water

Flavorings
Bitters (Angostura, Fee Brothers, Peychaud's)
Grenadine
Fruit, fresh
Fruit syrups
Rose's lime juice
Sugar (superfine, powdered)
Tabasco
Worcestershire sauce

CHECK THE PROOF
Proof gauges the strength of a spirit. The proof shown on the bottle is twice the percentage of alcohol—in other words, 100-proof liquor contains 50 percent alcohol.

Why check the proof when buying liquor and other spirits? Because a few drinks mixed with 80-proof liquor are much less likely to put you (or worse, your guests) under the table than the same drinks mixed with a 150-proof product. The same goes for wine, the strength of which is shown on the label as the percentage of alcohol—typically from 10 to 16 percent.

THE PERFECT DRINK

The next few pages tell you how to perform (mostly) easy tasks on your way to the perfect mixed drink. Remember that the quality of a cocktail is measured by the artfulness with which the flavors are blended and the freshness of the ingredients, not by the color or a fancy garnish.

TECHNIQUES

When it comes to mixing drinks, practice doesn't always make perfect. It is more important to simply pay attention to what you're doing. A drink whose ingredients have been mismeasured (or one that gets watered down while you prepare it) is just another drink—as opposed to the winner you aspire to create.

Shaken or Stirred?

Whether to shake a drink or to stir it is one of the finer points of mixing, and choosing one over the other is hardly going to make or break your cocktail. Still, common procedure is to shake drinks that contain any of the following: sugar, spice(s), cream, or fresh sour mix (page 28). Chilled drinks without the aforementioned ingredients are generally stirred, although shaking won't hurt them (not surprisingly, the idea that shaking will "bruise" gin is a myth).

Shaking and stirring both chill and slightly dilute a drink—and while a little dilution is desirable, too much will affect the taste. That's one reason why we recommend pouring the ingredients into the mixing glass or shaker *before* adding the ice—a departure from normal procedure. How much ice to add? Enough to fill the shaker about three-quarters full. And take note: When shaking or stirring, use only ice cubes, not crushed ice; the latter melts faster and can result in a too-watery drink.

Shaking

Once you've put the liquid ingredients (with the exception of club soda, Champagne, or any other sparkling beverages) in the mixing glass or shaker, add the ice. Fit the stainless steel shell over the glass of a Boston shaker or make sure the lid of a standard shaker is on tight. Then give your drink eight to ten vigorous shakes. (More shakes will risk diluting the drink, and fewer may leave it insufficiently blended.)

Two more points:

- Put plenty of pressure on both ends of the Boston shaker to keep it from springing a leak (or worse) as you shake.
- Mix no more than two drinks at once in the shaker. A drink's ingredients need some room to blend.

Stirring

While most of the recipes in this book specify a mixing glass for stirring, it matters not whether you use the mixing glass of a Boston shaker, a pitcher, or any other container. Just make sure it's large enough to keep the ingredients from sloshing over the sides as you stir.

Pour the specified ingredients into the mixing glass, then stir vigorously about 20 times with a stirring rod, barspoon, or any other long-handled spoon. Don't overdo it, or you could end up with a diluted drink.

Straining and Pouring

Pour your drink(s) immediately after shaking or stirring with ice—again, to keep them from getting watery.

Straining

Straining not only strains a straight-up drink off the ice but also keeps any muddled leaves or other solids out of your drink.

Pouring

Some of our iced drink recipes direct you to pour shaker ice into the drinking glass along with the drink. That's because ice becomes coated with the flavor of the ingredients during shaking, unlike ice waiting in the glass. Still, the choice is yours—you needn't follow the pouring directions to the letter.

Muddling

To muddle fruits or herbs is to crush or mash them with a wooden tool called—you guessed it—a muddler. What's the point? To release the ingredient's aromatic oils. Muddling is often done directly in the bottom of the drinking glass, as when a cherry and orange slice are muddled for an Old-Fashioned. Some recipes call for straining out the muddled plant material, while others consider the material part of the finished drink.

Blending

When blending frozen drinks or smoothies, use crushed ice, which not only "purees" faster but is easier to measure. The amount of ice used varies according to recipe. but it's important not to use too much. The more ice that goes into the blender, the slushier and more watered-down the drink.

Put the ingredients in the blender first; if you're adding fruit, process it before adding the ice, to avoid diluting the drink. Make sure the lid is on tight before you throw the switch, then process the contents until smooth, starting at slow speed and gradually increasing to medium.

Another tip: Frozen drinks and smoothies will keep their texture longer if you chill the drinking glass before filling it (page 24).

Floating and Layering

Some recipes call for floating cream or a spirit on top of the cocktail. Other drinks are layered—either intentionally or because the ingredients settled in the bottom of the glass are left unstirred. In fact, many of the cocktail recipes in this book don't call for stirring; a highball that has a nice dark color at the bottom and is light at the top is not only eye-pleasing but will mix itself as you sip.

Serious layering is the business at hand when making pousse-cafés (page 169), which call for layering a number of spirits atop one another. Naturally, this kind of layering works only when the spirit on top is lighter. To gauge the relative weight of spirits and liqueurs, check the alcohol volume on the label (see Check the Proof, page 19). The lower it is, the heavier the product: Low-proof products contain sugar and consequently are syrupy and weightier.

Floating

Float an ingredient by pouring it on top of your cocktail very slowly. Alternatively, use the tool required for layering drinks: a barspoon.

Layering

To layer a pousse-café is to top one ingredient with another according to weight to achieve a pretty rainbow effect. You could also layer a couple of spirits in any liqueur-based cocktail for an attention-getting presentation.

To layer ingredients, pour the heaviest in the glass first, then place the bowl of a barspoon (bottom up) at the edge of the liquid. Pour the next ingredient slowly down the neck (the part of the handle just above the bowl of the spoon) so that it gradually flows into the glass, creating a second layer. In the case of pousse-cafés, repeat until all ingredients are used.

Chilling Glasses

The simplest way to chill glasses: Put them in the refrigerator for 30 minutes or so, or in the freezer for 10. At parties, when fridge space is at a premium, try one of these methods: 1) Put crushed ice in the glass and let it stand for about 5 minutes, then discard the ice and wipe the glass dry. 2) Put ice cubes in the glass and fill it with water; after 3 or 4 minutes, dump the contents and wipe the glass dry.

Frosting Glasses

Give summery iced drinks that something extra by frosting the glasses. To frost a glass inside and out, dip a glass in cold water, shake off the excess, and put the glass in the freezer for at least half an hour.

Frosting Rims

When you want to frost the rim of a glass with sugar or salt, moisten the rim (the first step) in one of two ways: 1) Rub a wedge of citrus fruit used as a garnish around the rim or, 2) dip the rim of the glass in water, juice, or liquor and shake off the excess. (You could also dip your finger into a liquid and run it around the rim, but this shortcut is less effective.) Then simply dip the rim into a saucer of sugar or table salt (see also A Word from the Bartenders, page 133).

Steaming Glasses

To steam a glass is merely to heat it. The heat brings out a spirit's aroma—the reason brandies are often served in steamed glasses. To steam a glass easily, fill it with hot water and let it sit for a minute or two. Then discard the water and wipe the glass dry.

MIXERS ET CETERA

Here's a rundown on mixers and other nonalcoholic ingredients used in the recipes in this book, complete with tips for how to get the best out of them and what to look for when buying.

Apple, Pineapple, and Tomato Juices

Refrigerated apple and pineapple juices are almost always better for cocktails than the bottled variety. Tomato juice comes either bottled or canned, so be sure to choose a quality brand.

About Ice

In this guide, when we say "ice," we mean ice cubes. Crushed ice is specified as such and is listed with the recipe ingredients. Cubes don't melt as fast as crushed ice, which explains why they're the best choice when shaking or stirring mixed drinks.

To turn ice cubes into crushed ice, put them in a heavy plastic bag, wrap with a dishtowel, and pound away with a mallet or rolling pin. (You'll probably have to do the same with the bags of ice you buy at the supermarket.) Just don't overdo it: The smaller the pieces, the faster they melt. Inexpensive ice crushers are available and come in both electric and manual models.

A couple of tips for freezing and using ice:

- Keep ice from absorbing refrigerator odors by freezing it (preferably from bottled water) shortly before you use it.
- Use the ice left in the shaker only if making the same drink twice. Traces of the previous ingredients remain on the ice, and in most cases will do the new drink you're shaking no favors. (For fruit-juice ice cubes, see page 204.)

Bitters

Falling under the "bitters" umbrella are any aromatic mixtures that result from the distillation of herbs, seeds, bark, roots, and flowers. But this broad definition also includes such aperitifs and digestives as Campari and Fernet-Branca, which are drinks in their own right. The bitters called for in the recipe ingredients in this guide, such as Angostura bitters, are the type dashed into a drink as an accent.

In some towns, bitters products aren't all that easy to find. Specialty food markets and some liquor stores stock them, and you can always order bitters online.

Citrus Juices

The fresher the juice, the better the finished cocktail. Choose quality-brand refrigerated orange juice over bottled or frozen, and don't even consider taking a shortcut by buying lemon or lime juice in one of those squeezable fruit-shaped plastic containers.

Juicers for extracting juice from lemons, limes, and oranges range from handheld citrus presses and reamers to electric juicers (page 13).

Whether to strain the pulp out of orange juice is a matter of taste, although no-pulp orange juice will keep your drinking glass looking neater as you sip.

Cream and Milk

Our recipes specify either **light cream** or **heavy cream**. In a pinch, you may have to rely on **half and half** as a light cream substitute. The big "but": Half and half has about 50 percent of light cream's fat content, so you may want to use a richer mixture of heavy cream and whole milk instead. (See also Whipped Cream, page 31.)

When using **milk** in a recipe that calls for it, avoid anything but whole, or full fat; except for milk punches, shakes, and smoothies, the amount called for in a typical recipe should pose no waistline worries. A few of this book's recipes call for **skim (fat-free) milk,** but only when acidic ingredients may curdle the drink. To give more body to these drinks, choose one of the creamy-style fat-free milks sold at most supermarkets.

Cream of Coconut

Popular brands of this rich, sweet mixer include Coco Lopez, Coco Casa, and Goya. Do not confuse cream of coconut with coconut milk or even coconut cream, both of which are less rich. **Coconut water** is not creamy in the least, of course, though it does have the tiniest bit of saturated fat.

Fruit Purees and Nectars

You don't have to reach for the blender when mixing cocktails that call for a fruit puree. Bottled or frozen purees can be found in gourmet markets and online, and include those made by Boiron, Culinary Traditions, L'Epicerie, and Monin.

Nectars are generally thick fruit juices, such as peach or pear, that are sold canned, bottled, or—better yet—in the refrigerated section. Nectars that come in plastic squeeze bottles are meant to be added to drinks in small quantities as a flavoring.

Fruit Syrups

You probably won't find fruit syrups at the corner grocery, but they're available at specialty food stores and online. The most widely used is grenadine—once made from pomegranate but now usually artificially flavored. True fruit syrups come in a wide range of flavors, and include those made by Fee Brothers, Monin, Teisseire, and Torani.

Simple Syrup

This thickened sugar water has long been an ingredient in cocktails. Whip up a batch, refrigerate it, and use as needed.

The recipe:

1 cup superfine sugar
1 cup water (preferably bottled)

Combine the ingredients in a small saucepan. Place over medium-high heat and stir until the mixture comes to a boil. Reduce the heat and simmer for 3 to 4 minutes, stirring occasionally. Let the syrup cool to room temperature and spoon it into a jar. Seal the jar tightly and store in the refrigerator for up to 3 weeks.

Soft Drinks

Lemon-lime soft drinks such as Sprite and 7UP are the most commonly used in cocktails, although cola and root beer find a place in mixed drinks as well. To maximize the fizz, add any carbonated ingredient to your drink last and then give your drink a single (and gentle) stir.

Sorbet

Store-bought sorbet adds a velvety texture and extra flavor to drinks served straight up. In most recipes, a single scoop of half-thawed sorbet is added to the ingredients in a mixing glass or shaker. Take the sorbet out of the freezer a few minutes before using to give it a soft consistency.

Sour Mix, Fresh

Many of our recipes call for an ounce or so of fresh sour mix, which can be made in quantity and kept in the refrigerator for up to 3 weeks. For a pint of sour mix, you'll have to juice several lemons—but don't let that tempt you to buy inferior packaged juice.

Our recipe:

2 cups freshly squeezed lemon juice
½ cup superfine sugar
¼ cup pasteurized egg white

Combine the ingredients in a shaker and shake well. Pour the mix into an airtight container and store in the refrigerator for up to 3 weeks.

Spice

When spices are mixed into a drink, the drink is usually shaken to ensure that the spice doesn't clump. Nutmeg and cinnamon are two common cocktail spices, most frequently used in holiday drinks or mulled wines.

Sugar

Recipes that call for sugar specify **superfine sugar**, which dissolves faster than regular granulated sugar when shaken with liquids. Some drinks mixed directly in the glass call for **powdered sugar**, also known as confectioner's sugar, which dissolves even faster. (For frosting glass rims with sugar, see page 25.)

Water

Water, water, everywhere . . .

Not to put too fine a point on it, but **club soda** is carbonated with carbon dioxide, while **sparkling water** is naturally carbonated in a spring. **Seltzer** technically refers to the water that comes from the German town of Niederselters, but all three of these terms have become interchangeable. When using carbonated water of any type as a mixer, screw the cap back on the bottle tightly; it can lose its bubbles in an hour or two.

And **still water**? When a cocktail recipe calls for it, choose bottled water over tap water—unless, that is, your town's tap water is known for its taste and purity. Cocktail purists prefer distilled water to mineral water because it has no taste whatsoever.

GARNISHES

A garnish imparts a bit of extra flavor to a cocktail and gives it some flair to boot. The range of choices is wide, but make sure a garnish is in proportion to the glass: A fat strawberry perched on the rim of a delicate liqueur glass is impractical and looks silly.

Cherries

Most cherry-garnished recipes in this guide specify **maraschino cherries**, also called cocktail cherries—the sweet, bright-red fruits that come in a jar. Just drop them into the drink whole.

Chocolate

A candy store—especially one that specializes in chocolate—is the place to find the long, narrow **chocolate sticks** used to garnish drinks such as Two-for-One (page 126) and Peppermint Patty (page 168). **Chocolate shavings** can simply be scraped from a block of chocolate with a sharp knife or a cheese shaver.

Flowers

We don't plant flowers in drinks at The Four Seasons, but that doesn't mean you can't—especially if you're wild about flowers or enjoy gardening. Wild hibiscus and plumeria (the flower of Hawaiian leis) are popular and attractive choices, but you might also want to try edible flowers such as nasturtium, dandelion, calendula (a marigold cousin), sage blossom, and squash blossom.

A caveat: Use only flowers that you're sure have never been sprayed with pesticide. Also know what *not* to use. The shortlist of unsafe, even toxic, flowers includes crocus, chrysanthemum, daffodil, foxglove, hydrangea, lily of the valley, oleander, rhododendron (including azalea), and sweet pea.

Fruit Slices, Wedges, and Spirals

Melon, apple, and other fruits that are usually peeled for use as a garnish are ready to go, but you'll want to wash citrus fruits beforehand. Cut **fruit slices** from ¼- to almost ½-inch thick; if you want to perch a whole or halved slice on the glass rim, make a cut from the outer edge to the center.

To cut **wedges,** slice the fruit lengthwise in half, then lengthwise into quarters or eighths. (See also A Word from the Bartenders, page 56.) To cut long spirals of peel, begin at one end of the fruit and use a citrus stripper or sharp paring knife to cut around and down the fruit, creating a continuous spiral.

Fruit or Vegetable Spears

Firm-fleshed fruits such as pineapple and mango can be cut into spears and used to garnish tall iced drinks. With a sharp knife, cut the peeled fruit lengthwise into slices just under ½-inch thick. Then cut the slices into spears that are an inch or two taller than your rocks or highball glass.

Fruit, Whole or Halved

Small fruits such as strawberries and apricots can be used whole or halved as garnishes. Just drop them into the glass (minus any leaves or stems) or perch them on the rim of the glass. For the latter, cut a small slit in the bottom of the fruit to secure it on the rim.

Olives

Pitted green olives stuffed with pimiento are the standard cocktail garnish. But that doesn't mean you can't use olives stuffed with anything from a bit of anchovy to an almond (the former with a Bloody Mary and its variations, of course). Just make sure the stuffing isn't going to spoil the taste of your drink—a jalapeño-stuffed olive in a martini made with sweet vermouth isn't exactly a marriage made in heaven.

Threading an olive (or olives) with a cocktail toothpick isn't just for show. It makes the garnish easier to retrieve and nibble as you finish your drink.

Onions, Cocktail

The Gibson and its variations may be among the few cocktails that call for this garnish, but you can try cocktail onions in any savory drink (think Bloody Mary). These small, pickled pearl onions can be found in most grocery stores and in some liquor stores. Flush them with water before using them so the pickling brine doesn't mix with the drink—unless, that is, the onions are packed in vermouth.

Twists

Citrus peel twists are so named because they release a spritz of aromatic oil when twisted over a drink. You can also use twists to rub the rim of the glass for a bit of extra aroma. At The Four Seasons, twists are wider and shorter than the traditional sort. This larger piece of peel is not only easier to twist but also releases more citrus oil.

For a **traditional twist**, cut the fruit in half lengthwise. Use a sharp paring knife or a citrus stripper to cut the rind lengthwise into ¼-inch strips.

To cut a **Four Seasons–style twist** (as pictured in The Genie on page 90), use a sharp paring knife to cut an ovoid piece of rind about 2 inches by 1 inch, taking care to cut just beneath the colored part of the rind.

Hold the twist between the thumb and forefinger of both hands and give it a sharp twist over the drink; if you look closely, you'll see a fine burst of spray. Then drop the twist into the drink.

Whipped Cream

When topping a drink with whipped cream, there's no reason not to use the type in the can as your everyday topper. For after-dinner drinks served at dinner parties, however, fresh whipped cream crowning a hot drink will no doubt be noticed and appreciated by your guests. (Note that one cup of cream makes about two cups of whipped cream.)

WHAT? AND WHERE FROM?

While the cocktail was born and bred in America, it draws on ingredients from all corners of the world. And when a Four Seasons bar patron asks about cocktails, the question often revolves around the ingredients in a certain liqueur or spirit, and where the product originated. Products with an asterisk in this table are generic; those without an asterisk are brand names.

Product or brand	Main ingredients or flavorings	Origin
AGAVERO	agave	Mexico
ALIZÉ	Cognac with passion fruit	France
*APPLEJACK	apple brandy	United States
BAILEYS IRISH CREAM	Irish whiskey, cream	Ireland
*BANANE, CRÈME DE	banana	France
BÉNÉDICTINE	Cognac with botanicals, honey	France
*BLUE CURAÇAO	curaçao with artificial coloring	Curaçao
*CACAO, CRÈME DE	cocoa bean	France
CAMPARI	bitter herbs	Italy
*CASSIS, CRÈME DE	black currant	France
CHAMBORD	black raspberry	France
CHARTREUSE	herbs and spices	France
CHERRY HEERING	cherry	Denmark
COINTREAU	bitter and sweet dried orange peel	France
*CURAÇAO	dried peel of laraha citrus fruit, related to orange	Curaçao
CYNAR	artichoke	Italy
DRAMBUIE	aged malt whiskey, honey, botanicals	Scotland
DUBONNET	wine with herbs	France
FERNET-BRANCA	bitter herbs	Italy
*FRAMBOISE	red raspberry	France
FRANGELICO	hazelnut	Italy

GALLIANO	herbs, spices, flowers	Italy
GOLDSCHLÄGER	cinnamon schnapps with gold leaf	Switzerland
GRAND MARNIER	Cognac with bitter dried orange peel, spices	France
HARVEY'S BRISTOL CREAM	blend of Spanish cream sherries	England
IRISH MIST	aged Irish whiskey, honey	Ireland
JÄGERMEISTER	bitter herbs, spices, botanicals	Germany
KAHLÚA	coffee	Mexico
*KIRSCHWASSER (KIRSCH)	cherry	Germany
*KÜMMEL	cumin, botanicals	Netherlands
LILLEHAMMER	lingonberry	Norway
LILLET	blend of wines and fruit liqueurs	France
*LIMONCELLO	lemon rind	Italy
*MARASCHINO	marasca sour cherry	Croatia
MIDORI	honeydew melon	Japan
*NOYAUX, CRÈME DE	fruit pits	France
*OUZO	anise	Greece
PERNOD	star anise, botanicals	France
PIMM'S NO. 1	gin with herbs, spices, fruits	England
PUNT È MES	vermouth with orange, herbs	Italy
*SAMBUCA	anise, elderberry	Italy
*SAMBUCA NEGRA	sambuca flavored with coffee	Italy
SOUTHERN COMFORT	bourbon with orange, peach	United States
STREGA	herbs	Italy
TIA MARIA	rum with coffee	Jamaica
*TRIPLE SEC	sweet and bitter dried orange peel	Curaçao
TUACA	brandy-based liqueur reminiscent of butterscotch	Italy
UNICUM	bitter herbs	Hungary

SCOTCH

What is it about Scotch that makes it the choice of the sophisticated and the suave? For one thing, its fabled history, which began around A.D. 1300. For another, the subtle yet incomparable taste of malted barley tinged with peat smoke. (To "malt" barley is to control germination in a way that's far too technical to go into here; suffice to say that it helps convert starch into fermentable sugar.) The malted barley acquires its smokiness as it dries in a peat-burning kiln.

Prized **single malt Scotch** is made only from malted barley and at a single distillery. Yet close to 90 percent of the market is cornered by **blended Scotch**, made from up to 50 different types of Scotch selected by a master blender.

ARGYLL

Comforting as an old sweater

2 ounces Scotch
1 ounce calvados
½ ounce gin
1 teaspoon heather honey
Lemon twist for garnish

Combine spirits and honey in mixing glass. Add ice and shake. Strain into glass and garnish.

THE AULD RESTING CHAIR

Named for a traditional Scottish fiddling tune

2½ ounces Aberlour a'bunadh Scotch
1½ ounces B & B
1 or 2 splashes still water

Combine Scotch and liqueur in mixing glass. Add ice and stir to chill. Strain into glass and top with water.

AUTUMN LEAF

With the colors of fall

2 ounces Johnnie Walker Black Label
1 ounce Punt è Mes
1 ounce Kahlúa
Club soda
Orange twist for garnish

Combine Scotch, vermouth, and liqueur in mixing glass. Add ice, shake, and pour with ice into glass. Top with club soda to taste and garnish.

BENSON EXPRESS

The drink of a longtime regular

2½ ounces 25-year-old Macallan Scotch
Club soda on ice as a chaser

Pour Scotch into ice-filled rocks glass. Serve with club soda on the side.

BLUSHING SCOT

Tinted with red grenadine

2 ounces Scotch
1 ounce Godiva white chocolate liqueur
½ ounce light cream
¼ teaspoon grenadine

Combine ingredients in mixing glass. Add ice, shake, and strain into glass.

BOBBY BURNS MARTINI

A toast to Scotland's randy poet

2 ounces Scotch
1 ounce sweet vermouth
1 teaspoon Bénédictine
Lemon twist for garnish

Combine liquid ingredients in mixing glass. Add ice and stir to chill. Strain into glass and garnish.

COCK O' THE BEAVER

Named for the nineteenth-century Scottish soldiers who tipped their fur caps to the angels

3 ounces Glenlivet 12-year-old Scotch
1 ounce Southern Comfort
Orange twist for garnish

Combine Scotch and liqueur in mixing glass. Add ice and shake. Pour with ice into glass and garnish.

FANCY SCOTCH

The name of the orange liqueur triple sec means "triple dry," yet the taste is sweet.

2 ounces Scotch
½ ounce triple sec
½ ounce fresh sour mix
1 dash bitters of choice

Combine ingredients in mixing glass. Add ice, shake, and strain into glass.

FOUR SEASONS ROB ROY

Our twist on the original Rob Roy (page 39). Before straining the drink, moisten the rim of the glass with the orange twist.

3 ounces Scotch
1 teaspoon sweet vermouth
1 dash orange bitters
Orange twist for garnish
Maraschino cherry for garnish

Combine liquid ingredients in mixing glass. Add ice and stir to chill. Strain into glass and garnish.

FOUR SEASONS ROB ROY

FOUR SEASONS SUMMER BLOSSOM

With juice of the blood orange. The sweet exclamation point in this cocktail is a maraschino cherry marinated in Grand Marnier.

Maraschino cherry
½ ounce or more Grand Marnier
2 ounces Scotch
1 ounce Galliano
1 ounce blood orange juice

Place cherry in a shot glass and pour in Grand Marnier to cover; let soak for 8 to 12 hours. Combine Scotch, Galliano, and juice in mixing glass. Add ice and shake. Strain into glass and garnish with your extra-special little red fruit.

GODFATHER

Enjoy it or else.

2 ounces Scotch
1 ounce amaretto

Pour Scotch and liqueur into ice-filled rocks glass and stir.

GUINEVERE'S SMILE

Perchance sipped by the good folk of Camelot?

3 ounces Chivas Regal
1 ounce Baileys Irish Cream
1 to 3 black currants for garnish

Combine Scotch and liqueur in mixing glass. Add ice and shake. Strain into glass and garnish.

HOLE IN ONE

A post-round pick-me-up

2 ounces Scotch
½ ounce Noilly Prat sweet vermouth
½ ounce lemon juice
1 dash Angostura bitters
Maraschino cherry for garnish

Combine liquid ingredients in mixing glass. Add ice and stir to chill. Strain into glass and garnish.

A WORD FROM THE BARTENDERS

If you ever order a shaken cocktail at The Four Seasons and notice a bit of froth on the surface, don't worry. It's a *good* thing—a little pasteurized egg white in our fresh sour mix (page 28), which froths up as the shaker does its thing.

INVERNESS SHORES

Loch Lomond calls . . .
Crushed ice
3 ounces Glenmorangie 18-year-old Scotch
Bottled still water to taste

Fill a tulip glass with crushed ice and add Scotch. Top with water and stir.

IRISH RUSTY NAIL

Irish whiskey subs for the usual Drambuie.
1½ ounces Scotch
1½ ounces Irish whiskey

Combine whiskeys in ice-filled rocks glass and stir.

JOHN COLLINS

Tom Collins's Scottish cousin
2 ounces Scotch
1 ounce fresh sour mix
3 ounces club soda
Maraschino cherry for garnish
Orange slice for garnish

Combine Scotch and sour mix in mixing glass. Add ice, shake, and pour with ice into glass. Top with club soda and garnish.

THE MCCARVER

The right stuff
2½ ounces Glenmorangie 18-year-old Scotch
1½ ounces Grand Marnier
Club soda
Orange twist for garnish

Combine Scotch and liqueur in an ice-filled highball glass. Stir, top with club soda to taste, and garnish.

MIAMI BEACH COCKTAIL

For grapefruit lovers
1 ounce Scotch
½ ounce dry vermouth
1½ ounces grapefruit juice

Combine ingredients in mixing glass. Add ice, shake, and strain into glass.

PURPLE HEATHER HIGHBALL

PURPLE HEATHER HIGHBALL

The color comes from black currant
2½ ounces Scotch
1½ ounces crème de cassis
Club soda

Combine Scotch and liqueur in highball glass. Add ice, stir, and top with club soda to taste.

ROB ROY

A classic cocktail dating from the Gilded Age

2½ ounces Scotch
½ ounce sweet vermouth
Maraschino cherry for garnish

Combine Scotch and vermouth in mixing glass. Add ice and stir to chill. Strain into glass and garnish.

RUSTY NAIL

Two Scots in a glass

1½ ounces Scotch
1 ounce Drambuie

Pour Scotch and liqueur into ice-filled rocks glass and stir.

SCITALINA

Scotch with an Italian liqueur

Crushed ice
2 ounces Scotch
1 ounce Galliano
Orange twist for garnish

Fill a tulip glass with crushed ice and add Scotch and liqueur. Stir and garnish.

SCOTCH ALE

Ginger ale, that is

2 ounces Scotch
Ginger ale

Pour Scotch into ice-filled highball glass and top with ginger ale to taste.

SCOTCH ALEXANDER

Rich and velvety enough for a czar

1 ounce Dewars White Label Scotch
1 ounce white crème de cacao
1 ounce heavy cream
Nutmeg for sprinkling

Combine liquid ingredients in mixing glass. Add ice and shake. Strain into glass and sprinkle with nutmeg.

SCOTCH BLOSSOM

Orange flavor x 3. The French liqueur Cointreau is made from the dried peels of oranges grown in Curaçao, Spain, and Latin America.

3 ounces Scotch
½ ounce Cointreau
½ ounce orange juice
Orange peel spiral for garnish

Combine liquid ingredients in mixing glass. Add ice and stir to chill. Strain into glass and garnish.

SCOTCH BY THE POOL

A Four Seasons Pool Room favorite

3 ounces Scotch
3 dashes Angostura bitters
5 ounces club soda
Orange twist for garnish

Combine liquid ingredients in ice-filled highball glass. Stir and garnish.

Scotch and Soda

This classic cocktail is so simple it's not even a real recipe: Scotch, club soda, ice. Still, it is sacrosanct to Scotch purists. The variations below might seem heretical to some, but we'll take a cue from the French, shrug our shoulders, and say *à chacun son goût*—each to his own taste.

BASIC SCOTCH AND SODA

The original
2½ ounces Scotch
Club soda to taste

Pour Scotch into ice-filled rocks glass and top with club soda.

CORAL GABLES SCOTCH AND SODA

With a touch of orange-flavored liqueur based on Cognac
2½ ounces Scotch
¼ ounce Grand Marnier
Club soda

Pour Scotch into ice-filled rocks glass. Top with liqueur and add soda to taste.

SCOTCH COOLER

With a hint of mint
2½ ounces Scotch
1½ teaspoons white crème de menthe
Club soda

Pour Scotch into ice-filled rocks glass. Top with liqueur and add club soda to taste.

SCOTCH HIGHBALL

With two types of soda
2½ ounces Scotch
Ginger ale
Club soda
Lemon wedge for garnish

Pour Scotch into ice-filled highball glass. Top with equal parts ginger ale and club soda and garnish.

SCOTCH RICKEY

Scotch and soda for Limeys?
2½ ounces Scotch
Juice of half a lime
3 ounces club soda
Lime twist for garnish

Pour Scotch and juice into ice-filled rocks glass. Add club soda and garnish.

SCOTCH CABLEGRAM

Telegraphing good vibes

2 ounces Scotch

1 ounce fresh sour mix

Ginger ale to taste

Combine Scotch and sour mix in mixing glass. Add ice and shake. Pour with ice into glass and top with ginger ale.

SCOTCH CIDER

An apple for the Teacher('s)

2 ounces Teacher's Scotch

1 ounce apple brandy

Lime slice for garnish

Pour Scotch and brandy into ice-filled rocks glass. Stir and garnish.

SCOTCH GIMLET

A variation on the gin classic

2½ ounces Scotch

½ ounce lime juice

Lime slice for garnish

Pour Scotch and juice into ice-filled rocks glass. Stir and garnish.

SCOTCH MILK PUNCH

Off-limits to Junior

2 ounces Scotch

1 ounce whole milk

1 teaspoon superfine sugar

Nutmeg for sprinkling

Combine Scotch, milk, and sugar in mixing glass. Add ice and shake. Strain into glass and sprinkle with nutmeg.

SCOTCH MIST

Straight Scotch with plenty of ice

Crushed ice

2½ ounces Scotch

Lemon twist for garnish

Fill rocks glass half full of crushed ice and add Scotch. Top with more ice and garnish.

SCOTCH OLD-FASHIONED

Fruity and sweet

1 teaspoon superfine sugar

Orange slice

Maraschino cherry

1 dash bitters of choice

2½ ounces Scotch

1 splash still water

Muddle sugar, orange, cherry, and bitters in bottom of rocks glass. Add ice, pour in Scotch, and top off with water.

SCOTCH ON THE GRILL

A Four Seasons Grill Room specialty

3 ounces Scotch

½ ounce Cinzano sweet vermouth

3 dashes Angostura bitters

Lemon twist for garnish

Combine liquid ingredients in mixing glass. Add ice and stir to chill. Strain into glass and garnish.

SCOTCH ON THE ROCKS

The whiskey in all its naked glory

2½ ounces Scotch of choice

Fill rocks glass three-quarters full of ice and add Scotch.

SCOTCH RADKE

"The usual" for a Four Seasons regular is served neat—and doesn't come cheap.
2½ ounces Johnnie Walker Blue Label
Club soda on ice as chaser

Pour Scotch into ice-filled rocks glass. Serve with club soda on the side.

SCOTCH RADKE

SCOTCH SOUR

If you prefer, forgo the sour glass and serve this on the rocks.
2 ounces Scotch
1 ounce fresh sour mix
Maraschino cherry for garnish
Orange peel spiral for garnish

Combine Scotch and sour mix in mixing glass. Add ice and shake. Strain into sour glass or pour with ice into rocks glass and garnish.

SCOTCH STINGER

Minty mixology
2 ounces Scotch
1 ounce Cognac
1 ounce white crème de menthe
Mint sprig for garnish

Pour Scotch, brandy, and liqueur into ice-filled rocks glass. Stir and garnish.

SCOTCH STREET

Your route to pleasant potation
1½ ounces Scotch
½ ounce Southern Comfort
½ ounce fresh sour mix
Orange slice for garnish
Maraschino cherry for garnish

Combine liquid ingredients in mixing glass. Add ice and shake. Strain into glass and garnish.

SCOTTISH MAIDEN

With a streak of Italian
1 ounce Macallan 12-year-old Scotch
½ ounce Punt è Mes
½ ounce cherry brandy
Cherry with stem for garnish

Combine liquid ingredients in mixing glass. Add ice and shake. Strain into glass and garnish.

SUMMER SCOTCH COCKTAIL

Made with grapefruit juice and vermouth
2 ounces Scotch
½ ounce dry vermouth
2 ounces grapefruit juice
Lime peel spiral for garnish

Combine liquid ingredients in mixing glass. Add ice and stir to chill. Strain into glass and garnish.

TIPPERARY SCOTCH COCKTAIL

The original Tipperary calls for Irish whiskey.
1 ounce Scotch
1 ounce sweet vermouth
1 ounce green Chartreuse
Maraschino cherry for garnish

Combine liquid ingredients in mixing glass. Add ice and stir to chill. Strain into glass and garnish.

An American Landmark

One reason why The Four Seasons Restaurant is renowned worldwide is its architectural provenance. How many restaurants occupy space designed by two of architecture's leading lights?

It was Phyllis Bronfman Lambert, daughter of Seagram Company founder Samuel Bronfman, who enlisted the team of Mies van der Rohe and Philip Johnson to take on the task of designing a new Seagram headquarters in Manhattan. Having studied architecture at New York University, Lambert took great interest in her father's plans for the building. She strove to explain, she recalled, "what the business's responsibility could mean in terms of architecture, and to convince [my father] of the validity of the new architectural thinking."

The German-born American architect Mies van der Rohe was a driving force behind the International Style, with its unornamented, seemingly weightless glass-and-steel buildings of cantilever construction. His design of the Seagram Building (van der Rohe's sole building in New York) stands as one of his crowning achievements. Philip Johnson, then architecture director at New York's Museum of Modern Art and an acolyte of van der Rohe's, designed the building's spare and elegant interiors.

The fruit of their labors opened in 1958: a dramatic black-and-bronze "floating" skyscraper set 100 feet back from Park Avenue on a grand, wide-open plaza. And, to the good fortune of food lovers everywhere, an expansive space on the Seagram Building's first floor would be the site of a restaurant: The Four Seasons, a landmark for more than a half century. In fact, it was officially designated as such by New York City's Landmarks Preservation Commission in 1989—the only Manhattan restaurant ever to be so honored.

BOURBON

Ninety-nine percent of America's iconic whiskey (Congress declared bourbon the national spirit in 1964) is produced in a 900-square-mile area of Kentucky bluegrass country. The real thing is distilled from a mash of corn, barley, and rye, and must contain at least 51 percent corn. Aging in charred new oak barrels gives the spirit its hint of sweet vanilla.

Unlike Scotch, bourbon is never blended. At the same time, a very limited number of bourbons that are biding time in a distillery's barrels may be combined to yield bottlings of special character—so called **small batch bourbons**, the "class act" of the bunch in the minds of most bourbon connoisseurs.

ANCHORS AWEIGH

In a word, lush

2½ ounces bourbon

1 ounce Cointreau

2 teaspoons Hiram Walker peach brandy

2 teaspoons maraschino liqueur

2 ounces heavy cream

3 or 4 dashes maraschino cherry juice

Combine ingredients in mixing glass. Add ice, shake, and strain into glass.

BABYLON SOUR

Serve straight up or on the rocks

2½ ounces bourbon

1 ounce fresh sour mix

2 dashes bitters of choice

Combine ingredients in mixing glass. Add ice and shake. Strain into sour glass or pour with ice into rocks glass.

BEEKMAN PLACE

Inspired by the nearby good address

3 ounces Very Old Barton bourbon

1 ounce Southern Comfort

2 dashes orange bitters

Combine ingredients in mixing glass. Add ice, stir to chill, and strain into glass.

BOURBON AND SODA

Bourbon with a bit of fizz

2½ ounces bourbon

1 ounce club soda

Pour bourbon and club soda into ice-filled rocks glass and stir.

BOURBON AND SPRITE

Fizz plus lemon-lime

2½ ounces bourbon

1 ounce Sprite

Lime slice for garnish

Pour bourbon and soft drink into ice-filled rocks glass. Stir and garnish.

BOURBON BREEZE

Rustling the bluegrass

2 ounces bourbon

½ ounce blue curaçao

1 ounce lemon juice

Combine ingredients in mixing glass. Add ice, stir to chill, and pour with ice into glass.

BOURBON CREAM FLOAT

No ice cream, but still delish

2 ounces bourbon

2 ounces Godiva chocolate liqueur

½ ounce heavy cream

Pour bourbon into martini glass and float liqueur and cream on top.

BOURBON FRUIT FIZZ

A low-alcohol drink with the slightest hint of fruit. Take your pick of juice: citrus; apple or pear; tropical fruits; berry; or anything else that strikes your fancy.

1 ounce bourbon

1 splash fruit juice

Club soda

Pineapple spear for garnish

Pour bourbon into ice-filled rocks glass and add juice. Top with club soda to taste and garnish.

BOURBON GODFATHER

The Don tries on a southern accent.

2½ ounces bourbon
½ ounce amaretto

Pour bourbon and liqueur into ice-filled rocks glass and stir.

BOURBON JOHN COLLINS

Another drink named John Collins calls for Scotch (page 38)

2 ounces bourbon
1 ounce fresh sour mix
Club soda
Orange slice for garnish

Pour bourbon and sour mix into ice-filled highball glass. Top with club soda to taste and garnish.

BOURBON KISS 1

For the chocoholic. The "cacao" in the crème de cacao is cocoa.

2 ounces bourbon
½ ounce dark crème de cacao
½ ounce white crème de cacao

Combine ingredients in mixing glass. Add ice, stir to chill, and strain into glass.

BOURBON KISS 2

Alias the Bourbon Chocolate Martini

1½ ounces bourbon
½ ounce dark crème de cacao
½ ounce Godiva chocolate liqueur

Combine ingredients in mixing glass. Add ice, stir to chill, and strain into glass.

BOURBON LIME RICKEY

Lime juice–and–club soda cocktails are traditionally called rickeys.

2½ ounces bourbon
½ ounce lime juice
Club soda
Lime peel spiral for garnish

Pour bourbon and juice into ice-filled rocks glass. Top with club soda to taste and garnish.

BOURBON MANHATTAN

NYC meets Bourbon County, KY

3½ ounces bourbon
½ ounce dry vermouth
Maraschino cherry for garnish

Combine bourbon and vermouth in mixing glass. Add ice and shake. Strain into glass and garnish.

BOURBON MILK PUNCH

With a touch of cinnamon

2 ounces bourbon
2 ounces whole milk
1 teaspoon superfine sugar
⅛ teaspoon cinnamon
Cinnamon for sprinkling

Combine bourbon, milk, sugar, and ⅛ teaspoon cinnamon in mixing glass. Add ice and shake. Pour into glass and sprinkle with more cinnamon.

BOURBON MIST

Bourbon, ice, and more ice

Crushed ice
3½ ounces Ten High bourbon

Fill rocks glass with crushed ice and add bourbon. As ice settles, top up glass with more ice.

BOURBON OLD-FASHIONED

A classic cocktail heads south
1 teaspoon superfine sugar
Orange slice
Maraschino cherry
3 dashes Angostura bitters
2½ ounces Maker's Mark bourbon
1 ounce club soda

Muddle sugar, orange, cherry, and bitters in bottom of rocks glass. Add ice, pour in bourbon, and top with club soda.

BOURBON OLD-FASHIONED

BOURBON PIE

Tempting and rich
1 ounce bourbon
½ ounce dark crème de cacao
½ ounce crème de banane
½ ounce whole milk

Combine ingredients in mixing glass. Add ice, stir to chill, and strain into glass.

BOURBON SOUR

Tart but pleasing, whether straight up or on the rocks
3 ounces bourbon
1 ounce fresh sour mix
Orange slice for garnish
Maraschino cherry for garnish

Combine bourbon and sour mix in mixing glass. Add ice and shake. Strain into sour glass or pour with ice into rocks glass and garnish.

CAESAR

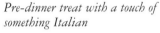

Pre-dinner treat with a touch of something Italian
3½ ounces bourbon
½ ounce Campari
Lemon slice for garnish

Pour bourbon and Campari into ice-filled rocks glass. Stir and garnish.

CUSTER'S LAST STAND

Does battle with boredom
½ ounce Jim Beam bourbon
½ ounce grenadine
1 ounce lemon juice
3 dashes bitters of choice
Lemon wedge for garnish

Pour liquid ingredients into ice-filled rocks glass. Stir and garnish.

D. L. COCKTAIL

Bartender Charles shares a recipe long kept on the down low.
2½ ounces bourbon
½ ounce sweet vermouth
½ ounce lemon juice

Pour ingredients into ice-filled rocks glass and stir.

DUBONNET MANHATTAN

White or red? Your pick.

3 ounces bourbon
½ ounce Dubonnet Blanc or Rouge
½ ounce dry vermouth

Combine ingredients in mixing glass. Add ice, shake, and strain into glass.

EDIE'S CHOICE

A bourbon stinger

2 ounces bourbon
½ ounce Cognac
½ ounce white crème de menthe

Pour ingredients into ice-filled rocks glass and stir.

EQUALIZER

"Dessert" after a big meal

2 ounces bourbon
½ ounce white crème de menthe
3 dashes Grand Marnier

Combine ingredients in mixing glass. Add ice, shake, and strain into glass.

FRENCH CONNECTION

Avec deux liqueurs française

1½ ounces bourbon
½ ounce Pernod
½ ounce dark crème de cacao
1 ounce heavy cream
Nutmeg for sprinkling

Combine liquid ingredients in mixing glass. Add ice and shake. Strain into glass and sprinkle with nutmeg.

THE GENERAL LEE

Grabs joy from the jaws of defeat

2 ounces bourbon
2 ounces brandy
½ ounce triple sec
Ginger ale
Orange slice for garnish

Pour bourbon, brandy, and liqueur into ice-filled highball glass. Top with ginger ale to taste and garnish.

HEADLESS JOCKEY

Kentucky riff on the Headless Horseman cocktail (page 91)

2 ounces bourbon
1 dash bitters of choice
Ginger ale

Pour bourbon and bitters into ice-filled rocks glass. Top with ginger ale to taste.

KENTUCKY KISS

Simple and smooth

2 ounces bourbon
4 ounces apricot nectar

Pour ingredients into ice-filled highball glass and stir.

LASER BEAM FIZZ

Pinpointed pleasure

2 ounces bourbon
1 ounce Drambuie
1 ounce peppermint schnapps
Club soda

Combine bourbon, liqueur, and schnapps in mixing glass. Add ice and shake. Pour with ice into glass and top with club soda to taste.

LOUISVILLE SLUGGER

Step up to the plate and sip.

1½ ounces bourbon
½ ounce orange juice
½ ounce pineapple juice
Club soda

Pour bourbon and juices into ice-filled rocks glass and top with club soda.

LULU'S FIZZ

Specialty of a Kentucky "hostess with the mostest"

2 ounces bourbon
2 ounces light rum
½ ounce fresh sour mix
3 dashes bitters of choice
Club soda
Maraschino cherry for garnish

Combine bourbon, rum, sour mix, and bitters in mixing glass. Add ice and shake. Pour with ice into rocks glass, top with club soda to taste, and garnish.

MANHATTAN COWBOY

A little bit country, a little bit man-about-town

2½ ounces Maker's Mark bourbon
½ ounce Southern Comfort
½ ounce orange juice
½ ounce lemon juice
Orange twist for garnish

Pour liquid ingredients into ice-filled rocks glass. Stir and garnish.

THE MIDTOWN

Named for our very large neighborhood

1 ounce bourbon
½ ounce Harvey's Bristol Cream sherry
½ ounce Grand Marnier

Combine ingredients in mixing glass. Add ice, shake, and strain into glass.

MISSION IMPOSSIBLE

But well worth undertaking

3 ounces bourbon
½ ounce lemon juice
1 dash bitters of choice
½ ounce still water
Lime slice for garnish

Combine liquid ingredients in mixing glass. Add ice and shake. Strain into glass and garnish.

Mint Julep

The Four Seasons is a world away from Kentucky horse country, but that doesn't mean our bartenders aren't well acquainted with the authentic recipe for this storied drink of the South. They also had enough Yankee gall to develop their own version—and, to the horror of transplanted Southerners, serve mint juleps in a highball or tulip glass rather than a silver or pewter julep cup. Less traditional? Without question. Less delightful? We think not.

CLASSIC MINT JULEP

For die-hard traditionalists

4 mint sprigs
1 teaspoon superfine sugar
2 teaspoons still water
Crushed ice
2½ ounces Kentucky Gentleman bourbon
Mint sprig for garnish

Muddle mint and sugar with water in bottom of julep cup or highball glass. Fill with crushed ice and add bourbon. Garnish with mint and serve with a straw.

DIXIE JULEP

Where's the mint? In the garnish.

2½ ounces bourbon
½ teaspoon superfine sugar
Crushed ice
3 mint sprigs for garnish

Combine bourbon and sugar in mixing glass. Add ice, shake, and strain into glass filled with crushed ice. Garnish with mint and serve with a straw.

FOUR SEASONS MINT JULEP

Either peppermint or spearmint will do.

6 mint sprigs
3 ounces bourbon
2 ounces fresh sour mix
Crushed ice

Muddle mint in bottom of mixing glass. Add bourbon and sour mix. Add ice and shake. Strain into glass filled with crushed ice, and serve with a straw.

MOCK MINT JULEP

No muddling required

Crushed ice
2 ounces bourbon
½ ounce white crème de menthe
Mint sprig for garnish

Fill tulip glass with crushed ice. Pour in bourbon and liqueur, stir, and garnish.

PLYMOUTH ROCK

Concoction unknown to the grog-loving Pilgrim fathers

2½ ounces bourbon
Juice of half a lemon
Juice of half a lime
2 dashes orange bitters
Club soda
Lime slice for garnish

Pour bourbon and juices into ice-filled highball glass. Add bitters and stir. Top with club soda to taste and garnish.

PORTIA'S CHOICE

Sweet 'n' sour

2 ounces bourbon
1 ounce sweet vermouth
1 ounce fresh sour mix
Club soda

Combine bourbon, vermouth, and sour mix in mixing glass. Add ice and shake. Pour with ice into rocks glass and top with club soda to taste.

PROHIBITION EXPRESS

Do not mix in the bathtub. The Italian liqueur sambuca, made from anise and elderberries, gives this drink its licoricy flavor.

2½ ounces bourbon
1 ounce sambuca

Pour bourbon and liqueur into ice-filled rocks glass and stir.

RUSTY SPIKE

The Rusty Nail (page 39) pointed southward

3 ounces bourbon
1 ounce Drambuie

Pour bourbon and liqueur into ice-filled rocks glass and stir.

SEX IN THE MOUNTAINS

When you've had it with Sex on the Beach (page 99)

1½ ounces bourbon
1 ounce peach schnapps
1 ounce orange juice
½ ounce cranberry juice

Combine ingredients in ice-filled rocks glass and stir.

SEX IN THE VALLEY

Ditto

1½ ounces bourbon
2 ounces peach schnapps
½ ounce triple sec
½ ounce pineapple juice
½ ounce cranberry juice

Pour ingredients into ice-filled rocks glass and stir.

SOUTHERN BREEZE

With the irresistible scent of fruit

Crushed ice
2 ounces bourbon
½ ounce Southern Comfort
½ ounce orange juice
½ ounce cranberry juice

Fill a tulip glass with crushed ice. Pour in ingredients and stir.

SOUTHERN CREAM PIE

Dig in
2½ ounces bourbon
1 teaspoon superfine sugar
½ ounce heavy cream
⅛ teaspoon nutmeg, plus extra
   for sprinkling

Combine bourbon, sugar, cream, and ⅛ teaspoon nutmeg in mixing glass. Add ice and shake. Strain into glass and sprinkle with more nutmeg.

SOUTHERN SETTLER

Meant for the morning after
2 ounces bourbon
1 ounce 7UP or Sprite
1 ounce club soda
2 dashes bitters of choice

Pour ingredients into ice-filled rocks glass and stir.

STATUE OF LIBERTY

In honor of Lady of the Harbor's French origins
3 ounces bourbon
½ ounce Cointreau
½ ounce grenadine
Maraschino cherry for garnish

Combine liquid ingredients in mixing glass. Add ice and stir to chill. Strain into glass and garnish.

SWEET BOURBON MANHATTAN

Savvy late-night choice
3½ ounces bourbon
½ ounce sweet vermouth
Maraschino cherry for garnish

Combine bourbon and vermouth in mixing glass. Add ice and stir to chill. Strain into glass and garnish.

TIM TAM

A toast to the thoroughbred that won the 1958 Kentucky Derby
2½ ounces Ten High bourbon
1 ounce fresh sour mix
1 ounce orange juice
Sprite or 7UP

Combine bourbon, sour mix, and juice in mixing glass. Add ice, shake, and pour with ice into glass. Add soft drink to taste and stir.

TNT

An explosion of orange and licorice
2½ ounces bourbon
½ ounce anisette
½ ounce orange liqueur

Pour ingredients into ice-filled rocks glass and stir.

THE Y'ALL COME

Southern hospitality on the rocks
2 ounces bourbon
2 ounces Southern Comfort
Club soda
Orange twist for garnish

Combine bourbon and liqueur in mixing glass. Add ice and shake. Pour with ice into glass, top with club soda to taste, and garnish.

WHISKEY COCKTAILS

S cotch and bourbon are hardly the only whiskeys on the block. At The Four Seasons Grill Room the bartenders make good use of other types from across the ocean, north of the border, or right here in the USA.

Old-fashioned **rye whiskey**, which has made a comeback in recent years, is grassy and a little sour when young, and tastes of caramel and spice with age. **Tennessee whiskey**, made at only two distilleries, is lighter-bodied and sweeter than bourbon thanks to its filtration through finely ground sugar-maple charcoal. **Irish whiskey** lacks the smokiness of Scotch but makes up for it with maltiness. **Canadian blended whiskey** is our northern neighbor's pride and joy, with virtually all Canadian distillers producing blends of grain whiskeys of different ages.

ACT TWO

A nightcap after the show?

2 ounces Canadian Club whiskey
2 ounces ruby port
1 ounce dark rum
4 or 5 dashes Angostura bitters

Combine ingredients in mixing glass. Add ice, shake, and strain into glass.

ALGONQUIN

Created at the eponymous hotel's Blue Bar by bartending legend David Grinstead, who ended his career at The Four Seasons

1½ ounces whiskey of choice
1 ounce dry vermouth
1 ounce pineapple juice
1 ounce club soda

Combine whiskey, vermouth, and juice in mixing glass. Add ice and stir to chill. Strain into glass, top with club soda, and stir.

BLACK ROCK

Named for the investment company in our 52nd Street block

1½ ounces Jameson Irish whiskey
½ ounce blue curaçao
½ ounce Cognac
Orange peel spiral for garnish

Combine liquid ingredients in mixing glass. Add ice and stir to chill. Strain into glass and garnish.

A WORD FROM THE BARTENDERS

Fruit garnishes aren't anything to skimp on. At The Four Seasons, we cut a wedge of lemon or lime no less than an inch wide; lime, lemon, and orange slices end up close to half an inch wide. The rationale? You'll flavor your drink all the more when you squeeze a citrus garnish and drop it into the glass. Presentation is well and good, but it's not going to thrill the palate.

BLACKSTONE

In honor of yet another neighborhood firm

2 ounces whiskey of choice
½ ounce dry sherry
½ ounce fresh sour mix
Maraschino cherry for garnish

Combine liquid ingredients in mixing glass. Add ice and shake. Strain into glass and garnish.

BOILERMAKER

A blast from your college past

12 ounces beer of choice, chilled
1 ounce whiskey of choice

Pour beer into highball glass, top with whiskey, and stir.

CATCH-22

Half Irish, half Scottish

1½ ounces Irish whiskey
1½ ounces Scotch

Pour whiskeys into ice-filled rocks glass and stir.

CATSKILL COCKTAIL

Mountain cherry picking

2½ ounces whiskey of choice
½ ounce Hiram Walker cherry brandy
Maraschino cherry for garnish

Pour whiskey and brandy into ice-filled highball glass. Stir and garnish.

CHARLES'S WARD EIGHT

A Four Seasons bartender reinterprets an old favorite (page 61).

2 ounces Canadian whiskey
½ ounce fresh sour mix
½ ounce grenadine
Crushed ice
Orange slice for garnish

Combine whiskey, sour mix, and grenadine in mixing glass. Add ice and shake. Strain into glass filled with crushed ice and garnish. Serve with a straw, if desired.

CITY STORMER

Mad swirl of whiskey and two liqueurs

1½ ounces whiskey of choice
½ ounce white crème de menthe
½ ounce dark crème de cacao

Pour ingredients into ice-filled rocks glass and stir.

COMMODORE

For imbibing on your yacht

2 ounces whiskey of choice
½ ounce Drambuie
1 ounce fresh sour mix
Orange slice for garnish

Combine liquid ingredients in mixing glass. Add ice and shake. Strain into ice-filled glass and garnish.

CONNOLLY

Created by—and named for—head bartender Greg

1½ ounces Jack Daniels Tennessee whiskey
½ ounce lime juice
½ ounce orange juice
Ginger ale
Lime wedge for garnish

Combine whiskey and juices in mixing glass. Add ice, shake, and pour with ice into glass. Top with ginger ale to taste and garnish.

DEE DEE'S MANHATTAN

Named for a customer who likes it tart

2 ounces rye whiskey
½ ounce sweet vermouth
1 ounce cranberry juice
2 drops lemon juice
Orange slice for garnish

Pour liquid ingredients into ice-filled rocks glass. Stir and garnish.

EAST RIVER COCKTAIL

Potent and olivey

2½ ounces whiskey of choice
½ ounce olive juice
3 olives for garnish

Pour whiskey and olive juice into ice-filled rocks glass. Stir and garnish.

CONNOLLY

THE 59TH STREET BRIDGE

Why the name? See page 64.
2 ounces whiskey of choice
½ ounce Drambuie
¼ ounce sloe gin

Combine ingredients in mixing glass. Add ice and shake. Strain into ice-filled glass and stir.

52ND STREET COCKTAIL

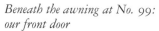

Beneath the awning at No. 99: our front door
2½ ounces whiskey of choice
½ ounce Southern Comfort
Maraschino cherry for garnish

Pour whiskey and Southern Comfort into ice-filled rocks glass. Stir and garnish.

FOUR SEASONS BLUE MONDAY

Our version of the classic vodka cocktail—a toast to the weekend that was
2 ounces whiskey of choice
½ ounce blue curaçao
½ ounce fresh sour mix
Maraschino cherry for garnish

Combine liquid ingredients in mixing glass. Add ice and shake. Strain into glass and garnish.

FOUR SEASONS SHAMROCK

Erin go bragh
2 ounces Irish whiskey
1 ounce dry vermouth
1 teaspoon green crème de menthe

Combine ingredients in mixing glass. Add ice, stir to chill, and strain into glass.

FOUR SEASONS WHISKEY SOUR

Our take on a classic
2½ ounces Crown Royal whiskey
1½ ounces fresh sour mix
Crushed ice
Orange slice for garnish
Maraschino cherry for garnish

Combine whiskey and sour mix in mixing glass. Add ice and shake. Strain into glass filled with crushed ice and garnish.

HERBY PEACH

With peach schnapps and a bittersweet Italian vermouth
2 ounces whiskey of choice
1 ounce peach schnapps
1 ounce Punt è Mes
Club soda

Combine whiskey, schnapps, and vermouth in mixing glass. Add ice and shake. Pour with ice into glass and top with club soda to taste.

HUDSON VIEW COCKTAIL

Savored by New Yorkers on both banks
2 ounces whiskey of choice
½ ounce dry vermouth
½ ounce orange juice

Combine ingredients in mixing glass. Add ice, shake, and strain into glass.

IRISH COOLER

A soft drink well spiked
2½ ounces Irish whiskey
12 ounces Sprite or 7UP
Lemon slice for garnish

Pour whiskey and soft drink into ice-filled highball glass. Stir and garnish.

IRISH FIXER

Tonic for the morning after. Irish Mist, based on an ancient formula, is flavored with honey and herbs.

2 ounces Irish whiskey
½ ounce Irish Mist
¼ ounce orange juice
¼ ounce lemon juice
Crushed ice

Combine liquid ingredients in mixing glass. Add ice, shake, and strain into glass filled with crushed ice.

L'ANISETTE

Whiskey with a touch of licoracy anisette

2½ ounces Canadian whiskey
½ ounce anisette
1 dash Fee Brothers orange bitters
Lemon twist for garnish

Combine liquid ingredients in mixing glass. Add ice and stir to chill. Pour with ice into glass and garnish.

LYNCHBURG LEMONADE

From Jack Daniels's hometown in Middle Tennessee

2 ounces Jack Daniels Tennessee whiskey
½ ounce triple sec
1 ounce fresh sour mix
1½ ounces Sprite or 7UP
Lemon peel spiral for garnish
Maraschino cherry for garnish

Combine whiskey, triple sec, and sour mix in mixing glass. Add ice and shake. Pour with ice into glass, add soft drink, and garnish. Serve with a straw.

MOONLIGHT JIG

MINTICELLO

Limoncello with mint

2 ounces whiskey of choice
1 ounce limoncello
1 ounce white crème de menthe
Club soda
Mint sprig for garnish

Combine whiskey and liqueurs in mixing glass. Add ice and shake. Pour with ice into glass, top with club soda to taste, and garnish.

MOONLIGHT JIG

Foot-stompin' good

2 ounces Irish whiskey
1 ounce Drambuie
1 ounce B & B
Crushed ice
Club soda
Orange slice for garnish

Combine whiskey and liqueurs in mixing glass. Add ice and shake. Pour into glass filled with crushed ice, top with club soda to taste, and garnish.

MOUNTED COP

In honor of New York's finest and their steeds

2 ounces whiskey of choice
½ ounce white crème de cacao
½ ounce heavy cream
Nutmeg for sprinkling

Combine liquid ingredients in mixing glass. Add ice and shake. Strain into glass and sprinkle with nutmeg.

OPENING NIGHT COCKTAIL

Curtain up, light the lights!

2 ounces whiskey of choice
1 ounce Cointreau
Lemon twist for garnish

Pour whiskey and liqueur into ice-filled rocks glass. Stir and garnish.

PARK AVENUE SOUR

An homage to the high-powered boulevard where our famous building stands

2 ounces whiskey of choice
1 ounce fresh sour mix
Maraschino cherry for garnish
Orange slice for garnish

Combine whiskey and sour mix in mixing glass. Add ice and shake. Strain into glass and garnish.

PARKING METER

Ticking with flavor

2½ ounces whiskey of choice
½ ounce lemon juice
1 dash Tabasco

Combine ingredients in mixing glass. Add ice, shake, and pour with ice into glass.

RUSTY SCREW

The Rusty Nail meets the Screwdriver.

1½ ounces whiskey of choice
1 ounce Drambuie
½ ounce orange juice
Orange slice for garnish

Pour liquid ingredients into ice-filled rocks glass. Stir and garnish.

RYE FIZZ

Bubbly and sweet. Pungent Angostura bitters was formulated in Venezuela by an immigrant German surgeon.

2½ ounces rye whiskey
½ teaspoon superfine sugar
1 dash Angostura bitters
Club soda
Lemon twist for garnish

Combine whiskey, sugar, and bitters in mixing glass. Add ice, shake, and strain into ice-filled glass. Top with club soda to taste and garnish.

SEASIDE

Whiskey with a touch of gin

1½ ounces whiskey of choice
½ ounce gin
½ ounce fresh sour mix
Crushed ice
3 sprigs fresh mint for garnish

Combine liquid ingredients in mixing glass. Add ice and shake. Strain into glass filled with crushed ice and garnish.

Rye Old-Timers

Some of America's best-known vintage cocktails are based on rye whiskey. They also have rich histories. Take the Manhattan, for example: In the Gilded Age it was a staple for the upper crust, and financier J. P. Morgan is said to have enjoyed a Manhattan every day after the stock market closed.

For other rye whiskey recipes in this chapter, see Dee Dee's Manhattan, page 57; Rye Fizz, facing page; and Whiskey Fizzer, page 63. Or choose rye for any of the recipes that leave the type of whiskey up to you.

DRY MANHATTAN

With dry vermouth and lemon
2¾ ounces rye whiskey
¼ ounce dry vermouth
Lemon twist for garnish

Combine whiskey and vermouth in mixing glass. Add ice and shake. Strain into glass and garnish.

OLD-FASHIONED

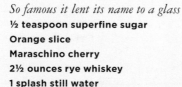

So famous it lent its name to a glass
½ teaspoon superfine sugar
Orange slice
Maraschino cherry
2½ ounces rye whiskey
1 splash still water

Muddle sugar, orange, and cherry in bottom of rocks glass. Add ice, pour in whiskey, and top with water.

SAZERAC

Created in the mid-1800s at the Sazerac Coffee House in New Orleans
1 ounce simple syrup (page 27)
3 to 5 dashes Peychaud's bitters
3 ounces rye whiskey
Absinthe for coating glass
Crushed ice
Lemon twist for garnish

Chill rocks glass while preparing drink. Combine syrup and bitters in mixing glass and stir. Add whiskey and ice and stir to chill. Discard ice in rocks glass and wipe dry. Add enough absinthe to coat the inside as glass is swirled. Fill glass with crushed ice, strain in whiskey mixture, and garnish.

SWEET MANHATTAN

With sweet vermouth and maraschino liqueur
2½ ounces rye whiskey
¼ ounce sweet vermouth
¼ ounce maraschino
Maraschino cherry for garnish

Combine liquid ingredients in mixing glass. Add ice and shake. Strain into glass and garnish.

WARD EIGHT

Named in the early 1900s for the political precinct of Roxbury, the Boston suburb
2 ounces rye whiskey
1 ounce lemon juice
½ ounce orange juice
2 or 3 dashes grenadine
Maraschino cherry for garnish

Combine liquid ingredients in mixing glass. Add ice and shake. Strain into glass and garnish.

7 AND 7

A simple yet classic pairing
2½ ounces Seagrams 7
12 ounces 7UP

Pour whiskey into ice-filled highball glass. Top with soft drink and stir.

SMITHTOWN

Named for Greg's Long Island hometown
1½ ounces Jameson Irish whiskey
½ ounce dry vermouth
½ ounce sweet vermouth
Lemon twist for garnish

Pour liquid ingredients into ice-filled rocks glass. Stir and garnish.

SUBWAY CAR

Usually fast, sometimes "sloe." Sloe gin is made from sloe plums, the fruit of the black thorn tree (Prunus spinosa).
2 ounces whiskey of choice
1 ounce sloe gin
Olive for garnish

Pour whiskey and sloe gin into ice-filled rocks glass. Stir and garnish.

TAXI CAB

Catch it!
2 ounces whiskey of choice
2 ounces orange juice
½ ounce lemon juice
Lemon peel spiral for garnish

Combine liquid ingredients in mixing glass. Add ice and stir to chill. Strain into glass and garnish.

TENNESSEE LIGHTNIN' FIZZ

Jack and mint on the rocks
2 ounces Jack Daniels Tennessee whiskey
1½ ounces green crème de menthe
Club soda
Mint sprig for garnish

Combine whiskey and liqueur in mixing glass. Add ice and shake. Pour with ice into glass, top with club soda to taste, and garnish.

VICK'S PICK

Light 'n' lemony
2 ounces whiskey of choice
Juice of half a lemon
1 teaspoon grenadine
½ teaspoon powdered sugar
Lemon peel spiral for garnish

Combine whiskey, juice, grenadine, and sugar in ice-filled white wine glass. Stir and garnish.

WHISKEY DRIVER

Not limited to golf days
2 ounces whiskey of choice
1½ ounces orange juice
Orange slice for garnish

Combine whiskey and juice in ice-filled rocks glass. Stir and garnish.

WHISKEY FIZZER

Effervescent and sweet

2½ ounces rye whiskey
½ teaspoon superfine sugar
1 dash Fee Brothers lemon bitters
Crushed ice
Club soda

Combine whiskey, sugar, and bitters in mixing glass. Add ice and shake. Strain into glass filled with crushed ice, top with club soda to taste, and stir.

WHISKEY GODFATHER

Hold the Brando impersonation.

1 ounce whiskey of choice
1 ounce amaretto

Pour whiskey and liqueur into ice-filled rocks glass and stir.

WHISKEY MINT COOLER

With a touch of lemon

¼ ounce lemon juice
5 mint leaves
2½ ounces whiskey of choice
Mint sprig for garnish

Muddle lemon juice and mint leaves in bottom of rocks glass. Add ice and pour in whiskey. Stir and garnish.

WHISKEY ORCHARD

Flavored with apple brandy

2 ounces whiskey of choice
1 ounce apple brandy
Apple slice for garnish

Pour whiskey and brandy into ice-filled rocks glass and garnish.

WHISKEY PRES

Short for Presbyterian—in barspeak, "light on the liquor"

2 ounces whiskey of choice
Club soda
Ginger ale

Pour whiskey into ice-filled highball glass. Top with equal parts club soda and ginger ale and stir.

WHISKEY STINGER

Minty and cool

2 ounces whiskey of choice
½ ounce brandy
½ ounce white crème de menthe

Pour ingredients into ice-filled rocks glass and stir.

WILL'S PEPPERMINT STICK

Will has a sweet tooth.

2 ounces whiskey of choice
1½ ounces peppermint tea
½ teaspoon superfine sugar
3 sprigs peppermint, crushed
Club soda
Peppermint sprig for garnish

Combine whiskey, tea, sugar, and crushed peppermint in mixing glass. Add ice and shake. Strain into glass, top with club soda to taste, and garnish.

A Bar Regular: The Creative Muse

The creative dynamos practicing their art behind the bar in The Four Seasons Grill Room continuously reaffirm that necessity is the mother of invention. "I'd like something with gin," says a visitor. Another volunteers that she loved a drink in Seattle last month but recalls only a couple of ingredients. So, as often as not, the bartenders find themselves inventing drinks on the spot. That the cocktails typically draw rave reviews is a tribute to the expertise of Greg Connolly, Charles Corpion, and John Varriano.

Of course, every new invention needs a name. Some of the drinks are named after Four Seasons regulars who have particular tastes, while others are named for customers who have requested a certain variation on a cocktail. A Mr. Hoerdemann ordered the Sidecar "his way" for so long that the Hoerdemann Howl (page 151) is now on the bar menu.

Other names come straight from the bartenders' fertile minds:

- Greg Connolly drives to and from The Four Seasons over the Queensboro Bridge, where traffic is notorious for slowing to a crawl. What better to call his sloe gin–based cocktail than the logjam magnet's colloquial name: The 59th Street Bridge (page 58)?
- Charles Corpion works wonders with rum, tequila, and other spirits, and he has a practical side as well—as the hot ginger-and-rum concoction named Dr. Corpion's Cold Chaser attests. (page 221).
- John Varriano, who has a background in art, not only paints but also appreciates the works of Pablo Picasso—hence the name for his cocktail laced with blue curaçao and, "for elegance," a splash of Pernod: The Blue Period (page 86).

Sir Charles, by John Varriano; oil on linen (48" x 40") 2009

GIN

It is believed that gin was invented by a Dutch chemist for medicinal purposes, but it was the English who introduced the spirit the Dutch knew as *genever* to the world. In fact, in the eyes of people everywhere, the juniper berry–flavored spirit we call gin is wrapped in the British flag—not surprising, since **London dry gin** sets the standard for excellence. Distilleries in the port cities of Liverpool, Bristol, and Plymouth produced fruitier, more aromatic versions of dry gin, but only **Plymouth gin** survives today.

Trivia tidbit: During the Franco-Dutch War of the late seventeenth century, British soldiers fought alongside Dutch soldiers, who fortified themselves with a nip of genever before going into battle—hence gin's old nickname of "Dutch courage."

THE ACADEMIC

A study in good taste

2 ounces gin
½ ounce Galliano
½ ounce orange juice

Combine ingredients in mixing glass. Add ice, stir to chill, and strain into glass.

ANDROMEDA

A galaxy of aromas and flavors

2 ounces gin
1 ounce Southern Comfort
½ ounce sloe gin
½ ounce Chambord
½ teaspoon blue curaçao

Pour ingredients into ice-filled rocks glass and stir.

ANGEL'S BREAST

White, whiter, whitest

2 ounces gin
1 ounce white crème de cacao
1 ounce Godiva white chocolate liqueur
1 ounce light cream

Combine ingredients in mixing glass. Add ice, shake, and strain into glass.

THE ANSONIA

Named for the architectural gem on New York City's Upper West Side

3 ounces gin
1 ounce lemon juice
1 ounce raspberry puree
Lemon slice for garnish

Combine ingredients in mixing glass. Add ice and shake. Strain into glass and garnish.

APOLLO

Fit for a Greek god

2½ ounces gin
1 ounce white crème de cacao
½ ounce blue curaçao

Combine ingredients in mixing glass. Add ice, stir to chill, and strain into glass.

ARCHBISHOP

A religious experience?

2½ ounces Seagram's Extra Dry gin
½ ounce Bénédictine
1 dash bitters of choice

Pour ingredients into ice-filled rocks glass and stir.

THE ARTHUR

A bow to Camelot's king

2½ ounces gin
½ ounce Grand Marnier
1 teaspoon lemon juice
Orange twist for garnish

Combine liquid ingredients in mixing glass. Add ice and stir to chill. Pour with ice into glass and garnish.

ASCOT

No silk neck scarf required

2½ ounces gin
½ ounce sweet vermouth
2 dashes Angostura bitters

Combine ingredients in mixing glass. Add ice, stir to chill, and strain into glass.

ASTORIA
SPECIAL

A warm toast to the Greek residents of Queens
3 ounces gin
½ ounce ouzo
White grape for garnish

Combine gin and ouzo in mixing glass. Add ice and shake. Strain into glass and garnish.

ASTOR
PLACE

Downtown haunt of fun-seekers
2½ ounces gin
½ ounce Galliano
1 dash bitters of choice

Combine ingredients in mixing glass. Add ice, stir to chill, and strain into glass.

ATHENA

For the goddess inside
2 ounces gin
1 ounce white crème de menthe
1 ounce light cream

Combine ingredients in mixing glass. Add ice, shake, and strain into glass.

AVENUE B

Way down in Alphabet City
2 ounces gin
1 ounce white crème de cacao
½ ounce Drambuie

Combine ingredients in mixing glass. Add ice, stir to chill, and strain into glass.

BEE LINE

Named for New York City's Sixth Avenue subway line
2 ounces gin
½ ounce peach schnapps
½ ounce apricot brandy

Combine ingredients in mixing glass. Add ice, stir to chill, and strain into glass.

BETTE'S
CHOICE

The favorite of a Grill Room regular
2½ ounces gin
½ ounce Pernod
½ teaspoon grenadine

Combine ingredients in mixing glass. Add ice, stir to chill, and strain into glass.

BILBO B.

One rich little Hobbit
2 ounces gin
1 ounce Scotch
½ ounce dark crème de cacao
½ ounce heavy cream

Combine ingredients in mixing glass. Add ice, shake, and pour with ice into glass.

BLEECKER
STREET

Named for Greenwich Village's street of dreams
2½ ounces gin
½ ounce Grand Marnier
½ ounce lime juice
½ teaspoon superfine sugar
Orange peel spiral for garnish

Combine gin, liqueur, juice, and sugar in mixing glass. Add ice and shake. Strain into glass and garnish.

BLOODY BRIT

Cheers, mate!

2½ ounces Beefeater dry gin

3 ounces tomato juice

5 dashes Worcestershire sauce

3 dashes Tabasco

Smoked or raw oyster for garnish

Pour liquid ingredients into ice-filled rocks glass, stir, and garnish.

BLUE SKY

Tinted with blue curaçao

2 ounces gin

½ ounce blue curaçao

½ ounce orange liqueur

Pour ingredients into ice-filled rocks glass and stir.

BRAVEHEART

British gin, Scottish whiskey

2½ ounces Gordon's gin

1 teaspoon Scotch

Lemon twist for garnish

Combine gin and Scotch in mixing glass. Add ice and stir to chill. Strain into glass and garnish.

BRONX TALE

A variation on the classic Bronx Cocktail, which calls for sweet and dry vermouth

2 ounces gin

1 ounce orange juice

1 teaspoon dry vermouth

Combine ingredients in mixing glass. Add ice, shake, and strain into glass.

BROOKLYN NITE

Good times across the bridge

2 ounces gin

1 ounce dark rum

1 ounce Cointreau

1 teaspoon lemon juice

Pour ingredients into ice-filled rocks glass and stir.

CAROUSEL

May set you spinning

2 ounces gin

1 ounce white crème de cacao

2 dashes grenadine

1 ounce light cream

Combine ingredients in mixing glass. Add ice, shake, and strain into glass.

CATAPULT

Hook feet around chair legs when sipping

2 ounces gin

1 ounce vodka

1 ounce Campari

1 ounce orange juice

Pour ingredients into ice-filled rocks glass and stir.

CENTURY

A timeless mix

2 ounces gin

1 ounce grapefruit juice

½ ounce Chambord

½ ounce triple sec

Combine ingredients in mixing glass. Add ice, shake, and strain into glass.

CHANDELIER

Icy scintillation

2 ounces gin
½ ounce dry vermouth
½ ounce Pernod
2 dashes orange bitters
Crushed ice

Combine ingredients in mixing glass. Add ice, stir to chill, and strain into glass filled with crushed ice.

THE CLOISTERS

Inspired by northern Manhattan's garden of delights

1½ ounces gin
½ ounce sweet vermouth
1 ounce Campari
1 teaspoon Bénédictine
1 teaspoon Pernod
2 dashes bitters of choice
Orange twist for garnish

Combine liquid ingredients in mixing glass. Add ice and stir to chill. Strain into glass and garnish.

COMMEDIA DELL'ARTE

An improvisational triumph

2 ounces gin
1 ounce Galliano
½ ounce sambuca negra

Combine ingredients in mixing glass. Add ice, stir to chill, and strain into glass.

THE CRATER

Puts you over the moon

2 ounces gin
1 ounce dark crème de cacao
½ ounce Chambord
½ ounce heavy cream

Combine ingredients in mixing glass. Add ice, shake, and strain into glass.

CRUSADER

Spread the word

2 ounces gin
1 ounce white crème de cacao
1 ounce green Chartreuse

Combine ingredients in mixing glass. Add ice, stir to chill, and pour with ice into glass.

DAMSEL

A beauty of British, Russian, and French descent

1 ounce Tanqueray gin
1 ounce vodka
1 ounce Cointreau
1 ounce orange juice
1 ounce cranberry juice
Orange twist for garnish

Combine liquid ingredients in mixing glass. Add ice and shake. Pour with ice into glass and garnish.

DEAR VERE

Favorite of a citizen of the world

2 ounces gin
½ ounce dry vermouth
1 teaspoon blue curaçao
2 dashes Angostura bitters

Combine ingredients in mixing glass. Add ice, stir to chill, and strain into glass.

DELANCEY

An olivey toast to the historic street on New York City's Lower East Side

2 ounces gin
1 ounce Absolut Peppar
1 ounce olive brine
3 olives for garnish

Combine liquid ingredients in mixing glass. Add ice and stir to chill. Strain into glass and garnish.

DELMONICO

A brandy-laced cocktail from America's first true restaurant, which opened in Manhattan in 1827 and went out of business for good during Prohibition

1½ ounces gin
½ ounce brandy
½ ounce sweet vermouth
2 dashes orange bitters

Combine ingredients in mixing glass. Add ice, stir to chill, and strain into glass.

DREAMY

For lovers of white chocolate

1 ounce gin
1 ounce vodka
1 ounce Godiva white chocolate liqueur
1 ounce white crème de cacao

Combine ingredients in mixing glass. Add ice, stir to chill, and pour with ice into glass.

EAST END AVENUE

Named for the upper-crusty Manhattan address

Crushed ice
1½ ounces gin
½ ounce dry sherry
1 ounce Lillet Blanc
Lemon twist for garnish

Fill glass with crushed ice and add the gin, sherry, and liqueur. Stir and garnish.

EDGAR'S BRITISH PEPPERMINT

The drink of a captain of industry with a historic link to The Four Seasons

1 tablespoon chopped peppermint leaves
1 tablespoon diced roasted red bell pepper
½ ounce fresh lime juice
1 teaspoon superfine sugar
3 ounces Hendrick's gin

Muddle peppermint, bell pepper, juice, and sugar in bottom of mixing glass. Add ice and gin. Shake and strain into glass.

EQUESTRIAN

Gin and tonic for the horsey set
2 ounces Bombay gin
2 ounces tonic water
1 dash Grand Marnier
2 dashes bitters of choice
Lime wedge for garnish

Pour liquid ingredients into ice-filled rocks glass. Stir and garnish.

FAIRY TALE

As enchanting as it sounds
Crushed ice
2 ounces gin
½ ounce apricot brandy
½ ounce peach schnapps
½ ounce Lillet Rouge
Orange twist for garnish

Fill glass with crushed ice and add liquid ingredients. Stir and garnish.

FAUST

Room temp, yet hot as the devil
3 ounces gin
2 or 3 dashes Tabasco
Chili pepper for garnish

Pour gin into martini glass and add Tabasco. Stir and garnish.

FLORENTINE

Best appreciated in a piazza in Florence. Cynar is a unique artichoke-based aperitif from Italy.
1½ ounces gin
1 ounce Campari
½ ounce grapefruit juice
½ ounce Cynar

Pour ingredients into ice-filled rocks glass and stir.

FRINGE BENEFITS

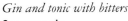

Guarantees a big tip for the bartender
1 ounce Tanqueray No. Ten gin
1 ounce Chambord
1 ounce orange juice
1 ounce cranberry juice

Combine ingredients in mixing glass. Add ice, shake, and strain into a glass.

GENTLE PINK

Gin and tonic with bitters
2 ounces gin
4 ounces tonic water
3 dashes Angostura bitters
Lemon twist for garnish

Pour liquid ingredients into ice-filled highball glass. Stir and garnish.

GIN AND TONIC

A classic among classics
2 ounces Gordon's gin
4 ounces tonic water
Lime wedge for garnish

Pour gin and tonic into ice-filled highball glass. Stir and garnish.

GIN DAISY

In cocktail lingo, "daisy" means slightly sour
3 ounces gin
1½ ounces fresh sour mix
3 dashes grenadine
Orange slice for garnish
Maraschino cherry for garnish

Combine liquid ingredients in mixing glass. Add ice and shake. Pour with ice into glass and garnish.

GIN FIZZER

Bubbly and tart

2½ ounces gin
1 ounce sour mix
4 ounces club soda

Combine gin and sour mix in mixing glass. Add ice and shake. Strain into glass and top with club soda.

GINGERLY

Gin and ginger

3 ounces gin
5 ounces ginger ale
Lemon wedge for garnish

Pour gin and ginger ale into ice-filled highball glass. Stir and garnish.

GIN GIBSON

The famous onion pickler

3 ounces gin
½ ounce dry vermouth
3 cocktail onions for garnish

Combine gin and vermouth in mixing glass. Add ice and stir to chill. Strain into glass and garnish.

GIN GIMLET

A prized antique

3 ounces gin
½ ounce Rose's lime juice
Lemon wedge for garnish

Combine gin and juice in mixing glass. Add ice and stir to chill. Strain into glass and garnish.

GIN MADRAS

Patterned for pleasure

3 ounces Bombay gin
2 ounces orange juice
2 ounces cranberry juice

Pour ingredients into ice-filled highball glass and stir.

GIN PRESBYTERIAN

Respectably light on the gin

2 ounces gin
3 ounces club soda
3 ounces ginger ale

Pour ingredients into ice-filled highball glass and stir.

GIN SOUR

A bracing draft

3 ounces gin
1 ounce fresh sour mix
Orange slice for garnish
Maraschino cherry for garnish

Combine gin and sour mix in mixing glass. Stir to chill, strain with ice into glass, and garnish.

GOLDEN DROP

With hints of dry vermouth and Scotch, the latter added with a dropper (page 15)

3½ ounces Tanqueray No. Ten gin
1 teaspoon dry vermouth
3 drops Scotch
Lemon peel spiral for garnish

Combine liquid ingredients in mixing glass. Add ice and stir to chill. Strain into glass and garnish.

The Gin Martini

Let us consider the gin martini versus the vodka martini. The former is the fabled original drink—but in the 1980s, vodka began to replace gin as the spirit of choice because it was found by many to be more drinkable. Martini die-hards dismiss the vodka martini as the social climber of the cocktail world, but drinkers across the nation have spoken—so it's your call, ladies and gents.

The Method The martinis on this page are prepared by the same method; only the garnishes differ. Combine liquid ingredients in a mixing glass. Add ice and shake. Strain into a chilled martini glass and garnish.

CHATEAU MARTINI

With a touch of raspberry

3 ounces gin
1 dash dry vermouth
½ ounce Chambord
Orange twist for garnish

DIRTY GIN MARTINI

Extra olive flavor

3 ounces gin
1 dash dry vermouth
½ ounce olive brine
3 stuffed olives for garnish

GIN MARTINI

The classic

3½ ounces Tanqueray No. Ten gin
1 teaspoon Cinzano Bianco dry
   vermouth
Stuffed olive or lemon twist for garnish

NOHO MARTINI

A lighter variation

2 ounces gin
1 teaspoon dry vermouth
2 ounces pineapple juice
½ ounce Chambord
Small pineapple chunk for garnish

PETER T.'S MARTINI

With a red vermouth offering "something different." Herby, bittersweet Punt è Mes has a hint of orange and is slightly syrupy.

3 ounces gin
1 dash dry vermouth
½ ounce Punt è Mes
Orange twist for garnish

SOHO MARTINI

A little more complex

2½ ounces gin
1 dash dry vermouth
½ ounce Chambord
1 ounce sour mix
1 or 2 raspberries for garnish

GRAND TOUR

A photogenic equal-parts cocktail
2 ounces gin
2 ounces Campari
2 ounces orange juice
Orange twist for garnish

Pour ingredients into ice-filled highball glass, stir, and garnish.

THE GREENIE

For the environmentalist in you
2 ounces Juniper Green organic gin
1 ounce green crème de menthe
2 dashes Fee Brothers mint bitters
Sprig of organic mint for garnish

Combine ingredients in mixing glass. Add ice and shake. Strain into glass and garnish.

GREEN DEVIL

Minty and tart
2 ounces gin
1 ounce green crème de menthe
1 ounce Rose's lime juice
Club soda
Lime slice for garnish

Combine gin, liqueur, and juice in mixing glass. Add ice and shake. Pour with ice into glass, top with club soda to taste, and garnish.

GREEN RIVER

"Green" as in Chartreuse. This herby, spicy liqueur was created by Carthusian monks in sixteenth-century France.
2½ ounces gin
½ ounce green Chartreuse
½ ounce yellow Chartreuse

Combine ingredients in mixing glass. Add ice, stir to chill, and strain into glass.

HARLEM NIGHTS

Jazz up your palate
2 ounces gin
1 ounce pineapple juice
½ ounce maraschino liqueur
Orange twist for garnish

Combine liquid ingredients in mixing glass. Add ice and shake. Strain into glass and garnish.

HAUNTED BRIDE

Named for a Grill Room bar patron who was second-guessing her engagement
1½ ounces gin
1 ounce dry vermouth
½ ounce Bénédictine
1 teaspoon Pernod
2 dashes bitters of choice

Combine ingredients in mixing glass. Add ice, stir to chill, and strain into glass.

HOMER'S CHOICE	*Was ouzo the Greek poet's muse?*
	2½ ounces gin
	1 ounce ouzo

Combine ingredients in mixing glass. Add ice, stir to chill, and strain into glass.

KATE'S FAVE	*The choice of a died-in-the-wool Anglophile*
	2 ounces Boodles gin
	1 ounce orange liqueur
	1 ounce Rose's lime juice

Pour ingredients into ice-filled rocks glass and stir.

KATHY'S KICK	*Yellow and herby*
	2 ounces gin
	1 ounce yellow Chartreuse
	Lemon twist for garnish

Combine gin and liqueur in mixing glass. Add ice and stir to chill. Strain into glass and garnish.

LATIN TWIST	*Gin with tequila and rum!*
	1 ounce gin
	1 ounce tequila
	1 ounce rum
	1 ounce Cointreau
	½ ounce blue curaçao
	Orange twist for garnish

Pour liquid ingredients into ice-filled highball glass, stir, and garnish.

THE MONK	*A drink on which to meditate*
	2 ounces gin
	1 ounce Bénédictine
	2 ounces orange juice

Pour ingredients into ice-filled rocks glass and stir.

NAPOLÉON	*Très français*
	3 ounces gin
	½ ounce Dubonnet Rouge
	½ ounce Grand Marnier

Combine ingredients in mixing glass. Add ice, stir to chill, and strain into glass.

NATURE GIRL	*Hangs out in the orange grove*
	2 ounces gin
	1 ounce triple sec
	1 teaspoon blue curaçao
	1 dash orange bitters

Combine ingredients in mixing glass. Add ice, stir to chill, and strain into glass.

NEGRONI	*The Campari classic, served straight up or on the rocks*
	2 ounces gin
	1½ ounces Campari
	½ ounce sweet vermouth
	Orange twist for garnish

Combine liquid ingredients in mixing glass. Add ice and stir to chill. Strain into martini glass or pour with ice into rocks glass and garnish.

ORANGE BLOSSOM

Grandmother of the well-loved Screwdriver

2 ounces Gordon's gin
2 ounces orange juice
1 teaspoon superfine sugar
Orange peel spiral for garnish

Combine gin, juice, and sugar in mixing glass. Add ice and shake. Strain into glass and garnish.

PARIS OPERA

A taste of the Right Bank

2 ounces gin
1 ounce Dubonnet Rouge
3 dashes orange bitters
Orange twist for garnish

Combine liquid ingredients in mixing glass. Add ice and stir to chill. Strain into glass and garnish.

THE PICADILLY

Close your eyes and think of England

1 ounce gin
1 ounce Harvey's Bristol Cream sherry
2 dashes Angostura bitters

Combine ingredients in mixing glass. Add ice, shake, and strain into glass.

PINK LADY

This vintage cocktail dates from the Art Deco era

2 ounces gin
1 ounce white crème de cacao
1 teaspoon grenadine
½ ounce heavy cream

Combine ingredients in mixing glass. Add ice, shake, and strain into glass.

PINK PANTHER

Topped with a bit of bubbly

2 ounces gin
1 ounce Campari
½ ounce grapefruit juice
½ ounce Champagne

Combine gin, Campari, and juice in mixing glass. Add ice and shake. Strain into glass and top with Champagne.

PINK PUSSYCAT

Crème de noyaux is an almondy pink liqueur made from fruit pits.

2 ounces gin
1 ounce crème de noyaux
3 ounces pineapple juice

Combine ingredients in mixing glass. Add ice and stir to chill. Pour with ice into rocks glass or strain into martini glass.

PINK ROSE

Served in a sugar-rimmed glass

1 teaspoon powdered sugar
1 lime wedge
2 ounces gin
1 ounce apricot brandy
1 ounce lime juice

Spread powdered sugar on a saucer; moisten rim of martini glass with lime wedge and dip into sugar. Combine gin, brandy, and juice in mixing glass. Add ice, stir to chill, and carefully strain into glass.

PINK SQUIRREL

A bit nutty

2 ounces gin

1 ounce crème de noyaux

1 teaspoon grenadine

1 ounce light cream

Combine ingredients in mixing glass. Add ice, shake, and strain into glass.

THE POOLSIDE

Gin teams with two liqueurs in this Pool Room favorite.

2 ounces gin

½ ounce amaretto

½ teaspoon blue curaçao

Orange twist for garnish

Pour liquid ingredients into ice-filled rocks glass, stir, and garnish.

QUEEN MUM

British to the core

2 ounces Boodles gin

3 ounces Pimm's No. 1

1 ounce orange juice

2 ounces ginger ale

Maraschino cherry for garnish

Pour gin, Pimm's, and juice into ice-filled highball glass. Top with ginger ale and garnish.

ROOT BEER HIGHBALL

The soft drink all dressed up

2 ounces gin

1 ounce fresh sour mix

1 teaspoon Galliano

3 ounces root beer

Orange twist for garnish

Combine gin, sour mix, and Galliano in mixing glass. Add ice, shake, and pour with ice into glass. Top with root beer, stir, and garnish.

SERAPHIM

RUBY ROYALE

Cherry red

2 ounces Barton London Extra Dry gin

½ ounce cherry puree

1 teaspoon sweet vermouth

Combine ingredients in mixing glass. Add ice, stir to chill, and strain into glass.

SERAPHIM

Hear the angels sing.

2 ounces gin

1 ounce dry vermouth

1 ounce crème de cassis

Lemon twist for garnish

Pour liquid ingredients into ice-filled rocks glass. Stir and garnish.

SEXY MAIDEN

The head-turner with the citrusy perfume

2½ ounces gin

1 ounce Cointreau

1 teaspoon blue curaçao

1 ounce fresh sour mix

1 ounce grapefruit juice

Combine ingredients in mixing glass. Add ice, shake, and strain into glass.

SINGAPORE SLING

Created in the early 1900s at the storied Raffles Hotel in Singapore

2½ ounces gin
½ ounce cherry brandy
1 ounce fresh sour mix
5 ounces club soda
Maraschino cherry for garnish
Orange peel spiral for garnish

Combine gin, brandy, and sour mix in mixing glass. Add ice and shake. Pour with ice into glass and top with club soda. Stir and garnish.

SOUTHSIDE COCKTAIL

Minty vintage cocktail from the Windy City

3 mint leaves
1 teaspoon superfine sugar
2 ounces gin
1½ ounces lemon juice
Mint sprig for garnish

Muddle mint leaves and sugar in bottom of mixing glass. Add gin and juice. Add ice and stir to chill. Strain into glass and garnish.

TOM COLLINS

One for the ages

2 ounces gin
1 ounce fresh sour mix
3 ounces club soda
Maraschino cherry for garnish
Orange slice for garnish

Combine gin and sour mix in mixing glass. Add ice and shake. Strain into ice-filled glass and top with club soda. Stir and garnish.

TRITON

Three liqueurs fly you to the moon: Neptune's.

2 ounces gin
1 ounce triple sec
1 ounce white crème de cacao
½ teaspoon blue curaçao

Combine ingredients in mixing glass. Add ice, stir to chill, and strain into glass.

How The Four Seasons Got Its Name

It was a book of haiku meditations on time and change that gave Joseph H. Baum the idea to name the new restaurant in the Seagram Building "The Four Seasons." A visionary young hotelier who joined Riker's Restaurant Associates (RA) in 1952, Joe Baum was among those charged with creating what would become a shrine to haute cuisine. The poetry struck a chord, he recalls, because "everything we wanted to do with the restaurant represented change. What is more foodlike and sophisticated than the seasons and what they bring to New York? . . . The theatrical season; the social season, the fall, spring, summer . . . The happy idea of the seasons lets us create an enduring style instead of a contemporary fashion."

RA asked personnel in all of their departments to offer ideas for names based on the seasons, reaping such contenders as "The Orbit of The Four Seasons," "The Symphony of The Four Seasons," "C'est la [sic] Saisons," and "Season-o-Rama" (the last two no doubt quickly discarded). The name eventually chosen was shorn of excess, in perfect keeping with the simplicity and elegance of the 24,000-square-foot space in architect Mies van der Rohe's celebrated building.

VODKA

Traditionally distilled from grains, potatoes, or sugar-beet molasses (and nowadays almost any plant matter under the sun), **clear vodka** has eclipsed gin in cocktail after cocktail. Vodka's purity—no aroma, little taste—makes it the perfect foil for liqueurs and other tools of the bartender's trade.

It is believed that vodka originated in Russia in the fourteenth century and quickly spread to the Ukraine, Poland, Lithuania, Poland, and Scandinavia. **Flavored vodkas** eventually emerged with the simple addition of medicinal herbs or taste-enhancing fruits and spices—a far cry from some of the out-there vodka flavorings seen today (see A Word from the Bartenders, page 89).

ABRA CADABRA

Works its magic sip by sip

2 ounces vodka
½ ounce peach schnapps
½ ounce apricot brandy
1 ounce pineapple juice

Combine ingredients in mixing glass. Add ice, stir to chill, and strain into glass.

THE ALCHEMIST

Goes for the gold

2 ounces vodka
1 ounce Goldschläger
1 ounce sambuca
Club soda

Combine vodka and liqueurs in mixing glass. Add ice and shake. Pour with ice into glass and top with club soda to taste.

AMBROSIA

Fruity and rich

2 ounces vodka
1 ounce apricot schnapps
1 ounce peach nectar
½ ounce light cream

Combine ingredients in mixing glass. Add ice, shake, and strain into glass.

ANNA KARENINA

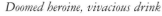

Doomed heroine, vivacious drink

2 ounces vodka
2 ounces cranberry juice
4 ounces club soda
Lime wedge for garnish

Pour vodka and juice into ice-filled highball glass. Top with club soda and garnish.

APPLE MARTINI

With sour apple schnapps

2 ounces vodka
1½ ounces DeKuyper Pucker sour apple schnapps
½ ounce lemon juice
Apple slice for garnish

Combine liquid ingredients in mixing glass. Add ice and stir to chill. Strain into glass and garnish.

BANANARAMA

Mellow yellow

2 ounces vodka
1 ounce crème de banane
½ ounce white crème de cacao
½ ounce light cream
2 drops yellow food coloring

Combine ingredients in mixing glass. Add ice, shake, and strain into glass.

BANANA SPLIT

Roll up your sleeves and dig in.

1 ounce vodka
1 ounce crème de banane
1 ounce Godiva white chocolate liqueur
½ ounce strawberry syrup
½ ounce heavy cream
Strawberry for garnish

Combine liquid ingredients in mixing glass. Add ice and shake. Strain into glass and garnish.

BIRTH OF VENUS

Inspired by the sensual Botticelli painting

2 ounces vodka

1 ounce Cointreau

1 teaspoon blue curaçao

1 ounce peach juice

1 ounce Champagne

Combine vodka, liqueurs, and juice in mixing glass. Add ice and stir to chill. Strain into glass, top with Champagne, and stir.

BLACK RUSSIAN

A coffee-flavored White Russian (page 104)

2 ounces Smirnoff vodka

1 ounce coffee liqueur

1 dash lemon juice

Pour vodka and liqueur into ice-filled rocks glass. Add dash of lemon juice and stir.

BLOODY BULLSHOT

Take one for a hangover and call us in the morning.

2 ounces vodka

2 ounces beef broth

1 ounce tomato juice

1 teaspoon Worcestershire sauce

¼ teaspoon lemon juice

3 dashes Tabasco

Combine ingredients in mixing glass. Add ice, shake, and pour with ice into glass.

BLOODY MARY

Queen of the brunch

2 ounces vodka

4 ounces tomato juice

1 tablespoon Worcestershire sauce

1 dash Tabasco

Lime slice for garnish

Pour liquid ingredients into ice-filled rocks glass. Stir and garnish.

BLUE BANANA

Buzzy and beautiful

2 ounces vodka

1 ounce crème de banane

1 ounce white crème de cacao

½ teaspoon blue curaçao

Crushed ice

Combine liquid ingredients in mixing glass. Add ice, shake, and strain into glass filled with crushed ice.

BLUEBERRY TART

Stoli brain food?

1½ ounces Stolichnaya Blueberi

1 ounce cranberry juice

½ ounce lemon juice

½ ounce simple syrup (page 27)

Club soda

2 or 3 fresh blueberries for garnish

Combine vodka, juices, and syrup in mixing glass. Add ice and shake. Pour with ice into glass, top with club soda to taste, and garnish.

BLUEBIRD

Simple and eye-pleasing

3 ounces vodka
1 ounce blue curaçao
Orange peel spiral for garnish

Combine vodka and liqueur in mixing glass. Add ice and stir to chill. Strain into glass and garnish.

BLUE INCA

Flavored with tequila and rum

2 ounces vodka
1 ounce silver tequila
1 ounce light rum
1 ounce blue curaçao

Combine ingredients in mixing glass. Add ice, stir to chill, and strain into glass.

THE BLUE PERIOD

Bartender John's salute to Picasso

2 ounces Ketel One vodka
1 ounce Southern Comfort
½ ounce Pernod
½ ounce blue curaçao
½ ounce Chambord

Combine ingredients in mixing glass. Add ice, stir to chill, and strain into glass.

BRIGHT STAR

Inspired by the late legends who crossed The Four Seasons threshold, from Marilyn Monroe to Princess Diana

1½ ounces vodka
½ ounce pineapple juice
½ ounce Southern Comfort
½ ounce Chambord
½ ounce blue curaçao

Combine ingredients in mixing glass. Add ice, stir to chill, and strain into glass.

BULLSHOT

Beefed-up and muy picante

2 ounces vodka
2 ounces beef broth
1 teaspoon Worcestershire sauce
¼ teaspoon lemon juice
3 dashes Tabasco
Lime slice for garnish

Combine liquid ingredients in mixing glass. Add ice and shake. Pour with ice into glass and garnish.

BUTTERFLY WING

Graceful and gorgeous

1 ounce Belvedere vodka
1 ounce Cointreau
½ ounce peach schnapps
1 tablespoon orange sorbet
1 tablespoon pineapple sorbet
Crushed ice
Orange twist for garnish

Combine vodka, liqueurs, and sorbets in mixing glass. Shake, pour into glass filled with crushed ice, and garnish.

BUTTERFLY
WING

CANDY CANE

Christmas cheer

1 ounce vodka
1 ounce peppermint schnapps
½ ounce white crème de menthe
½ ounce white crème de cacao

Combine ingredients in mixing glass. Add ice, stir to chill, and strain into glass.

CAPE COD

One of the classics, originally called the Cape Codder

2 ounces vodka
3 ounces cranberry juice

Pour vodka and juice into ice-filled rocks glass and stir.

CAPRI

As seductive as the isle

1 ounce vodka
2 ounces Campari
1 ounce grapefruit juice
1 ounce apricot brandy
3 ounces club soda

Combine vodka, Campari, juice, and brandy in mixing glass. Add ice and shake. Pour with ice into glass, top with club soda, and stir.

CATHERINE THE GREAT

Russian Empress smitten by France and Italy. The latter is home to the aperitif Campari, named for the Milanese restaurateur who created it.

2 ounces vodka
2 ounces Campari
½ ounce Pernod
3 ounces club soda

Pour vodka, Campari, and Pernod into ice-filled highball glass and stir. Top with club soda and stir.

CELLO'S DREAM

Heady confection named for bartender John's Yorkshire terrier

1 ounce vodka
1 ounce white crème de cacao
1 ounce Godiva white chocolate liqueur
½ ounce Chambord
½ ounce light cream

Combine ingredients in mixing glass. Add ice, shake, and strain into glass.

CHELSEA

In honor of Manhattan's artiest nabe
2 ounces vodka
1 ounce Bols apricot brandy
1 ounce peach juice
4 ounces club soda

Pour vodka, brandy, and juice into ice-filled highball glass. Top with club soda and stir.

CHERRY PIE

How do you spell yum*?*
2 ounces vodka
1 ounce brandy
1 ounce cherry brandy

Combine ingredients in mixing glass. Add ice, stir to chill, and pour with ice into glass.

CHINATOWN

Next door to Manhattan's Little Italy
2 ounces vodka
1 ounce sambuca
1 ounce fresh peach juice
4 ounces club soda
Lychee for garnish

Pour vodka, sambuca, and juice into ice-filled highball glass. Top with club soda and garnish.

CÎROC ROCKS

With Cîroc grape vodka
3 ounces Cîroc vodka
½ ounce Grand Marnier
½ ounce fresh sour mix
1 splash Champagne
3 red grapes for garnish

Combine vodka, liqueur, and sour mix in mixing glass. Add ice, shake, and strain into glass. Top with Champagne and garnish.

COOPER UNION

A big toast to New York City's tuition-free institution of higher learning
2 ounces vodka
1 ounce Southern Comfort
½ ounce Cointreau
½ ounce lemon juice

Combine ingredients in mixing glass. Add ice, stir to chill, and strain into glass.

COSMOPOLITAN

A lovable blast from the Nineties
2 ounces vodka
1 ounce Cointreau
½ ounce cranberry juice
½ ounce fresh sour mix
Lemon twist for garnish

Combine liquid ingredients in mixing glass. Add ice and shake. Strain into glass and garnish.

CREAMSICLE

Built for grown-ups
2 ounces vodka
1 ounce triple sec
1 ounce orange juice
1 ounce heavy cream

Combine ingredients in mixing glass. Add ice, shake, and strain into glass.

CREAMY DREAM

Visions of orange and black currant
2 ounces vodka
1 ounce Grand Marnier
½ ounce crème de cassis
½ ounce light cream

Combine ingredients in mixing glass. Add ice, shake, and strain into glass.

DELILAH

As tempting as its biblical namesake
2 ounces Stolichnaya Ohranj
1 ounce Cointreau
1 ounce white crème de cacao
½ teaspoon grenadine

Combine ingredients in mixing glass. Add ice, stir to chill, and strain into glass.

DIRTY MARY

In cocktail lingo, "dirty" usually describes a drink made with olive brine.
2½ ounces vodka
3 ounces tomato juice
½ ounce olive brine
4 dashes Worcestershire sauce
3 dashes Tabasco
3 olives for garnish

Pour liquid ingredients into ice-filled highball glass, stir, and garnish.

DITZY BLONDE

Adorable as they come
2 ounces vodka
1 ounce Johnnie Walker Gold Label
1 ounce Drambuie

Combine ingredients in mixing glass. Add ice, stir to chill, and strain into glass.

DRY SHERRY MARTINI

An interesting twist
2 ounces vodka
½ ounce dry vermouth
½ ounce dry sherry
Lemon twist for garnish

Combine liquid ingredients in mixing glass. Add ice and shake. Strain into glass and garnish.

FLIGHT OF THE BUMBLEBEE

With a bit of a zzzsting
1 teaspoon honey
2 ounces strong ginger tea, warm
1 ounce vodka
1 ounce Harvey's Bristol Cream sherry
½ ounce Cointreau

Dissolve honey in warm tea. When tea is cool, combine with other ingredients in mixing glass. Add ice, shake, and strain into glass.

FLIRTINI

Hardly relegated to singles night
1½ ounces vodka
½ ounce triple sec
½ ounce cranberry juice
½ ounce lemon juice
½ teaspoon superfine sugar
1 ounce Champagne
Orange twist for garnish

Combine vodka, liqueur, juices, and sugar in mixing glass. Add ice and shake. Strain into glass and top with Champagne. Stir and garnish.

FRENCH MARTINI

C'est si bon!

2 ounces vodka
1 ounce Chambord
1½ ounces pineapple juice

Combine ingredients in mixing glass. Add ice, stir to chill, and strain into glass.

FRUIT SALAD

With all kinds of goodies

1½ ounces vodka
1 ounce Southern Comfort
½ ounce Galliano
½ ounce apricot puree
½ ounce cranberry juice
Maraschino cherry for garnish

Combine liquid ingredients in mixing glass. Add ice and stir to chill. Strain into glass and garnish.

THE GENIE

Your wish for cassis come true

2 ounces vodka
1 ounce dry vermouth
1 ounce crème de cassis
Lemon twist for garnish

Pour liquid ingredients into ice-filled rocks glass. Stir and garnish.

GODCHILD

A creamy delight

1 ounce vodka
1 ounce amaretto
1 ounce heavy cream

Combine ingredients in mixing glass. Add ice, shake, and strain into glass.

THE GENIE

GODMOTHER

Gentler than the Godfather

2 ounces Tito's Handmade vodka
2 ounces amaretto

Pour vodka and liqueur into ice-filled rocks glass and stir.

GOLDEN GONDOLA

Venice, vicariously

2 ounces vodka
½ ounce Strega
2 teaspoons crème de banane
1 ounce orange juice

Combine ingredients in mixing glass. Add ice, shake, and pour with ice into glass.

GREG'S CHOCOLATE MARTINI

Use the best chocolate syrup you can find.

2½ ounces vodka
½ ounce Van Gogh chocolate liqueur
½ ounce chocolate syrup
Chocolate shavings for garnish

Combine liquid ingredients in mixing glass. Add ice and shake. Strain into glass and garnish.

GREYHOUND

No-salt grandfather of the Salty Dog (page 98)

2 ounces vodka
3 ounces grapefruit juice

Pour vodka and juice into ice-filled rocks glass and stir.

HARVEY WALLBANGER

There's life in the old boy yet.

2 ounces vodka
3 ounces orange juice
1 ounce Galliano

Pour vodka and juice into ice-filled rocks glass, stir, and float liqueur on top.

HEADLESS HORSEMAN

Drink of choice up in Sleepy Hollow?

2 ounces vodka
1 dash Fee Brothers lemon bitters
Ginger ale

Combine vodka and bitters in an ice-filled highball glass. Top with ginger ale to taste and stir.

HIGH NOTE

Hits the high C

3 ounces vodka
1 splash orange juice
1 splash cranberry juice
Orange wedge for garnish

Pour liquid ingredients into rocks glass filled with ice. Stir and garnish.

ICE AGE

Très cool

2 ounces vodka
1 ounce white crème de menthe
1 ounce Jägermeister
Crushed ice

Combine liquid ingredients in mixing glass. Add ice, stir to chill, and strain into glass filled with crushed ice.

ICY DOG

A variation on the Greyhound

2 ounces vodka
1 ounce grapefruit juice
1 ounce peach schnapps
Crushed ice

Combine liquid ingredients in mixing glass. Add ice, stir to chill, and strain into glass filled with crushed ice.

A WORD FROM THE BARTENDERS

No law dictates which glass you use for a cocktail, of course. Yes, it's more practical to serve iced drinks in roomy highball or rocks glasses, but only the worst stickler will insist that a sour be served in a sour glass or liqueur in tailor-made liqueur glasses.

At The Four Seasons, women are frequently served drinks in stem glasses, no matter the cocktail. This makes for a more artistic presentation, and—in our experience, at least—women are more likely than even the most meticulous gentleman to keep a stem glass upright and upspilt.

THE IMPRESARIO

An intriguing production
1 ounce vodka
1 ounce Cynar
1 ounce Campari
1 ounce orange juice
3 ounces club soda

Combine vodka, Cynar, Campari, and juice in mixing glass. Add ice and shake. Pour with ice into glass, top with soda, and stir.

ISLAND DELIGHT

Slip on your flip-flops and enjoy.
2 ounces Skyy Vanilla vodka
1 ounce light rum
1 ounce triple sec
3 ounces mango juice
½ teaspoon grenadine
Orange slice for garnish

Pour liquid ingredients into ice-filled highball glass. Stir and garnish.

ITALIAN LEMONADE

Lemony through and through
2 ounces lemon-flavored vodka
1 ounce limoncello
2 ounces fresh lemon juice
½ teaspoon superfine sugar
Club soda
Lemon peel spiral for garnish

Combine vodka, liqueur, juice, and sugar in mixing glass. Add ice, stir to chill, and pour with ice into glass. Top with club soda to taste and garnish. Serve with a straw.

JUBILEE

Gaiety in a glass
2 ounces vodka
½ ounce Cointreau
1 ounce fresh sour mix
2 mint leaves, crushed
Mint sprig for garnish

Combine vodka, liqueur, sour mix, and mint leaves in mixing glass. Add ice and shake. Strain into glass and garnish.

KARAMAZOV

A hats-off to Dostoyevsky's immortal Russian brothers
3 ounces Smirnoff vodka
1 ounce sambuca
4 ounces club soda

Pour vodka and liqueur into ice-filled highball glass. Top with club soda and stir.

LA GIOCONDA

A Mona Lisa of a drink
1 ounce vodka
1 ounce Campari
1 ounce peach schnapps
1½ ounces Champagne
Orange twist for garnish

Combine vodka, Campari, and schnapps in mixing glass. Add ice, stir to chill, and strain into glass. Top with Champagne and garnish.

THE LATINO

A spirited triple treat of vodka, tequila, and rum

1 ounce vodka
1 ounce tequila
1 ounce rum
4 ounces club soda
Lime wedge for garnish

Pour vodka, tequila, and rum into ice-filled highball glass. Top with club soda and garnish.

THE LIMEY

Not quite as English as it sounds

2 ounces vodka
1 ounce Grand Marnier
2 ounces Rose's lime juice
3 ounces club soda
Lime wedge for garnish

Pour vodka, liqueur, and juice into ice-filled highball glass. Top with club soda and garnish.

LINCOLN CENTER

Operatic

1 ounce Grey Goose vodka
1 ounce Campari
1 ounce peach juice
½ ounce peach schnapps
1 teaspoon Pernod

Pour ingredients into ice-filled rocks glass and stir.

MELON BALL

Vodka with honeydew and more

2 ounces vodka
1 ounce Midori
1 ounce orange juice
1 ounce cranberry juice

Pour ingredients into ice-filled rocks glass and stir.

MERRY BERRY

The berry? Raspberry.

2 ounces Stolichnaya Razberi
1 ounce Chambord
½ ounce sloe gin
½ ounce lemon juice

Combine ingredients in mixing glass. Add ice, stir to chill, and strain into glass.

METROPOLITAN

Seriously sophisticated

1½ ounces Absolut Kurant
1 ounce Cointreau
½ ounce Chambord
1 ounce fresh sour mix
1 ounce cranberry juice
Lemon peel spiral for garnish

Combine liquid ingredients in mixing glass. Add ice and shake. Strain into glass and garnish.

MOSCOW MULE

The 1940s cocktail that popularized vodka in North America

2 ounces vodka
Juice of half a lime
Ginger beer
Lime wedge for garnish

Pour liquid ingredients into ice-filled rocks glass and garnish.

MOUNT ETNA	*A semi-fiery eruption*

2 ounces Absolut Peppar
1 ounce tomato juice
1 ounce sambuca
2 dashes Tabasco

Combine ingredients in mixing glass. Add ice, stir to chill, and strain into glass.

MUDSLIDE *Dangerously delicious*

1 ounce vodka
1 ounce Baileys Irish Cream
1 ounce dark crème de cacao

Combine vodka and Baileys in mixing glass. Add ice, stir to chill, and strain into glass. Tilt the glass slightly and rotate it while slowly drizzling crème de cacao down the sides.

NO-FRILLS
VODKA MARTINI

NEON LIGHT *"Are we all lit?"* (Auntie Mame)

1½ ounces vodka
½ ounce yellow Chartreuse
2 teaspoons Galliano
2 teaspoons blue curaçao
½ teaspoon lemon juice
Maraschino cherry for garnish

Combine liquid ingredients in mixing glass. Add ice and stir to chill. Strain into glass and garnish.

NO-FRILLS VODKA MARTINI *For those who like it simple*

3 ounces vodka
1 teaspoon dry vermouth
Lemon twist or 3 olives for garnish

Combine vodka and vermouth in mixing glass. Add ice and stir to chill. Strain into glass and garnish.

NUTS 'N' BERRIES *A favorite in California*

2 ounces vodka
1 ounce Frangelico
½ ounce Chambord
½ ounce dark crème de cacao
½ ounce light cream

Combine ingredients in mixing glass. Add ice, shake, and strain into glass.

OPHELIA *Drives you mad with delight*

2 ounces Stolichnaya Ohranj
1 ounce white crème de cacao
4 ounces club soda
Orange twist for garnish

Pour vodka and liqueur into ice-filled highball glass. Top with club soda and garnish.

The Fresher Martini

Fresh is back, and these vodka martinis aren't above following trends. All are made with muddled fruit, and our tasty sour mix (page 28) shows the vermouth who's boss. Note: If you find any of the drinks too tart for your taste, add a little simple syrup (page 27) to the mix.

BLACK CHERRY MARTINI

Or go with fresh red cherries, if you like

4 or 5 black cherries, pitted
½ ounce fresh sour mix
3 ounces vodka
1 splash dry vermouth
Black cherry with stem for garnish

Muddle cherries and sour mix in bottom of mixing glass. Add ice and spirits. Shake, strain into glass, and garnish.

LYCHEE MARTINI

Featuring the fragrant fruit from Asia

1 lychee (canned or fresh), diced
½ ounce fresh sour mix
3 ounces vodka
1 splash dry vermouth
Half a lychee for garnish

Muddle lychee and sour mix in bottom of mixing glass. Add ice and spirits. Shake, strain into glass, and garnish.

MANGO MARTINI

In India the mango symbolizes love

1 cube (1½ inches) mango pulp, diced
½ ounce fresh sour mix
3 ounces vodka
1 splash dry vermouth
Small chunk of mango for garnish

Muddle mango and sour mix in bottom of mixing glass. Add ice and spirits. Shake and strain into glass. To garnish, make a small slice in the mango chunk and secure it on rim of glass.

PINEAPPLE MARTINI

Sweet, sour, and fresh

1 cube (1½ inches) pineapple, diced
½ ounce fresh sour mix
3 ounces vodka
1 splash dry vermouth
Small pineapple chunk for garnish

Muddle pineapple and sour mix in bottom of mixing glass. Add ice and spirits. Shake and strain into glass. To garnish, make a small slice in the pineapple chunk and secure it on rim of glass.

ORANGE DELIGHT

Orange as can be

½ teaspoon powdered sugar
Orange twist
2 ounces orange-flavored vodka
1 ounce Cointreau
1 ounce orange juice

Spread sugar on a saucer; moisten rim of glass with orange twist and dip rim into sugar. Combine liquid ingredients in mixing glass. Add ice and stir to chill. Strain carefully into glass and garnish with the twist.

PASSIONATE PEACH

Gold and bubbly

2 ounces vodka
1 ounce Cointreau
1 ounce passion fruit juice
4 ounces club soda

Pour vodka, liqueur, and juice into ice-filled highball glass. Top with club soda and stir.

PAUL'S FIRE ISLAND PUNCH

Punched up with lime

3 ounces Ketel One vodka
½ ounce fresh lime juice
Lime twist for garnish

Combine vodka and juice in mixing glass. Add ice and shake. Strain into glass and garnish.

PERCOLATOR

Perks you right up

1 ounce vodka
1 ounce Cognac
1 ounce Grand Marnier
½ ounce white crème de cacao
Splash of club soda

Combine vodka, Cognac, and liqueurs in mixing glass. Add ice and stir to chill. Strain into glass and top with soda.

THE POLITICIAN

Even-steven portions of vodka, tonic, and soda

2 ounces vodka
2 ounces tonic water
2 ounces club soda
Lime wedge for garnish

Pour vodka and tonic into ice-filled highball glass. Top with club soda and garnish.

POMEGRANATE MARTINI

To your health! Look for pomegranate puree at specialty food stores or online.

2½ ounces vodka
1 teaspoon sweet vermouth
½ ounce pomegranate puree
Orange twist for garnish

Combine liquid ingredients in mixing glass. Add ice and shake. Strain into glass and garnish.

THE POTION

Sweet temptation. Chambord is a black raspberry liqueur of intense flavor and French origin.

2 ounces vodka
1 ounce Chambord
1 ounce lemon juice
½ teaspoon superfine sugar

Combine ingredients in mixing glass. Add ice, shake, and strain into glass.

PURPLE PASSION

An oldie but goodie

2 ounces vodka
3 ounces red grape juice
3 ounces grapefruit juice
½ teaspoon superfine sugar

Combine ingredients in mixing glass. Add ice, stir to chill, and strain into glass.

RASMOPOLITAN

A Cosmo jazzed up with raspberry

2 ounces raspberry-flavored vodka
1 ounce Cointreau
1 ounce cranberry juice
1 ounce fresh sour mix
Lemon twist for garnish

Combine liquid ingredients in mixing glass. Add ice and shake. Strain into glass and garnish.

THE RASPUTIN

For your favorite hypnotic monk

2 ounces vodka
1 ounce Frangelico
½ ounce dark crème de cacao
½ ounce light cream

Combine ingredients in mixing glass. Add ice, shake, and strain into glass.

THE REAL MAN

A Four Seasons managing partner's tribute to his counterpart

2 ounces Cîroc vodka
2 ounces Campari
½ ounce pineapple juice
Orange twist for garnish

Pour liquid ingredients into ice-filled rocks glass. Stir and garnish.

RENDEZVOUS

A meeting of four kindred spirits

1 ounce vodka
1 ounce brandy
1 ounce Grand Marnier
1 ounce crème de cassis

Combine ingredients in mixing glass. Add ice, stir to chill, and strain into glass.

ROSY GLOW

Rose-colored glasses in a glass

2 ounces vodka
2 ounces Campari
1 ounce peach schnapps
2 ounces orange juice
Orange slice for garnish

Combine liquid ingredients in mixing glass. Add ice and shake. Pour with ice into glass and garnish.

ROYAL RUSH

Berries red and black

2 ounces Stolichnaya Razberi
1 ounce Absolut Kurant
1 ounce Chambord
Club soda
Raspberry for garnish

Combine vodkas and liqueur in mixing glass. Add ice, shake, and pour with ice into glass. Top with club soda to taste and garnish.

RUSSIAN ALEXANDER

Sumptuousness worthy of the Romanovs

2 ounces vodka
1 ounce dark crème de cacao
1 ounce light cream
Nutmeg for sprinkling

Combine liquid ingredients in mixing glass. Add ice and shake. Strain into glass and sprinkle with nutmeg.

RUSSICANO

Vodka takes its turn in the Americano, one of the earliest Campari cocktails.

2 ounces vodka
2 ounces Campari
1 ounce Cinzano Rosso vermouth
3 ounces club soda
Orange wedge for garnish

Pour vodka, Campari, and vermouth into ice-filled highball glass. Top with club soda and garnish.

SALTY DOG

Left its Greyhound ancestor (page 91) in the dust

¼ teaspoon salt
Lime wedge
2 ounces vodka
5 ounces grapefruit juice

Spread salt on a saucer; moisten rim of glass with lime wedge and dip rim into salt. Combine vodka, remaining salt on saucer, and juice in mixing glass. Shake, carefully pour with ice into glass, and garnish with lime.

SCREWDRIVER

The unadorned classic

2 ounces vodka
4 ounces orange juice

Pour vodka and juice into ice-filled rocks glass and stir.

SEA BREEZE

Fresh and fruity

2 ounces vodka
2 ounces grapefruit juice
2 ounces cranberry juice

Pour ingredients into ice-filled rocks glass and stir.

SEA BREEZE

SECTION EIGHT

Inspired by an especially crazy night at the Four Seasons bar.

1½ ounces vodka
1 ounce Hennessy Cognac

Pour vodka and Cognac into ice-filled rocks glass and stir.

SEX IN THE POOL

A jokey reference to the high-octane flirting in our Pool Room

2 ounces vodka
1 ounce white crème de cacao
½ teaspoon blue curaçao
½ teaspoon Grand Marnier
Half a fig for garnish

Combine liquid ingredients in mixing glass. Add ice and stir to chill. Strain into glass and garnish.

SEX ON THE BEACH

Naughtily named cocktail from the mustachioed and pantsuited Seventies

2 ounces vodka
1 ounce peach schnapps
1½ ounces orange juice
1½ ounces cranberry juice

Pour ingredients into ice-filled rocks glass and stir.

SILVER LINING MARTINI

An homage to a much-missed publishing imprint. Aquavit, from Scandinavia, is a potent, colorless liquor distilled from potatoes or grain. It is then distilled a second time and flavored with caraway seeds, coriander, or dill.

2 large pimiento-stuffed Spanish olives
½ ounce aquavit or dry sherry, plus extra for the glass
2 ounces Chopin vodka, chilled

Place olives in a 3-ounce shot glass and pour in aquavit or sherry to cover; let soak for 8 to 12 hours. Pour a small amount of aquavit or sherry into well-chilled martini glass; swirl once and discard. Add chilled vodka and garnish with the olives.

SLOW COMFORTABLE SCREW

Relax! We're talkin' a Screwdriver made with sloe gin and Southern Comfort.

2 ounces vodka
1 ounce sloe gin
1 ounce Southern Comfort
3 ounces orange juice

Pour ingredients into ice-filled highball glass and stir.

SNOW STORM

Sparkly white

2 ounces vodka
1 ounce Godiva white chocolate liqueur
1 ounce white crème de cacao
Crushed ice

Combine liquid ingredients in mixing glass. Add ice, stir to chill, and strain into glass filled with crushed ice.

SOUTHERN SKIES

Romance takes flight!
1 ounce vodka
1 ounce light rum
1 ounce blue curaçao
1 ounce pineapple juice

Combine ingredients in mixing glass. Add ice, stir to chill, and strain into glass.

SPICY MARY

Hot as Hades
2½ ounces Absolut Peppar
3 ounces tomato juice
4 dashes Worcestershire sauce
3 dashes Tabasco
Salt and pepper to taste
Lime slice for garnish

Combine liquid ingredients, salt, and pepper in ice-filled highball glass. Stir and garnish.

SUBURBAN

A salute to our local bridge-and-tunnel customers
2 ounces vodka
1 ounce Hiram Walker peach schnapps
1 ounce apricot brandy
2 ounces orange juice
2 ounces club soda
Orange slice for garnish

Pour vodka, schnapps, brandy, and juice into ice-filled highball glass. Top with club soda and garnish.

SUMMER COOLER

Time to get your mint on
3 mint sprigs
1 teaspoon superfine sugar
1 ounce lemon juice
2½ ounces vodka
Mint sprig for garnish

Muddle 3 mint sprigs, sugar, and juice in bottom of mixing glass and add vodka. Add ice and shake. Strain into glass and garnish.

SUMMER SNAP

Two snaps up
2 ounces vodka
½ ounce white crème de menthe
1 ounce apricot brandy
½ ounce lemon juice
Mint sprig for garnish

Combine liquid ingredients in mixing glass. Add ice and stir to chill. Strain into glass and garnish.

SWISS ALPS

Think snow and chocolate
1 ounce Chopin vodka
1 ounce Godiva white chocolate liqueur
1 ounce white crème de cacao
1 ounce light cream
Chocolate shavings for garnish

Combine liquid ingredients in mixing glass. Add ice and shake. Strain into glass and garnish.

FLE

A velvety treat for the holidays

2 ounces vodka

1 ounce dark crème de cacao

½ teaspoon Chambord

1 ounce heavy cream

Combine ingredients in mixing glass.
Add ice, shake, and strain into glass.

'S
KA
KTAIL

The favorite of a grande dame from Tonga

2 ounces Stolichnaya Vanil

1 ounce white crème de cacao

½ ounce Godiva white chocolate liqueur

½ ounce sambuca

Combine ingredients in mixing glass.
Add ice, stir to chill, and strain into
glass.

OPA

*Singing the praises of Italy (amaretto and
Galliano) and France (Cointreau)*

1½ ounces vodka

½ ounce amaretto

½ ounce Cointreau

½ ounce Galliano

1 ounce orange juice

1 ounce pineapple juice

2 dashes bitters

Combine ingredients in mixing glass.
Add ice, stir to chill, and strain into
glass.

VODKA AND TONIC

Outran Gin and Tonic in the stretch

2 ounces Tito's Handmade vodka

Tonic water

Lime wedge for garnish

Pour vodka into ice-filled highball
glass. Fill with tonic water to taste,
stir, and garnish.

VODKA COLLINS

Russian take on a British classic

2 ounces vodka

1 ounce fresh sour mix

3 ounces club soda

Maraschino cherry for garnish

Orange slice for garnish

Combine vodka and sour mix in
mixing glass. Add ice, shake, and
strain into glass. Top with club soda
and garnish.

VODKA GIBSON

*By definition, a martini garnished
with cocktail onions*

3 ounces vodka

1 teaspoon dry vermouth

3 cocktail onions for garnish

Combine vodka and vermouth in
mixing glass. Add ice and stir to chill.
Strain into glass and garnish.

VODKA GIMLET

For lime lovers

2½ ounces vodka

1½ ounces Rose's lime juice

Lime wedge for garnish

Pour vodka and juice into ice-filled
rocks glass. Stir and garnish.

TANNHAUSER

Wagnerian in its richness. Jägermeister (first syllable pronounced YAYG) is a German liqueur with a bitter but intriguing herbiness.

2 ounces vodka
1 ounce dark crème de cacao
½ ounce Jägermeister
½ ounce light cream

Combine ingredients in mixing glass. Add ice, shake, and strain into glass.

THREE-PEAR HIGHBALL

Perfection for pear lovers
2 ounces Absolut Pears
1 ounce Poire William
1 ounce Hiram Walker pear schnapps
Club soda
Pear sliver for garnish

Pour vodka and liqueurs in ice-filled highball glass. Top with club soda to taste and garnish.

THUNDERCLOUD *A delectable Four Seasons specialty*

2 ounces vodka
½ ounce Chambord
½ ounce blue curaçao
½ ounce heavy cream

Combine ingredients in mixing glass. Add ice, shake, and strain into glass.

TOPAZ

Shimmering with orange
2 ounces Smirnoff vodka
1 ounce orange juice
1 ounce apricot brandy

Combine ingredients in mixing glass. Add ice, stir to chill, and strain into glass.

TRIXIE'S TROPICAL DREAM

TOP BANANA

For the tap dancer i
2 ounces vodka
2 ounces crème de l
4 ounces orange jui
Orange slice for gar

Combine liquid in glass. Add ice and with ice into glass

TRIXIE'S TROPICAL DREAM

Clink glasses with T nearest palm.
2 ounces vodka
2 ounces light rum
1 ounce blue curaçac
Orange peel spiral fc

Combine ingredien Add ice, stir to chi and garnish.

A V
Whe
Vod
vor
a pc
gue:
this

TRU

VIK
VO
CO

VIV
EU

VODKA GINGERLY

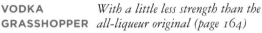

With ginger ale and mint
2 ounces vodka
½ ounce white crème de menthe
1 ounce fresh sour mix
4 ounces ginger ale
Orange slice for garnish

Combine vodka, liqueur, and sour mix in mixing glass. Add ice, shake, and pour with ice into glass. Top with ginger ale and garnish.

VODKA GRASSHOPPER

With a little less strength than the all-liqueur original (page 164)
1 ounce vodka
1 ounce green crème de menthe
1 ounce white crème de cacao

Combine ingredients in mixing glass. Add ice, stir to chill, and strain into glass.

VODKA MADRAS

Equal parts vodka, cranberry, and orange
2 ounces vodka
2 ounces cranberry juice
2 ounces orange juice

Pour ingredients into ice-filled rocks glass and stir.

VODKAMEISTER

Vodka and Jäg
2 ounces vodka
1 ounce Jägermeister
Club soda
Orange peel spiral for garnish

Combine vodka and liqueur in mixing glass. Add ice, shake, and pour with ice into glass. Top with club soda to taste and garnish.

VODKA NEGRONI

In this variation on a classic Campari cocktail, vodka stands in for the gin.
2½ ounces vodka
1½ ounces Campari
½ ounce sweet vermouth

Combine ingredients in mixing glass. Add ice, stir to chill, and strain into glass.

VODKA ORANGE BLOSSOM

Orange-flavored vodka makes this classic cocktail all the orangier.
2 ounces Stolichnaya Ohranj
1 ounce Cointreau
1 ounce orange juice
2 dashes orange bitters
Orange peel spiral for garnish

Combine ingredients in mixing glass. Add ice and stir to chill. Strain into glass and garnish.

VODKA SOUR

Serve straight up or on the rocks.
2½ ounces vodka
1½ ounces fresh sour mix
Orange slice for garnish
Maraschino cherry for garnish

Combine vodka and sour mix in mixing glass. Add ice and shake. Strain into sour glass or ice-filled rocks glass and garnish.

VODKA STINGER

Stinger = a drink with brandy and crème de menthe

2½ ounces vodka
½ ounce brandy
½ ounce white crème de menthe

Combine ingredients in mixing glass. Add ice, stir to chill, and strain into glass.

THE WARSAW

An elegant cocktail made with Polish potato vodka

2 ounces Lukusowa vodka
1 ounce Mr. Boston blackberry brandy
1 ounce dry vermouth
1 teaspoon lemon juice

Combine ingredients in mixing glass. Add ice, shake, and strain into glass.

WHITE RUSSIAN

A valiant survivor of the cocktail wars

2 ounces vodka
1 ounce white crème de cacao
1 ounce light cream

Combine ingredients in mixing glass. Add ice, shake, and pour with ice into glass.

WICKED MONK

Wicked good

1½ ounces vodka
1 ounce Frangelico
½ ounce blue curaçao
½ ounce Southern Comfort

Combine ingredients in mixing glass. Add ice, stir to chill, and strain into glass.

WOO WOO

And whoop de doo!

2 ounces vodka
1 ounce peach schnapps
4 ounces cranberry juice

Pour ingredients into ice-filled highball glass and stir.

THE XENIA

Full of passion

2 ounces Skyy passion fruit vodka
1 ounce passion fruit nectar
1 teaspoon Cointreau
Lemon twist for garnish

Combine liquid ingredients in mixing glass. Add ice and shake. Strain into glass and garnish.

XYLOPHONE

Plays a blue note

2 ounces vodka
½ ounce DeKuyper blueberry liqueur
½ ounce fresh sour mix

Combine ingredients in mixing glass. Add ice, shake, and strain into glass.

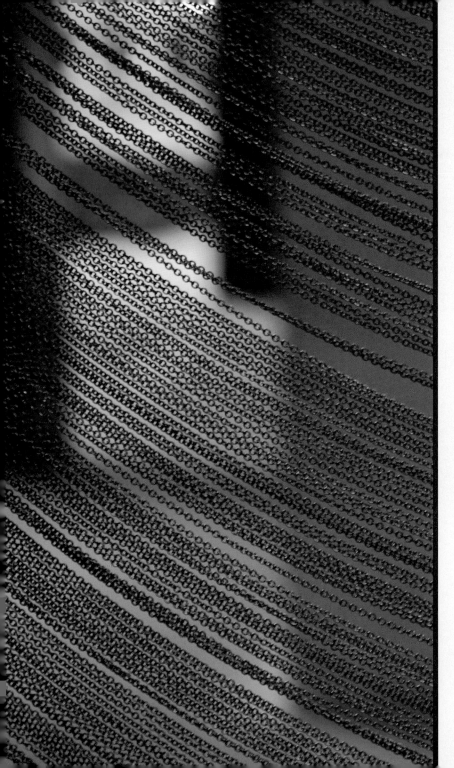

The Magic Curtains

Customers raising a glass at the bar in The Four Seasons may think they've had one too many when they notice the gentle undulations of the curtains covering the towering windows. But what they are witnessing is one of the bar's unique charms—a phenomenon that appeared as if by magic.

When the restaurant was taking shape in the late 1950s, the windows (which are 18 to 22 feet high) posed a serious challenge. Fabric curtains would fade and wear in the bright sunlight streaming in from the street. An artisan came up with the solution: curtains made of anodized aluminum beads.

The artisan was Marie Nichols, who fashioned the curtains by turning millions of beads into chains. The finished curtains were matchless—but on the day they were installed the workmen noticed something very odd, even worrisome. They quickly placed a call to Philip Johnson, the architect in charge, who arrived to find the bronze-hued draperies rippling from top to bottom.

Mystified, Johnson thought the movement must have been caused by air currents, or perhaps the trains rumbling beneath Lexington Avenue. In any event, he knew a phone call to Joe Baum of Restaurant Associates was in order. On viewing the spectacle, Baum declared it "beautiful." Johnson, too, came to love the mysterious rippling—caused, he mused, simply by "the shock of New York." Today, neither those who first saw the "magic curtains" nor the countless people who have since wined and dined in their shadow could imagine the elegant Pool and Grill Rooms without them.

RUM

Rum can be distilled in any country warm enough to grow sugar cane, but the North American market is cornered by rums from the Caribbean. **Light rums**, distilled in Puerto Rico, Barbados, and a few other subtropical isles, are clear and best used for fruit-based cocktails. Regardless of their country of origin, **gold rums** are amber-colored because they're aged longer. Most **dark rums** come from tropical isles like Jamaica, Haiti, and Martinique; they are heavier and richer from still longer aging. (See also A Word from the Bartenders, page 112.)

Competing with ordinary molasses-based rum in the twenty-first century is **pure cane rum**, distilled from sugar cane juice or syrup. Because of its clean taste, some rum lovers see pure cane rum—also known as *rhum agricole*—as the new vodka.

ALMOND JOY

Feed that sweet tooth!
Crushed ice
2 ounces light rum
½ ounce Coco Lopez cream of coconut
½ ounce amaretto
½ ounce chocolate liqueur

Fill a rocks glass with crushed ice and add liquid ingredients. Stir.

ANGELA'S CHOICE

Apple with a touch of spice
2 ounces Bacardi silver
½ ounce Berentzen apple liqueur
½ ounce Southern Comfort
Dash of ground cinnamon
Orange slice for garnish

Combine liquid ingredients and cinnamon in mixing glass. Add ice and shake. Strain into glass and garnish.

APPLE FIZZ

On the pleasantly sour side
2 ounces Meyer's rum
½ ounce sour apple schnapps
Club soda

Pour rum and schnapps into ice-filled rocks glass. Top with club soda to taste and stir.

APPLE PIE

Apt choice for Mom
2 ounces light rum
½ ounce calvados
½ teaspoon cinnamon
Apple slice for garnish

Combine rum, brandy, and cinnamon in mixing glass. Add ice and shake. Strain into ice-filled glass and garnish.

APPLESAUCE

The perfect autumn pleaser
2 ounces light rum
1 tablespoon apple puree
1 ounce applejack
1 teaspoon cinnamon
Apple slice for garnish

Combine rum, apple puree, applejack, and cinnamon in mixing glass. Add ice and shake. Strain into glass and garnish.

BANANA CREAM PIE

As yummy as it sounds
2 ounces light rum
½ ounce crème de banane
½ ounce Godiva white chocolate liqueur
½ ounce white crème de cacao

Combine ingredients in mixing glass. Add ice, stir to chill, and strain into glass.

BASTARD CHILD

Named for the offspring of Spanish sailors, post-1492?
1 ounce light rum
1 ounce sambuca
1 ounce Frangelico

Pour ingredients into ice-filled rocks glass and stir.

BLUE HAWAII

BLUE HAWAII

Sip while watching Elvis's 1961 film?

1 ounce light rum
1 ounce blue curaçao
2 ounces pineapple juice
1 ounce cream of coconut
Pineapple wedge for garnish

Pour liquid ingredients into ice-filled rocks glass and garnish.

BROOKLYN BRIDGE

A bow to the borough beyond the bridge

2 ounces light rum
¼ ounce white crème de menthe
¼ ounce white crème de cacao
Orange twist for garnish

Combine liquid ingredients in mixing glass. Add ice and stir to chill. Pour with ice into glass and garnish.

CANDY APPLE

Take a bite

2 ounces dark rum
½ ounce Bols sour apple schnapps
½ ounce Cherry Heering
½ ounce lemon juice

Combine ingredients in mixing glass. Add ice, stir to chill, and strain into glass.

BIG HIT

Made with a popular overproof rum. Standard rum is 80-proof—i.e., 40 percent alcohol by volume (abv). The abv for 151-proof rum is 75 percent.

2 ounces Bacardi 151
½ ounce Cointreau
½ ounce fresh sour mix
Lemon twist for garnish

Combine liquid ingredients in mixing glass. Add ice and shake. Strain into glass and garnish.

BLISSFUL BROTHER

Pure cane rum + a liqueur from the abbey

Crushed ice
2½ ounces Clément pure cane rum
1 ounce Bénédictine
Lemon twist for garnish

Fill a martini glass with crushed ice and add rum and liqueur. Stir and garnish.

CARESSING BREEZE	*Sweet!*
	2 ounces Bacardi rum
	1 ounce vodka
	2 ounces peach nectar
	½ ounce light cream
	1 teaspoon superfine sugar

Combine ingredients in mixing glass. Add ice, shake, and pour with ice into glass.

CARIBBEAN COCKTAIL	*A tropical cornucopia*
	2 ounces light rum
	½ ounce Malibu rum
	½ ounce orange liqueur
	½ ounce crème de banane
	½ ounce pineapple juice
	Coconut wedge for garnish

Pour liquid ingredients into ice-filled rocks glass, stir, and garnish.

CARIBBEAN TWILIGHT	*With dark rum. Monsieur Peychaud of New Orleans first formulated his bitters in 1837.*
	2 ounces dark rum
	½ ounce orange liqueur
	½ ounce lemon juice
	1 dash Peychaud's bitters
	Orange twist for garnish

Combine liquid ingredients in mixing glass. Add ice and shake. Strain into glass and garnish.

CARLITO'S WAY	*The creation of Four Seasons bartender Charles*
	2½ ounces 10 Cane pure cane rum
	½ ounce triple sec
	½ ounce lemon juice
	½ ounce lime juice
	Lemon twist for garnish

Pour liquid ingredients into ice-filled rocks glass. Stir and garnish.

CARTHUSIAN MONK	*Carthusian monks gave the world Chartreuse, France's aromatic liqueur.*
	2 ounces light rum
	½ ounce yellow Chartreuse
	Club soda
	Lemon twist for garnish

Pour rum and liqueur into ice-filled rocks glass. Top with club soda to taste and garnish.

CHOCOLATE-COVERED ORANGE	*Peel off some pleasure.*
	2 ounces light rum
	½ ounce Cointreau
	½ ounce Godiva chocolate liqueur
	Orange peel spiral for garnish

Combine liquid ingredients in mixing glass. Add ice and stir to chill. Strain into glass and garnish.

CHOCOLATE MINT COCKTAIL

Serve straight up or on the rocks.

2 ounces light rum
½ ounce white crème de menthe
½ ounce chocolate liqueur
Mint sprig for garnish

Combine liquid ingredients in mixing glass. Add ice and stir to chill. Strain into martini glass or pour with ice into rocks glass and garnish.

CHOCOLATE TWISTER

Spinning your way

2 ounces dark rum
½ ounce sambuca
½ ounce chocolate liqueur

Pour ingredients into ice-filled rocks glass and stir.

THE COLISEUM

Let the (fun and) games begin

2 ounces light rum
½ ounce Campari
½ ounce Cointreau
½ ounce fresh sour mix
Lemon twist for garnish

Combine liquid ingredients in mixing glass. Add ice and shake. Strain into ice-filled glass and garnish.

CUBA LIBRE

Better known as rum and Coke

2½ ounces Bacardi
1½ ounces Coca-Cola Classic
Lime wedge for garnish

Pour rum and cola into ice-filled rocks glass and garnish.

DAN'S DESERT INN

A former Vegas barman's specialty

2½ ounces light rum
½ ounce orange liqueur
½ ounce Dubonnet Blanc

Combine ingredients in mixing glass. Add ice, shake, and strain into glass.

DAIQUIRI

The nonfrozen original. For frozen daiquiris, see pages 114–15.

2½ ounces Bacardi Light
2 ounces fresh lime juice
1 teaspoon superfine sugar

Combine ingredients in mixing glass. Add ice, shake, and strain into glass.

DOÑA DIEGO

Get to know her.

2 ounces La Favorite pure cane rum
1 ounce B & B
Orange twist for garnish

Pour rum and liqueur into ice-filled rocks glass. Stir and garnish.

DONKEY EXPRESS

With a little sloe gin

2 ounces light rum
½ ounce sloe gin
½ ounce triple sec
Lime wedge for garnish

Pour liquid ingredients into ice-filled rocks glass. Stir and garnish.

EASTERN EXPRESS

A ginger-flavored fizz
2 ounces light rum
½ ounce orange liqueur
Ginger ale
Orange twist for garnish

Pour rum and liqueur into ice-filled rocks glass. Add ginger ale to taste and garnish.

THE 1812

Man the torpedoes
2 ounces Bacardi silver
½ ounce peach schnapps
½ ounce Southern Comfort
Orange twist for garnish

Combine liquid ingredients in mixing glass. Add ice and stir to chill. Strain into glass and garnish.

EXTREME SOUR APPLE

The Sour Apple Cocktail (page 124) gets sourer.
2 ounces dark rum
½ ounce sour apple schnapps
½ ounce lemon juice
Green apple slice for garnish

Pour liquid ingredients into ice-filled rocks glass. Stir and garnish.

A WORD FROM THE BARTENDERS

Know what you're buying when you pick a molasses-based or pure cane rum from the shelf. Light rums (also called silver or white) are clear and are best used for fruit-based cocktails. Gold, or *oro*, rums are aged longer and can be enjoyed neat on the rocks. Dark rums (also labeled as black or *añejo*) are the aristocrats of the bunch and, like brandy, are often drunk from a snifter.

THE FIDEL

No cigar required
2 ounces light rum
½ ounce DeKuyper melon liqueur
½ ounce Cointreau
½ ounce mango juice
½ ounce orange juice
½ ounce pineapple juice
1 splash cranberry juice
Pineapple spear for garnish

Pour rum, liqueurs, and mango, orange, and pineapple juices into ice-filled highball glass. Stir, add cranberry juice, and garnish.

FOREIGN LEGION

Pulpy OJ gives this hats-off to France a nice texture.
2 ounces light rum
½ ounce Dubonnet Rouge
½ ounce orange juice

Combine ingredients in mixing glass. Add ice, shake, and strain into glass.

FOUR SEASONS HURRICANE

Pineapple stands in for the passion fruit of the New Orleans original.
Crushed ice
2 ounces light rum
½ ounce blue curaçao
½ ounce pineapple juice
½ ounce lemon juice
Club soda
Pineapple wedge for garnish

Fill a highball glass with crushed ice and add rum, liqueur, and juices. Top with club soda and garnish.

FRANGELICO RUM FIZZ

FRANGELICO RUM FIZZ

The answer to a hazelnut lover's prayer. Frangelico is traced to the seventeenth-century Christian monks of Italy's Piedmont region.

Crushed ice
2 ounces dark rum
1 ounce Frangelico
Club soda

Fill a white wine glass with crushed ice and add rum and liqueur. Top with club soda to taste and stir.

FRENCH ISLAND

In this case, Martinique
2 ounces Depaz Blue pure cane rum
1 ounce Pernod
Club soda

Pour rum and liqueur into ice-filled rocks glass. Top with club soda to taste and stir.

FOUR SEASONS PARADISE COCKTAIL

The original Paradise Cocktail calls for brandy.
2 ounces light rum
½ ounce Cointreau
½ ounce Pernod

Pour ingredients into ice-filled rocks glass and stir.

FOXY SQUIRREL

For almond-crazy bipeds
2 ounces light rum
½ ounce amaretto
½ ounce crème de noyaux
½ ounce Chambord

Combine ingredients in mixing glass. Add ice and stir to chill. Strain into martini glass or pour with ice into rocks glass.

FROTHY LIME

Fresh-from-the-fruit juice only, please
2½ ounces light rum
1½ ounces lime juice
1 dash Fee Brothers lemon bitters
Club soda
Lime peel spiral for garnish

Pour rum and juice into ice-filled highball glass. Add bitters and top with club soda to taste. Stir and garnish.

Frozen Daiquiris

Frozen daiquiris were all the rage in the 1950s, but were elbowed out of the way by an ambitious Mexican cousin—the frozen Margarita. And it's time these cocktails made a comeback. Legend has it that an American engineer invented the daiquiri in 1896 in the Cuban town of the same name.

The Method To make a frozen daiquiri, combine the liquid ingredients in a blender with crushed ice—roughly equal parts ice and liquid. Blend until smooth, pour into glass, and garnish.

**APRICOT-
GUAVA
DAIQUIRI**

A happy marriage of apricot brandy and guava nectar
2 ounces light rum
1 ounce fresh sour mix
½ ounce apricot brandy
½ ounce guava nectar
Apricot half for garnish

**KIWI
SURPRISE**

Pleasantly tart
2 ounces light rum
1½ ounces fresh sour mix
½ ounce Bols kiwi liqueur
Kiwi slice for garnish

**BANANA
DAIQUIRI**

With banana-flavored liqueur
2 ounces light rum
1 ounce fresh sour mix
½ ounce crème de banane

**MANGO
DAIQUIRI**

Flavored with what's been called the king of fruits
2 ounces light rum
1 ounce fresh sour mix
1 ounce mango puree

**THE
MARY LOU**

She came, she saw, she drank
2 ounces light rum
1 ounce fresh sour mix
½ ounce crème de cassis

SAN JUAN DAIQUIRI

Perfect for a lazy day in the sun
2 ounces light rum
1 ounce fresh sour mix
½ ounce Grand Marnier
Orange twist for garnish

SOUR RASPBERRY

Graced with Chambord
2 ounces light rum
1 ounce fresh sour mix
½ ounce Chambord

SEÑOR ZEUS

A Greco-Latin treat
2 ounces light rum
1 ounce fresh sour mix
½ ounce ouzo

STRAWBERRY DAIQUIRI

An old favorite
2 ounces light rum
½ ounce Bols strawberry liqueur
1 ounce fresh sour mix

SHARMA DAIQUIRI

Peachy-keen karma
2 ounces light rum
½ ounce DeKuyper Pucker
   peach schnapps
1 ounce fresh sour mix

WATERMELON DAIQUIRI

Pretty and pink
2 ounces light rum
½ ounce Marie Brizard
   watermelon liqueur
1½ ounces fresh sour mix

FRUITY MIST

With apricot and guava. Maraska apricot liqueur is made in Croatia.
Crushed ice
2 ounces light rum
1 ounce Maraska apricot liqueur
½ ounce guava juice

Fill a tulip glass with crushed ice and add liquid ingredients. Stir.

GEORGIA SPRITZER

A peach and lemon-lime delight
2 ounces light rum
½ ounce peach schnapps
7UP or Sprite
Lime slice for garnish

Pour rum and schnapps into ice-filled highball glass. Top with soft drink to taste and garnish.

THE GISELLE

A Brazilian beauty
2½ ounces Leblon pure cane rum
Juice of 1 lime
½ ounce ginger beer
1 tablespoon shaved fresh ginger

Combine ingredients in mixing glass. Add ice, shake, and strain into glass.

GOLDEN ISLE

An invitation to relaxation
2 ounces Niesson pure cane rum
½ ounce Cointreau
Tonic water
Lime wedge for garnish

Pour rum and liqueur into ice-filled rocks glass. Top with tonic to taste and garnish.

THE GRAPE-STA

Put some hip in your hop.
2 ounces light rum
½ ounce DeKuyper Grape Pucker
½ ounce lemon juice
½ teaspoon superfine sugar
Lemon twist for garnish

Combine rum, liqueur, juice, and sugar in mixing glass. Add ice and shake. Strain into glass and garnish.

HAWAIIAN SOUR

Your chance to try pineapple liqueur
2 ounces light rum
½ ounce Malibu pineapple liqueur
½ ounce fresh sour mix
Pineapple wedge for garnish

Combine ingredients in mixing glass. Add ice and shake. Strain into sour glass or pour with ice into rocks glass and garnish.

HAZELNUT COOLER

Got Frangelico?
2 ounces light rum
½ ounce Frangelico

Pour rum and Frangelico into ice-filled rocks glass and stir.

HONEYPIE

For honeydew melon lovers
2 ounces light rum
½ ounce Midori
½ ounce orange liqueur
½ ounce lemon juice

Combine ingredients in mixing glass Add ice, shake, and strain into glass.

ICED HAZELNUT CREAM

Frangelico and Baileys on the rocks

2 ounces dark rum
1 ounce Frangelico
1 ounce Baileys Irish Cream
1 ounce club soda
Chocolate stick for garnish

Pour rum and liqueurs into ice-filled rocks glass. Top with club soda, stir, and garnish.

ISLA DE VIEQUES

Made with a premium Puerto Rican rum

2 ounces Bacardi Ciclón
1 ounce Chambord
2 ounces orange juice
Club soda
Orange twist for garnish

Pour rum, liqueur, and juice into ice-filled highball glass. Stir and garnish.

ITALIAN COOLER

Rum plus an herby liqueur

2 ounces light rum
½ ounce Strega

Pour rum and liqueur into ice-filled rocks glass and stir.

JAMAICAN THRILL

Zing!

1½ ounces Myer's dark rum
1½ ounces coffee liqueur
3 ounces pineapple juice
Crushed ice

Combine liquid ingredients in mixing glass. Add ice and shake. Strain into glass filled with crushed ice.

JOLLY GREEN GIGANTE

Rum with crème de menthe

1½ ounces dark rum
½ ounce green crème de menthe
1 dash Fee Brothers mint bitters

Pour ingredients into ice-filled rocks glass and stir.

JUBILEE COOLER

Mint, lemon-lime, and a bit of fizz

2 ounces light rum
½ ounce lemon juice
3 sprigs mint, crushed
½ ounce club soda
½ ounce Sprite or 7UP
Mint sprig for garnish

Combine rum, juice, and mint in mixing glass. Add ice and stir. Strain into ice-filled glass and top with club soda and soft drink. Stir and garnish.

LE BARBANCOURT

Made with prized (and pricey) Barbancourt pure cane rum from Haiti

2 ounces Barbancourt Three Star
  pure cane rum
½ ounce Cointreau
½ ounce lime juice

Pour ingredients into ice-filled rocks glass and stir.

LEMON FIZZ

Start squeezing.

2½ ounces light rum
1½ ounces fresh lemon juice
Club soda
Lemon slice for garnish

Pour rum and juice into ice-filled rocks glass. Top with club soda to taste and garnish.

LIBERTY FIZZ

Freedom from boredom
2 ounces light rum
½ ounce Galliano
Club soda

Pour rum and liqueur into ice-filled highball glass. Top with club soda to taste and stir.

LIME IN THE SUN

Imbibe while working on your tan
2 ounces light rum
½ ounce orange liqueur
7UP or Sprite
Orange slice for garnish

Pour rum and liqueur into ice-filled rocks glass. Top with soft drink to taste and garnish.

MAI TAI

Tiki, tiki, tiki!
1½ ounces Myers's rum
½ ounce triple sec
½ ounce amaretto
½ ounce grenadine
½ ounce lime juice

Pour ingredients into ice-filled highball glass and stir.

THE MATILDA

Laced with flavors of cream and orange
2 ounces light rum
½ ounce Harvey's Bristol Cream sherry
½ ounce Grand Marnier
1 dash Angostura bitters

Pour rum and liqueurs into ice-filled rocks glass. Add bitters and stir.

MAI TAI

MIAMI COCKTAIL

Con licor de naranja
2 ounces dark rum
½ ounce Southern Comfort
½ ounce orange liqueur
Club soda
Orange twist for garnish

Pour rum, Southern Comfort, and liqueur into ice-filled rocks glass. Top with club soda to taste and garnish.

MOJITO

The manna from Havana
2 mint sprigs
1 teaspoon superfine sugar
1 ounce lime juice
2 ounces light rum
Crushed ice
1 or 2 splashes sparkling water

Muddle mint, sugar, and juice in bottom of rocks glass. Pour in rum, add crushed ice, and top with sparkling water.

NEGRUMI

A Four Seasons riff on the Negroni, with two aperitifs

2 ounces light rum

2 ounces Campari

2 ounces Punt è Mes

Orange twist for garnish

Combine liquid ingredients in mixing glass. Add ice and stir to chill. Strain into glass and garnish.

NUT TWOFER

Hazelnut and almond in one

2 ounces light rum

1 ounce Frangelico

1 ounce amaretto

1 ounce club soda

Pour rum and liqueurs into ice-filled rocks glass. Top with club soda and stir.

NUTTY ISLANDER

The kind of nuttiness we like

2 ounces rum

½ ounce crème de noyaux

Pour rum and liqueur into ice-filled rocks glass and stir.

OLD SAN JUAN

A salute to Puerto Rico's capital city

2 ounces Bacardi Limón

½ ounce lemon juice

½ ounce Cointreau

½ ounce blue curaçao

2 ounces Bacardi 151

Combine Bacardi Limón, juice, and liqueurs in mixing glass. Add ice and shake. Pour contents into glass and top with Bacardi 151.

ORANGE BUBBLER

Pulpy or no-pulp OJ? Your call.

2½ ounces light rum

1½ ounces orange juice

½ teaspoon grenadine

Club soda

Orange slice for garnish

Pour rum, juice, and grenadine into ice-filled rocks glass. Top with club soda to taste and garnish.

PAGO PAGO

Named after the capital of American Samoa. How to say it? PAHNG-oh PAHNG-oh

2 ounces light rum

1 teaspoon white crème de cacao

1 teaspoon green Chartreuse

½ ounce pineapple juice

1 teaspoon fresh lime juice

Crushed ice

Combine liquid ingredients in mixing glass. Add ice, shake, and strain into glass filled with crushed ice.

PEACH FIXER

A bracing hangover soother

2 ounces light rum

½ ounce peach schnapps

½ ounce Southern Comfort

Club soda

Pour rum, schnapps, and liqueur into ice-filled highball glass. Top with club soda to taste and stir.

PEPPERMINT PATTY SOUR

Minty, but not too sweet
2 ounces light rum
½ ounce green crème de menthe
½ ounce fresh sour mix
Mint sprig for garnish

Combine liquid ingredients in mixing glass. Add ice and shake. Strain into glass and garnish.

THE PETITIONER

Let's just call this one a gold digger of a drink.
12 ounces cold Amstel Light beer
1 ounce Captain Morgan rum
Lime slice for garnish

Pour beer and rum into highball glass, stir, and garnish.

PIÑA COLADA

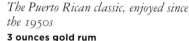

The Puerto Rican classic, enjoyed since the 1950s
3 ounces gold rum
2 ounces cream of coconut
4 ounces pineapple juice
Pineapple spear for garnish
Maraschino cherry for garnish

Combine liquid ingredients in mixing glass. Add ice and shake. Strain into glass and garnish.

PINEAPPLE EXPRESS

Hop aboard.
2 ounces Bacardi Black
1 ounce Malibu rum
2 ounces pineapple juice
Pineapple spear for garnish

Combine liquid ingredients in ice-filled rocks glass, stir, and garnish.

PINEAPPLE FIZZ

Take your pick of sweetened or unsweetened pineapple juice.
2½ ounces light rum
3 ounces pineapple juice
Club soda
Pineapple spear for garnish

Pour rum and juice into ice-filled highball glass. Top with club soda to taste and garnish.

POLLY'S CHOICE

The favorite of a wit from Down Under
2 ounces gold rum
½ ounce apricot brandy
½ ounce fresh sour mix
Lemon peel spiral for garnish

Combine liquid ingredients in mixing glass. Add ice and shake. Strain into martini glass or pour with ice into rocks glass, and garnish.

RAVEL'S BOLERO

Thumpingly good
2 ounces light rum
1 ounce peach schnapps
½ ounce apple brandy
¼ ounce dry vermouth
¼ ounce sweet vermouth

Combine ingredients in mixing glass. Add ice, stir to chill, and strain into glass.

RAVISHING HAZEL

Lashed with hazelnut liqueur and heavy cream
2½ ounces rum
½ ounce Frangelico
½ ounce heavy cream

Combine ingredients in mixing glass. Add ice, shake, and strain into glass.

ROWAN'S RED ROSE

Fruit and rum with a cherry on top
2½ ounces Myers's rum
1 ounce orange juice
1 ounce cranberry juice
Crushed ice
1 teaspoon Cherry Heering

Combine rum and juices in mixing glass. Add ice and shake. Pour into glass filled with crushed ice, and float liqueur on top.

ROYAL SOUR

Fit for a king
2 ounces Barton Gold rum
½ ounce Chambord
½ ounce fresh sour mix
Lemon twist for garnish

Combine liquid ingredients in mixing glass. Add ice and shake. Strain into glass and garnish.

RUM JUBILEE

RUM JUBILEE

A celebration of Mentha piperita, or peppermint
2 ounces light rum
½ ounce lemon juice
3 sprigs peppermint, crushed
Peppermint sprig for garnish

Combine rum, juice, and crushed peppermint in mixing glass. Add ice and stir to chill. Strain into glass and garnish.

RUM LEMON DROP

Tingles the tongue
2 ounces light rum
1 ounce fresh sour mix
Lemon twist for garnish

Combine rum and sour mix in mixing glass. Add ice and shake. Pour with ice into glass and garnish.

RUM LOVER'S FRUIT CUP

Overproof Bacardi with three tart juices
2 ounces Bacardi 151
1 ounce orange juice
½ ounce cranberry juice
½ ounce lemon juice

Combine ingredients in mixing glass. Add ice, shake, and strain into glass.

RUMMY MEDITATION

With liqueur straight from the abbey
2 ounces light rum
1 ounce Bénédictine
Orange twist for garnish

Combine rum and liqueur in mixing glass. Add ice and stir to chill. Strain into glass and garnish.

RUM MUDSLIDE

Rum subs for vodka.

2 ounces light rum
2 ounces Baileys Irish Cream
2 ounces Kahlúa

Pour rum and Baileys into ice-filled rocks glass and stir. Tilt the glass slightly and rotate it while slowly drizzling Kahlúa down the sides.

RUMMY MINT FIZZ

Elegant effervescense

2 ounces light rum
½ ounce white crème de menthe
Club soda

Pour rum and liqueur into ice-filled rocks glass. Top with club soda to taste and stir.

RUM NUTSHAKER

The nuts in play: coconut and almond. Malibu rum is white rum with a powerful coconut flavor.

2 ounces Malibu rum
1 ounce crème de noyaux
½ ounce Kahlúa

Combine ingredients in ice-filled rocks glass and stir.

RUM OLD-FASHIONED

Who needs whiskey?

1 teaspoon superfine sugar
Orange slice
Maraschino cherry
4 dashes bitters of choice
2 ounces gold rum
Club soda

Muddle sugar, orange, cherry, and bitters in bottom of rocks glass. Add ice, pour in rum, and top with club soda to taste.

RUM PRESBYTERIAN

For when you'd like it light

2½ ounces light rum
½ ounce club soda
½ ounce ginger ale

Pour rum into ice-filled rocks glass. Top with club soda and ginger ale and stir.

RUM RICO

Rich straight up or on the rocks

2 ounces light rum
1 ounce Malibu rum
1 ounce cranberry juice
1 ounce crème de banane
Orange twist for garnish

Combine liquid ingredients in mixing glass. Add ice and stir to chill. Strain into martini glass or pour with ice into rocks glass, and garnish.

RUM SANGRIA

Rum and port replace the usual red wine.

2 ounces light rum
½ ounce ruby port
½ ounce dark crème de menthe
½ ounce club soda
Citrus slices of choice for garnish

Pour rum, port, and liqueur into ice-filled rocks glass. Top with club soda and garnish.

RUMS AWEIGH

Three rums in one

1½ ounces Bacardi Light
1½ ounces Myers's dark rum
1½ ounces Captain Morgan rum
Club soda

Combine rums in ice-filled rocks glass, stir, and top with club soda to taste.

RUM SCREWDRIVER

Simplicity itself

1½ ounces light rum
5 ounces orange juice

Pour rum and juice into ice-filled rocks glass and stir.

RUM SHAKER

Hold on tight.

2 ounces dark rum
½ ounce Cointreau
1 ounce fresh sour mix
3 dashes orange bitters
Crushed ice

Combine liquid ingredients in mixing glass. Add ice and stir to chill. Strain into glass filled with crushed ice.

RUM STINGER

Minty refreshment

2 ounces light rum
½ ounce brandy
½ ounce white crème de menthe
Mint sprig for garnish

Pour rum and brandy into ice-filled rocks glass. Top with liqueur and garnish.

RUM TWISTER

With the scent of mint and chocolate

2 ounces light rum
¼ ounce white crème de menthe
¼ ounce crème de cacao
Lemon twist for garnish

Combine liquid ingredients in mixing glass. Add ice and stir to chill. Strain into glass and garnish.

ST. BARTS

A toast to the upscale isle

2 ounces La Favorite pure cane rum
½ ounce Cointreau
Club soda
Orange twist for garnish

Pour rum and liqueur into ice-filled rocks glass. Top with club soda to taste and garnish.

SEÑORA CAESAR

An exotic beauty

2 ounces light rum
½ ounce Galliano
½ ounce fresh sour mix
Lemon twist for garnish

Combine liquid ingredients in mixing glass. Add ice and shake. Strain into glass and garnish.

SEÑORA MCGILLICUDDY

With an Irish brogue

2 ounces light rum
½ ounce Irish Mist
½ ounce fresh sour mix
Lemon twist for garnish

Combine liquid ingredients in mixing glass. Add ice and shake. Strain into glass and garnish.

SEÑOR MARIPOSA

With brandy and citrus

2 ounces gold rum
½ ounce brandy
1 tablespoon tangerine juice
1 tablespoon lemon juice
1 dash grenadine

Combine ingredients in mixing glass. Add ice, stir to chill, and strain into glass.

SHIPWRECK

Malibu Mango rum to the rescue
1 ounce light rum
1 ounce Malibu Mango rum
Pineapple juice
1 ounce Barcardi 151
Pineapple spear for garnish

Pour light rum and Malibu rum into ice-filled highball glass, then top with pineapple juice to taste. Stir, float Bacardi on top, and garnish.

SOUR APPLE COCKTAIL

Pucker up.
1 ounce light rum
½ ounce DeKuper Pucker sour apple schnapps
Apple slice for garnish

Pour rum and liqueur into ice-filled sour glass. Stir and garnish.

SOUR EMPEROR

Green with envy?
2 ounces gold rum
½ ounce Midori
½ ounce fresh sour mix

Combine ingredients in mixing glass. Add ice, shake, and strain into glass.

SOUR THORN

Named for the blackthorn tree, whose sloe plums give us sloe gin.
2 ounces light rum
½ ounce sloe gin
½ ounce fresh sour mix
Maraschino cherry for garnish

Combine liquid ingredients in mixing glass. Add ice and shake. Strain into glass and garnish.

THE SOUTHERN BELLE

Pretty as you please
2 ounces light rum
1½ ounces peach schnapps
1½ ounces Southern Comfort
Peach slice for garnish

Combine liquid ingredients in mixing glass. Add ice and stir to chill. Strain into glass and garnish.

SQUIRREL'S NEST

Nutty 'n' nice
2 ounces dark rum
½ ounce amaretto
½ ounce crème de noyaux

Combine ingredients in mixing glass. Add ice, shake, and strain into glass.

STARBURST

A three-fruit explosion
2 ounces light rum
½ ounce apricot brandy
½ ounce orange juice
½ ounce cranberry juice

Pour ingredients into ice-filled highball glass and stir.

SUCCULENT MELON

The honeydew and pineapple get intimate.
2 ounces light rum
½ ounce Gaetano melon liqueur
½ ounce pineapple juice
Club soda
Lemon twist for garnish

Pour rum, liqueur, and juice into ice-filled rocks glass. Top with club soda to taste and garnish.

Spiked Soft Drinks

Add effervescence to rum with club soda if you like, but rum also blends well with soft drinks of different flavors. Serve these informal cocktails on ice, but don't let them sneak up on you.

The Method Simplicity itself. Pour rum into ice-filled glass, top with soft drink to taste, and garnish. If only the preparation for all drinks were so easy! (For Rum and Coke, see Cuba Libre, page 111.)

RUM AND CEL-RAY

With the piquant celery-flavored soft drink
2 ounces rum
Dr. Brown's Cel-Ray soda
Celery sliver for garnish

RUM AND GINGER

Ginger ale, of course
2 ounces rum
Canada Dry ginger ale
Lemon wedge for garnish

RUM AND CREAM SODA

Rum peps up a mellow old-timer.
2 ounces rum
A & W cream soda
Orange slice for garnish

RUM AND LIME

A tasty soda gets serious.
2 ounces rum
Stewart's key lime soda
Lime wedge for garnish

RUM AND RC

Moon pie optional
2 ounces rum
Royal Crown cola
Lemon wedge for garnish

RUM AND DR. PEPPER

Dr. Pepper was formulated in Waco, Texas, in the 1880s.
2 ounces rum
Dr. Pepper
Lime slice for garnish

RUM AND ROOT BEER

The earliest root beers were slightly alcoholic, so why not honor tradition?
2 ounces rum
Hires root beer
Lemon slice for garnish

TIJUANA EXPRESS

A rummy chocolate sundae
1½ ounces dark rum
½ ounce dark crème de cacao
Whipped cream for topping

Combine rum and liqueur in mixing glass. Add ice and shake. Strain into glass and top with whipped cream.

TOWER OF BABEL

May have you speaking in tongues
½ ounce rum
½ ounce vodka
½ ounce gin
½ ounce Cointreau
½ ounce Chambord
1 ounce coconut water
1 ounce pineapple juice

Combine ingredients in mixing glass. Add ice, shake, and pour with ice into glass.

TROPICAL BREEZE 1

One drink, four fruit juices
1½ ounces Mount Gay rum
½ ounce orange juice
½ ounce pineapple juice
½ ounce cranberry juice
2 drops lemon juice

Pour ingredients into ice-filled highball glass and stir.

TROPICAL BREEZE 2

More honeydewy
2 ounces light rum
½ ounce melon liqueur
½ ounce pineapple juice
½ ounce lemon juice
Pineapple spear for garnish

Pour liquid ingredients into ice-filled highball glass. Stir and garnish.

TWO-FOR-ONE

Light and dark rums plus chocolate
2 ounces light rum
2 ounces dark rum
½ ounce crème de menthe
½ ounce Cointreau
½ ounce Van Gogh chocolate liqueur
Chocolate stick for garnish

Combine ingredients in mixing glass. Add ice and shake. Strain into martini glass or pour with ice into rocks glass, and garnish.

VERY BERRY BERRY

A crush of currants and raspberries
2 ounces light rum
¼ ounce crème de cassis
¼ ounce Absolut Kurant vodka
¼ ounce Chambord
Raspberry for garnish

Combine liquid ingredients in mixing glass. Add ice and stir to chill. Strain into glass and garnish.

VIRGIN SKIES

With a rum from the U.S. Virgin Islands
2 ounces Cruzan Single Barrel Estate rum
½ ounce Midori
½ ounce pineapple juice
½ ounce grapefruit juice
Splash of cranberry juice
Pineapple spear for garnish

Combine rum, liqueur, pineapple juice, and grapefruit juice in ice-filled rocks glass and stir. Top with cranberry juice and garnish.

WHITE ISLAND

With Kahlúa and cream

2 ounces gold rum

½ ounce Kahlúa

½ ounce heavy cream

Combine ingredients in mixing glass. Add ice, shake, and strain into ice-filled glass.

THE WINDSURFER

Sweeps you away. Tia Maria is a Jamaican coffee liqueur said to have been formulated on the island in the mid-1600s.

1½ ounces light rum

1 ounce Tia Maria

1 ounce heavy cream

Combine ingredients in mixing glass. Add ice, shake, and strain into glass.

ZOMBIE

Be. Afraid.

1½ ounces light rum

1 ounce Jamaica rum

1 ounce apricot brandy

2 ounces orange juice

1 ounce unsweetened pineapple juice

1 teaspoon superfine sugar

½ cup crushed ice

1 ounce Bacardi 151

Pineapple spear for garnish

Maraschino cherry for garnish

Combine light rum, Jamaica rum, brandy, juices, sugar, and ice in blender. Blend at low speed for one minute, then strain into frosted glass. Float Bacardi on top and garnish.

Quality Goods

No one would call the drinks coming from behind the bar of The Four Seasons stuffy. To the contrary, the house-originated cocktails are clever and breezy—yet there's no mistaking the quality that goes into them. We use only Cognac, not generic brandy; only Cointreau, not garden-variety triple sec; only a freshly opened bottle of club soda for each drink, not soda water from a bar gun, which may be flat. All citrus juice is freshly squeezed, so that most customers who order, say, vodka with grapefruit juice volunteer that it's the best they've ever had. Even the citrus peel twists (page 31) are different: not as comely, perhaps, but superior to a regular twist as a flavoring.

Are we saying that you must buy only the best to make the perfect drink? Of course not. The reliance of Greg, Charles, and John on expensive ingredients is understandable, given their commitment to Four Seasons customers. You might want buy and keep a bottle or two of the better stuff for parties, but even home bartenders on the tightest budget can mix knock-out drinks so long as they choose the right recipe, pay attention to what they're doing, and remember that "fresh is best."

TEQUILA

This spirit is the gift of the blue agave, a huge succulent that grows in Mexico's desert reaches. The types of tequila preferred north of the border are **silver tequila** and **gold tequila**—the latter simply silver tequila with caramel or other flavoring. The crown jewel of tequilas is **añejo**, aged for one to three years and often likened to fine Cognac.

The *jimadores*, who harvest agave plants to distill Mexico's national spirit, carry vast stores of knowledge passed down for generations. They painstakingly cut the *piña* (the pineapple-like center of the plant), shred it, and press out the juice. After fermenting in vats, the juice is distilled to a milky liquid called *ordinario*. The *ordinario* is distilled for a second time, and *¡y mira!*—clear, or silver, tequila.

THE ALAMO

ALOHA

Laced with coconut-flavored rum
2 ounces tequila
1 ounce Malibu rum
Pineapple spear for garnish

Pour tequila and rum into ice-filled rocks glass. Stir and garnish.

APRICOT MARGARITA

With apricot brandy and Cointreau
1½ ounces tequila
½ ounce Mr. Boston apricot brandy
½ ounce Cointreau
1 splash Rose's lime juice
Lime wedge for garnish

Combine liquid ingredients in mixing glass. Add ice and shake. Strain into glass and garnish.

ARTICHOKE HIGH

With an artichoke-flavored aperitif!
2 ounces silver tequila
1 ounce Cynar

Pour tequila and Cynar into ice-filled rocks glass and stir.

AZTECA

Made with a little of the best-selling rum in Mexico
2 ounces silver tequila
1 ounce Bacardi Solera
2 teaspoons orange juice
Orange slice for garnish

Combine liquid ingredients in mixing glass. Add ice, shake, and strain into glass.

ABILENE LARIAT

Ropes you right in
2 ounces tequila
1 ounce Jim Beam bourbon
1 ounce lime juice
Lime slice for garnish

Pour liquid ingredients into ice-filled rocks glass. Stir and garnish.

AFTER THE RAIN

Silver droplets, superb taste
2 ounces silver tequila
1 ounce anisette

Pour tequila and liqueur into ice-filled rocks glass and stir.

THE ALAMO

A drink to remember
2 ounces tequila
1 ounce amaretto
1 splash orange juice
Lime twist for garnish

Pour liquid ingredients into ice-filled rocks glass. Stir and garnish.

BLOODY MARIA

Mary's saucy Mexican cousin

2 ounces tequila
4 ounces tomato juice
1 tablespoon Worcestershire sauce
1 or 2 dashes Tabasco
Lime slice for garnish

Pour liquid ingredients into ice-filled highball glass. Stir and garnish.

BLUE MARGARITA

Sunny skies all the way

1 ounce silver tequila
½ ounce blue curaçao
½ ounce brandy
½ ounce lemon juice
Lemon wedge for garnish

Combine liquid ingredients in mixing glass. Add ice and shake. Strain into glass and garnish.

BORDER CROSSING

Zips you across the Rio Grande

1½ ounces tequila
½ ounce orange juice
½ ounce pineapple juice
½ ounce Chambord
Club soda
Orange peel spiral for garnish

Pour tequila, juices, and liqueur into ice-filled rocks glass. Top with club soda to taste and garnish.

BRAVE BULL

The Mexican liqueur Kahlúa tastes of roasted coffee with a hint of chocolate.

2 ounces gold tequila
1 ounce Kahlúa
Lemon twist for garnish

Pour tequila and Kahlúa into ice-filled rocks glass. Stir and garnish.

CACTUS

Tasty and prickle-free

2 ounces gold tequila
1 ounce coffee liqueur
Club soda
Lemon twist for garnish

Pour tequila and liqueur into ice-filled highball glass. Top with club soda to taste and garnish.

CALIFORNIA SKY

Down Tijuana way

1½ ounces silver tequila
½ ounce light rum
½ ounce blue curaçao
½ ounce fresh sour mix
Maraschino cherry for garnish
Orange slice for garnish

Combine liquid ingredients in mixing glass. Add ice and shake. Strain into glass and garnish.

THE CHAPULTEPEC

Pushes your spirits uphill

2 ounces José Cuervo Oranjo tequila
1 ounce Grand Marnier
Orange slice for garnish

Combine tequila and liqueur in mixing glass. Add ice and shake. Strain into glass and garnish.

CHOCOLATE TEQUILA MARTINI

It had to happen.

3 ounces Tanteo chocolate tequila
1 teaspoon sweet vermouth
Mini marshmallow for garnish

Combine tequila and vermouth in mixing glass. Add ice and stir to chill. Strain into glass and garnish.

COCONUT CREAM

As rich as it gets

1½ ounces tequila
½ ounce Malibu rum
½ ounce white crème de cacao
½ ounce heavy cream
Coconut slice for garnish

Combine liquid ingredients in mixing glass. Add ice and shake. Strain into glass and garnish.

COSTA MESA

Dreamed up by a Texan transplanted to Paris

2 ounces silver tequila
4 ounces cranberry juice
Club soda
Lime wedge for garnish

Pour tequila and juice into ice-filled highball glass. Top with club soda to taste and garnish.

CREMA FRÍA

Tequila, vanilla, and cream on the rocks

2 ounces silver tequila
½ ounce Smirnoff Vanilla vodka
½ ounce heavy cream

Combine ingredients in mixing glass. Add ice, shake, and pour with ice into glass.

CRESCENT MOON

A drink for romantics

2 ounces silver tequila
1 ounce Pernod
Lemon twist for garnish

Pour tequila and liqueur into ice-filled rocks glass, stir, and garnish.

CRYSTAL PALACE

Tinted gold

Crushed ice
1 ounce silver tequila
1 ounce Crown Royal whiskey
1 ounce Galliano

Fill a rocks glass with crushed ice and add tequila, whiskey, and liqueur. Stir.

DIAMOND IN THE ROUGH

With an icy sparkle

2 ounces Gran Patrón Platinum tequila
2 ounces lychee juice
Juice of half a lime
1 ounce cranberry juice
1 teaspoon superfine sugar
Crushed ice

Combine liquid ingredients and sugar in mixing glass. Add ice and shake. Strain into glass filled with crushed ice.

DIVINO

Divine, thanks in part to the citrus-flavored tequila

1 ounce José Cuervo Citrico tequila
1 ounce vodka
1 ounce fresh sour mix
Lemon peel spiral for garnish

Combine ingredients in mixing glass. Add ice and shake. Strain into glass and garnish.

THE EXPLORER *In search of El Dorado*

2 ounces gold tequila
1 ounce peach schnapps
½ ounce crème de cassis

Pour ingredients into ice-filled rocks glass and stir.

FOUR SEASONS MARGARITA *Our take on one of America's favorite cocktails*

2 ounces gold tequila
1 ounce Cointreau
1 ounce fresh sour mix
1 splash Rose's lime juice
Lime wedge for garnish

Combine liquid ingredients in mixing glass. Add ice and shake. Strain into glass and garnish.

FROSTED ROSE *Named for its rosy color*

2½ ounces gold tequila
1 ounce grenadine
Lemon peel spiral for garnish

Combine tequila and grenadine in ice-filled rocks glass. Stir and garnish.

FROSTED ROSE

FROSTY WITCH *Casts a spell*

1½ ounces silver tequila
½ ounce amaretto
½ ounce pineapple juice
Orange wedge for garnish

Pour ingredients into ice-filled rocks glass. Stir and garnish.

GENTLE JUAN *Coffee flavor without the jangled nerves*

2 ounces tequila
1 ounce Tia Maria
Lemon twist for garnish

Pour tequila and liqueur into ice-filled rocks glass, stir, and garnish.

GOLD LEAF *The leaf? Mint.*

2 ounces José Cuervo Gold
1 ounce white crème de menthe
Mint sprig for garnish

Combine liquid ingredients in mixing glass. Add ice and stir to chill. Strain into glass and garnish.

A WORD FROM THE BARTENDERS

A with-salt margarita doesn't have salt in the drink itself, only on the rim of the glass. To salt the rim, spread a tablespoon of salt in a saucer; moisten the rim of glass with a lime wedge and dip the rim into the salt. Some tequila fans prefer coarse salt, others finer salt—but neither choice makes one with-salt margarita more "authentic" than the other.

GRAPPA TEQUILA

Tequila with an Italian eau-de-vie

2 ounces silver tequila
1 ounce grappa

Pour tequila and grappa into an ice-filled rocks glass and stir.

GREEN IGUANA

Melony and tart

2 ounces silver tequila
1 ounce Gaetano melon liqueur
½ ounce fresh sour mix
Lemon slice for garnish

Combine ingredients in mixing glass. Add ice and shake. Strain into glass and garnish.

THE GUADALUPE

A tequila 'n' rum fizz

1½ ounces gold tequila
1 ounce rum
Ginger ale
Mint sprig for garnish

Pour tequila and rum into ice-filled highball glass. Add ginger ale to taste and garnish.

GULF OF MEXICO

With blue curaçao

2 ounces silver tequila
1 ounce blue curaçao
½ ounce fresh sour mix

Combine ingredients in mixing glass. Add ice, shake, and strain into glass.

HONEYDEW

Tequila with a touch of melon

2 ounces silver tequila
2 ounces Midori
1 splash Rose's lime juice
Club soda
Lemon wedge for garnish

Pour tequila, liqueur, and juice into ice-filled highball glass. Top with club soda to taste and garnish.

HOT SOUR

Pepper-flavored vodka supplies the heat.

1½ ounces tequila
1½ ounces Absolut Peppar vodka
½ ounce fresh sour mix
Lemon slice for garnish

Combine liquid ingredients in mixing glass. Add ice and shake. Strain into glass and garnish.

ICE PICK

Iced tea spiked with a pineapple- and coconut-flavored tequila

2 ounces José Cuervo Tropiña tequila
6 ounces tea of choice, sweetened to taste
Lemon wedge for garnish

Pour tequila and tea into ice-filled highball glass, stir, and garnish.

ICICLE

Straight tequila on ice

Crushed ice
2½ ounces silver tequila
Lime slice for garnish

Fill a rocks glass with crushed ice and add tequila. Garnish.

IRISH ECHO

Erin go bueno
1½ ounces tequila
1½ ounces Irish Mist
Lemon twist for garnish

Pour tequila and liqueur into ice-filled rocks glass, stir, and garnish.

KENTUCKY HOMBRE

Equal parts bourbon and tequila
1½ ounces gold tequila
1½ ounces bourbon

Pour tequila and bourbon into ice-filled rocks glass and stir.

LA BAMBA

Chicano rock on the rocks?
1½ ounces gold tequila
¾ ounce Cointreau
1½ ounces pineapple juice
1½ ounces orange juice
2 dashes grenadine
Lime peel spiral for garnish

Combine liquid ingredients in mixing glass. Add ice and shake. Pour with ice into glass and garnish.

LA GRANADA

Granada = *pomegranate*
2 ounces silver tequila
2 ounces pomegranate juice
Club soda
Lemon wedge for garnish

Pour tequila and juice into ice-filled highball glass. Top with club soda to taste and garnish.

MARGARITA DE GUAYABA

Guayaba *is Spanish for guava.*
1½ ounces tequila
1 ounce guava nectar
1 splash Rose's lime juice
Lime slice for garnish

Combine liquid ingredients in mixing glass. Add ice and shake. Strain into glass and garnish.

MELON MARGARITA MARTINI

Flavored with Midori honeydew liqueur
1½ ounces tequila
½ ounce Midori
½ ounce Cointreau
1 splash Rose's lime juice
Lime wedge for garnish

Combine liquid ingredients in mixing glass. Add ice and shake. Strain into glass and garnish.

MELON MARGARITA MARTINI

Frozen Margaritas

Many margarita aficionados—especially those in warmer climes—prefer the drink frozen. If that means you, get out the ice and blender and try these recipes. Then check out the eight other margaritas in this chapter and freeze away, if you wish.

The Method To freeze a margarita, combine the liquid ingredients in a blender with ½ cup crushed ice. Blend well at high speed, then simply pour the contents into a margarita, or tulip, or martini glass, and garnish. Serve with a straw, if desired.

CHOCORITA

With chocolate-flavored tequila
2 ounces Tanteo chocolate tequila
½ ounce Cointreau
1 splash Rose's lime juice
Chocolate stick for garnish

GINGER MARGARITA

Deliciously assertive
1½ ounces gold tequila
½ ounce DeKuyper ginger brandy
½ ounce ginger schnapps
Piece of candied ginger for garnish

CINNAMON APPLE MARGARITA

All the better in autumn
1½ ounces gold tequila
½ ounce cinnamon schnapps
½ ounce apple cider
1 splash Rose's lime juice
Ground cinnamon for sprinkling

MANGO MARGARITA

Tropical yet frosty
1½ ounces tequila
½ ounce mango puree
½ ounce Cointreau
1 splash Rose's lime juice
Mango slice for garnish

COFFEE MARGARITA

Muy Mexicana
1½ ounces gold tequila
½ ounce Kahlúa
½ ounce Cointreau
1 splash Rose's lime juice
Lime slice for garnish

NUTS TO YOU MARGARITA

Wash down some almonds and hazelnuts
1½ ounces gold tequila
½ ounce amaretto
½ ounce Frangelico
1 splash Rose's lime juice
Orange slice for garnish

PASSION FRUIT MARGARITA

With a touch of passion fruit–flavored Cognac. Look for passion fruit puree at gourmet markets or online.

1½ ounces gold tequila
½ ounce Alizé Gold Passion Cognac
½ ounce passion fruit puree
1 splash Rose's lime juice
Lemon slice for garnish

VANILLARITA

Anything but plain

1½ ounces silver tequila
½ ounce Absolut Vanilia vodka
½ ounce Cointreau
1 splash Rose's lime juice
Lime wedge for garnish

WHITE FRUIT MARGARITA

Flavored with apple and pear

1½ ounces silver tequila
½ ounce Absolut Pears vodka
½ ounce sour apple schnapps
Pear slice for garnish

MEXICANA

An old standby

2 ounces gold tequila
1 ounce pineapple juice
1 ounce fresh sour mix
1 teaspoon grenadine
Maraschino cherry for garnish

Combine liquid ingredients in mixing glass. Add ice and shake. Strain into glass and garnish.

MEXICAN BANDIT

May steal your heart—and head

1 ounce gold tequila
1 ounce Myers's rum
1 ounce sambuca
Lime slice for garnish

Combine liquid ingredients in mixing glass. Add ice and shake. Strain into glass and garnish.

MEXICAN DOCTOR

Will fix you right up

2 ounces gold tequila
1 teaspoon grenadine
2 dashes Fee Brothers lime bitters
Splash of Sprite or 7UP
Maraschino cherry for garnish

Pour tequila and grenadine into ice-filled rocks glass. Add bitters and soft drink, and garnish.

MEXICAN EGG CREAM

Mexico meets Brooklyn.

2 ounces 1921 Tequila Cream
1 ounce white crème de cacao
Club soda

Pour tequila and liqueur into ice-filled highball glass. Top with club soda to taste and stir.

MEXICAN HOLIDAY

Enjoy on Cinco de Mayo
2 ounces tequila
1 ounce Harvey's Bristol Cream sherry

Pour tequila and sherry into ice-filled rocks glass and stir.

MEXICAN $TINGER

With Cognac and mint
2 ounces Silver Patrón tequila
½ ounce Remy Martin VSOP Cognac
1 splash white crème de menthe
Lemon twist for garnish

Combine liquid ingredients in ice-filled rocks glass. Stir and garnish.

MEZCAL HIGHBALL

Tequila's agave relative, on ice
2 ounces Monte Alban mezcal
Juice of half a lime
Club soda
Lime wedge for garnish

Pour mezcal and juice into ice-filled highball glass and stir. Top with club soda to taste and garnish.

MEZCAL MARTINI

A taste of Old Mexico
3 ounces mezcal
1 ounce sweet vermouth
3 jalapeño-stuffed olives for garnish

Combine mezcal and vermouth in mixing glass. Add ice and shake. Strain into glass and garnish.

MIND ERASER

Silver Patrón only, por favor. To sugar the lime slice you'll perch on the rim of the glass, spread a teaspoon of granulated sugar on a saucer and press slice into it on both sides.
2½ ounces Silver Patrón tequila
1½ ounces fresh lime juice
½ teaspoon superfine sugar
Crushed ice
Sugared lime slice for garnish

Combine tequila, juice, and sugar in mixing glass. Shake, strain into glass filled with crushed ice, and garnish.

MONTEREY SUNSET

Beautiful scene, beautiful drink
2 ounces gold tequila
½ ounce crème de cassis
Club soda
Lemon slice for garnish

Pour tequila and liqueur into ice-filled highball glass. Top with club soda to taste and garnish.

MUSIC TREE

Feel the beat.
2 ounces gold tequila
1 ounce blue curaçao
Pineapple juice
Lemon twist for garnish

Pour liquid ingredients into ice-filled highball glass. Stir and garnish.

NEW YORK SKYLINE

Mexico comes to Gotham.

2 ounces silver tequila
1 ounce cranberry juice
½ ounce lime juice
1 ounce club soda
Lime slice for garnish

Pour tequila and juices into ice-filled highball glass. Top with club soda and garnish.

PEACH MARGARITA

Peachy keen

1½ ounces tequila
½ ounce peach schnapps
½ ounce Cointreau
1 splash Rose's lime juice
Fresh peach wedge for garnish

Combine liquid ingredients in mixing glass. Add ice and shake. Strain into glass and garnish.

RAINDROP

Flavored with sambuca

2 ounces Sauza silver tequila
1 ounce sambuca
3 coffee beans for garnish

Pour tequila and liqueur into ice-filled rocks glass. Stir and garnish.

RASPBERRY MARGARITA

Sans seeds

1½ ounces gold tequila
½ ounce framboise
½ ounce Cointreau
1 splash Rose's lime juice
Raspberry for garnish

Combine liquid ingredients in mixing glass. Add ice and shake. Strain into glass and garnish.

RAINDROP

RED APPLE

With sour apple schnapps and a little black raspberry

1 ounce tequila
1 ounce sour apple schnapps
½ ounce Chambord
Apple slice for garnish

Pour liquid ingredients into ice-filled rocks glass. Stir and garnish.

ROSITA

Pretty as a red rose

2 ounces tequila
1 ounce Campari
½ ounce Cointreau

Pour ingredients into ice-filled rocks glass. Stir and garnish.

RUSTY STAKE

Nail, schmail

1½ ounces gold tequila
1½ ounces Drambuie
Lemon twist for garnish

Pour tequila and liqueur into ice-filled rocks glass. Stir and garnish.

SLOE TEQUILA

Follow up with a siesta?
2 ounces tequila
1 ounce sloe gin
½ ounce fresh sour mix

Combine ingredients in mixing glass. Add ice, shake, and strain into glass.

SOUTH OF THE BORDER

Another coffee-flavored favorite
2 ounces gold tequila
¾ ounce Tia Maria
½ ounce fresh sour mix

Combine ingredients in mixing glass. Add ice, shake, and strain into glass.

SPANISH IMPRESSIONIST

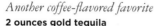

A palette of golden browns
2 ounces gold tequila
½ ounce Tio Pepe sherry

Pour tequila and sherry into ice-filled rocks glass and stir.

SPRING BREAK

A toast to Acapulco-bound college students
2 ounces tequila
1 ounce pineapple juice
1 ounce tangerine juice

Pour ingredients into ice-filled highball glass and stir.

STIFF PEAR

Tequila with a pear eau-de-vie
2 ounces gold tequila
1 ounce Poire William

Combine tequila and eau-de-vie in mixing glass. Add ice, shake, and strain into glass.

STRAWBERRY MARGARITA

To freeze or not to freeze?
1½ ounces tequila
½ ounce strawberry schnapps
½ ounce Cointreau
1 splash Rose's lime juice
Strawberry for garnish

Combine liquid ingredients in mixing glass. Add ice and shake. Strain into glass and garnish.

STRAWBERRY WHIP

The secret's in the schnapps.
2 ounces tequila
1 ounce triple sec
1 ounce strawberry schnapps
Strawberry for garnish

Pour liquid ingredients into ice-filled rocks glass. Stir and garnish.

TEN HIGH

Deserves a double high-five from vanilla lovers
2 ounces gold tequila
1 ounce Tuaca
Lime twist for garnish

Pour tequila and liqueur into ice-filled rocks glass. Stir and garnish.

TEQUILA AND PIMM'S

A jolly good cup
2 ounces silver tequila
1 ounce Pimm's No. 1
Lemon wedge for garnish

Pour tequila and Pimm's into ice-filled rocks glass. Stir and garnish.

TEQUILA AND TONIC

A no-nonsense tipple for tequila lovers

2 ounces tequila
Tonic water
Lime slice for garnish

Pour tequila into ice-filled rocks glass. Top with tonic to taste and garnish.

TEQUILA ANGEL

With silver wings

2 ounces Patrón Silver
1 ounce white crème de cacao
Lemon slice for garnish

Combine tequila and liqueur in ice-filled highball glass. Stir and garnish.

TEQUILA APRICOT COOLER

Fizzy refreshment

2 ounces tequila
1 ounce apricot brandy
Club soda
Fresh apricot half for garnish

Pour tequila and liqueur into ice-filled highball glass. Top with club soda to taste and garnish.

TEQUILA AZUL

Viva el blueberry!

2 ounces silver tequila
1 ounce blueberry puree
½ ounce blue curaçao
1 to 3 fresh blueberries for garnish

Combine liquid ingredients in mixing glass. Add ice and shake. Strain into glass and garnish.

TEQUILA CANYON

TEQUILA CANYON

With colorful layers of fruit juice

1½ ounces silver tequila
¼ ounce triple sec
4 ounces cranberry juice
½ ounce orange juice
½ ounce pineapple juice
Lime peel spiral for garnish

Pour tequila, liqueur, and cranberry juice into ice-filled highball glass. Top with orange juice, then with pineapple juice, and garnish. Serve with a straw.

TEQUILA CLOUDS

With a silver lining, of course

1½ ounces silver tequila
½ ounce white crème de menthe
Sprite or 7UP
Lemon twist for garnish

Pour tequila and liqueur into ice-filled highball glass. Top with soft drink to taste and garnish.

TEQUILA COLLINS

Tom heads southwest.
2 ounces tequila
1 ounce fresh sour mix
Club soda
Maraschino cherry for garnish
Orange slice for garnish

Combine tequila and sour mix in mixing glass. Add ice, shake, and pour with ice into glass. Top with club soda to taste and garnish.

TEQUILA GIMLET

With a touch of lime
1½ ounces tequila
½ ounce Rose's lime juice
Lime slice for garnish

Pour tequila and juice into ice-filled rocks glass, stir, and garnish.

TEQUILA GREYHOUND

Tequila subs for vodka in this Latino version of an old favorite.
2 ounces tequila
Grapefruit juice

Pour tequila into ice-filled rocks glass. Top with juice to taste and stir.

TEQUILA MANHATTAN

Tequila replaces rye whiskey.
2½ ounces gold tequila
1 ounce sweet vermouth
Lime peel spiral for garnish

Combine tequila and vermouth in mixing glass. Add ice and shake. Pour with ice into glass and garnish.

TEQUILA MOCKINGBIRD

Tweet away.
2 ounces silver tequila
½ ounce green crème de menthe
Juice of one lime
Lime slice for garnish

Combine liquid ingredients in mixing glass. Add ice and shake. Pour with ice into glass and garnish.

TEQUILA OLD-FASHIONED

The classic cocktail redefined
½ teaspoon superfine sugar
1 orange slice, peeled
1 maraschino cherry
1 dash bitters of choice
2 ounces gold tequila
1 splash still water

Muddle sugar, orange, cherry, and bitters in bottom of rocks glass. Add ice, pour in tequila, and top with water.

TEQUILA PRES

Tequila lite
2 ounces tequila
Ginger ale
Club soda
Lime twist for garnish

Pour tequila into ice-filled highball glass, top with equal parts ginger ale and club soda to taste, and garnish.

TEQUILA SCREWDRIVER

Way more potent than its vodka cousin
2 ounces tequila
4 ounces orange juice
Orange slice for garnish

Combine tequila and juice in ice-filled rocks glass. Stir and garnish.

TEQUILA SOUR

Serve straight up or on ice.

2 ounces tequila
3 ounces fresh sour mix
Lime slice for garnish

Combine tequila and sour mix in mixing glass. Add ice and shake. Strain into sour glass or pour with ice into rocks glass, and garnish.

TEQUILA SUNRISE

Immortalized in song by the Eagles

2 ounces silver tequila
½ ounce grenadine
3 ounces orange juice

Combine ingredients in ice-filled highball glass and stir.

TEQUILA SUNSET

A pleasant end to the day

2½ ounces silver tequila
½ ounce Rose's lime juice
½ ounce Chambord
Lime slice for garnish

Combine liquid ingredients in ice-filled rocks glass, stir, and garnish.

TEQUILA VERDE

Minty fresh

2 ounces silver tequila
1 ounce green crème de menthe
Mint sprig for garnish

Combine tequila and liqueur in ice-filled rocks glass, stir, and garnish.

A WORD FROM THE BARTENDERS

Unlike tequila, which is made from blue agave, the rougher-edged mezcal (which as a rule comes with a worm in the bottle) is produced from several different agave species. To see how mezcal compares in a cocktail to the real thing, prepare the Mezcal Martini on page 138; then mix the same drink using tequila. Sip one, then the other, as a taste test—and then pray you don't end up under the table.

VERA CRUZ

A salute to Mexico's intriguing southern state

2 ounces tequila
1 ounce white crème de menthe
1 splash club soda
Mint sprig for garnish

Pour tequila and liqueur into ice-filled highball glass. Top with club soda and garnish.

WONKY DONKEY

Steady there, boy.

1½ ounces tequila
1½ ounces Mount Gay rum
Lime slice for garnish

Pour tequila and rum into ice-filled rocks glass. Stir and garnish.

BRANDY

What might be called **standard brandy** is distilled from grape wine, while **fruit brandies** are made from the fermented mash of apples or other fruits, and are identified by the fruit at the source—e.g., blackberry brandy. Dutch traders discovered the spirit in Italy and introduced it to Northern Europeans. The traders also gave it its name—*brandewijn* (burnt wine), for the heating of the wine during distillation.

The finest standard brandy is **Cognac**, distilled in and around the eponymous French town. Two other Gallic stars in the brandy galaxy are grape wine–based **Armagnac** and Normandy's **calvados**, made from apple cider. Even so, France hardly has a lock on brandy. The spirit is distilled in countries around the world—including the United States, where almost all brandy distillers call California home.

ARMAGNAC
WITH MINT

APPLE BRANDY RICKEY

With the requisite lime

1½ ounces apple brandy
1 splash Rose's lime juice
Club soda
Lime wedge for garnish

Pour brandy into ice-filled rocks glass. Add juice and club soda to taste, and garnish.

APRICOT FIZZ

Apricot brandy is one of The Four Seasons bartenders' favorite mixers.

2 ounces apricot brandy
1 ounce fresh sour mix
4 ounces club soda

Combine brandy and sour mix in mixing glass. Add ice, shake, and pour with ice into glass. Top with club soda and stir.

APRICOT KISS

For Scotch lovers

2 ounces apricot brandy
1 ounce Scotch
½ ounce sweet vermouth

Pour ingredients into ice-filled rocks glass and stir.

APRICOT SOUR

Tart and refreshing

3 ounces apricot brandy
1 ounce fresh sour mix
Orange slice for garnish
Maraschino cherry for garnish

Combine brandy and sour mix in mixing glass. Add ice and shake. Strain into glass and garnish.

ARMAGNAC WITH MINT

Armagnac brandy is triple-distilled, leaving it with a lower alcohol content than Cognac.

2 ounces Armagnac
1 ounce dry vermouth
1 ounce green crème de menthe

Combine ingredients in mixing glass. Add ice, stir, and strain into glass.

BARCELONA BABY

Flavored with orange and apricot, fruits that thrive in the fair Castilian capital

2 ounces apricot brandy
1 ounce gin
1 ounce orange juice
½ teaspoon sweet vermouth

Combine ingredients in mixing glass. Add ice, shake, and strain into glass.

BLACKBERRY BLAST

With a touch of white chocolate

2 ounces Hiram Walker blackberry brandy

1 ounce Godiva white chocolate liqueur

1 ounce Baileys Irish Cream

Pour ingredients into ice-filled rocks glass and stir.

BLACKJACK

Two brandies plus cream

1½ ounces brandy

1 ounce blackberry brandy

1 ounce heavy cream

Combine ingredients in mixing glass. Add ice, shake, and strain into glass.

BLISSFUL BANANA

Cognac teams up with a dreamy banana liqueur.

2 ounces Cognac

1 ounce crème de banane

Combine ingredients in mixing glass. Add ice, stir to chill, and strain into glass.

BRANDY ALEXANDER

Classic and ultra-rich

1½ ounces Cognac

1 ounce white crème de cacao

1 ounce heavy cream

Nutmeg for sprinkling

Combine liquid ingredients in mixing glass. Add ice and shake. Strain into glass and sprinkle with nutmeg.

BRANDY AND SODA

See also Harmony, page 151.

2 ounces brandy

5 ounces club soda

Orange peel spiral for garnish

Pour brandy into ice-filled highball glass. Top with club soda and garnish.

BRANDY À L'ANANAS

Translation: brandy with pineapple

1½ ounces brandy

1 ounce pineapple juice

1 splash grenadine

Crushed ice

Maraschino cherry for garnish

Combine liquid ingredients in mixing glass. Add ice and stir to chill. Strain into glass filled with crushed ice and garnish.

BRANDY CANDY CANE

No Santa cap required

2 ounces brandy

½ ounce green crème de menthe

½ ounce grenadine

Maraschino cherry for garnish

Pour liquid ingredients into ice-filled rocks glass. Stir and garnish.

A WORD FROM THE BARTENDERS

Here's a guide to deciphering the initials you'll see on some Cognac bottles—to be exact, older Cognacs. The list below runs from youngest to oldest.

V.S. Very Special—Aged 2 to 4 years

V.S.O.P. Very Superior Old Pale—Aged 4 to 6 years

X.O. Extra old—Indicates the oldest Cognac made by a particular house, as do the words "Extra" or "Reserve." It is aged for a least 6 years, but usually around 20 years.

BRONZE BULLET

Fortified with B & B, a mix of brandy and Bénédictine liqueur

2 ounces brandy
1 ounce B & B
Maraschino cherry for garnish

Pour brandy and liqueur into ice-filled rocks glass. Stir and garnish.

BURNT CHERRY

A cherry triple whammy

2 ounces cherry brandy
½ ounce maraschino liqueur
½ ounce Cointreau
½ ounce lemon juice
1 tablespoon powdered sugar
Maraschino cherry for garnish

Combine liquid ingredients and sugar in mixing glass. Add ice and shake. Strain into glass and garnish.

CAFÉ MYSTIQUE

Coffee-flavored brandy with port

2 ounces DeKuyper coffee brandy
1½ ounces tawny port
½ teaspoon Cointreau
3 coffee beans for garnish

Combine liquid ingredients in mixing glass. Add ice and stir to chill. Strain into glass and garnish.

CENTRIFUGE

Swirling with flavor

2 ounces brandy
1 ounce sambuca negra
¼ ounce fresh sour mix

Combine ingredients in mixing glass. Add ice, shake, and strain into glass.

CHARMED

The enchantress is Madeira.

2 ounces brandy
1 ounce Madeira
½ ounce Cointreau

Combine ingredients in mixing glass. Add ice, stir to chill, and strain into glass.

CHOCOLATE-COVERED CHERRY

As tempting as it sounds

1½ ounces cherry brandy
1½ ounces dark crème de cacao
½ ounce Kahlúa
½ ounce heavy cream
Cherry with stem for garnish

Combine liquid ingredients in mixing glass. Add ice and shake. Strain into glass and garnish.

CLASSIC STINGER

Fashionable in British literary circles of the 1930s

2 ounces brandy
1 ounce white crème de menthe
Ice water as chaser

Pour brandy and liqueur into ice-filled rocks glass and stir. Serve with a glass of ice water on the side.

THE CLUB BOUNCER

Licoracy drink that doesn't mess around

1½ ounces brandy
½ ounce anisette
1 dash bitters of choice

Pour brandy and liqueur into ice-filled rocks glass. Add bitters and stir.

Calvados Cocktails

The most famous of the apple brandies comes from a region of Lower Normandy, where juice from choice apples is fermented into apple cider, double-distilled, and aged in oak barrels. *À votre santé!*

**APPLE
TRIPTYCH**

A work of art
2 ounces calvados
2 ounces DeKuyper apple schnapps
1 ounce apple juice

Combine ingredients in mixing glass. Add ice, shake, and strain into glass.

**CALVADOS
AU CITRON**

Apple brandy with lemon
2 ounces calvados
1 ounce lemon juice
½ ounce simple syrup (page 27)
Lemon slice for garnish

Combine liquid ingredients in mixing glass. Add ice and shake. Strain into glass and garnish.

**CALVADOS
COOLER**

With equal parts brandy and gin
2 ounces calvados
2 ounces gin
½ ounce lemon juice
½ ounce grenadine
Club soda
Lemon twist for garnish

Combine calvados, gin, juice, and grenadine in mixing glass. Add ice, shake, and pour with ice into glass. Top with club soda to taste and garnish.

**JACQUES
ROSE**

A calvados version of the Jack Rose, a classic applejack cocktail from the Prohibition era
1½ ounces calvados
Juice of half a lime
1 teaspoon grenadine

Combine ingredients in mixing glass. Add ice, shake, and strain into glass.

**POMME
ROUGE**

Simple and satisfying
2 ounces calvados
2 ounces Dubonnet Rouge
Lemon twist for garnish

Combine brandy and Dubonnet in mixing glass. Add ice and shake. Pour with ice into glass and garnish.

COGNAC JAPONAIS

A great Cognac shares the glass with a Japanese honeydew melon liqueur.

Crushed ice
2½ ounces Martell Cordon Bleu Cognac
1½ ounces Midori

Fill a tulip glass with crushed ice and pour in Cognac and liqueur. Stir.

CREAMY NUT

Nut as in nutmeg. Dark crème de cacao is a chocolate-flavored liqueur with a hint of vanilla. (White crème de cacao is the liqueur's clear form and is slightly less intense in flavor.)

2 ounces Armagnac
1 ounce dark crème de cacao
1 ounce light cream
¼ teaspoon grated nutmeg, plus extra for sprinkling

Combine liquid ingredients and ¼ teaspoon nutmeg in mixing glass. Add ice and shake. Strain into glass and sprinkle with nutmeg.

ELIXIR OF LOVE

Inspired by Donizetti's opera

1 ounce apricot brandy
1 ounce cherry brandy
1 ounce sweet vermouth
1 ounce peach juice

Combine ingredients in mixing glass. Add ice, shake, and strain into glass.

FIFTH AVENUE

Old guard and pricey

1½ ounces Cognac
1 ounce 25-year-old Macallan Scotch

Pour brandy and whiskey into ice-filled rocks glass and stir.

FIGHTING IRISH

A toast to the footballers of Notre Dame

2 ounces brandy
1 ounce Irish whiskey
Lemon twist for garnish

Pour brandy and whiskey into ice-filled rocks glass. Stir and garnish.

FOUR SEASONS SIDECAR

Spares no expense

2 ounces Hennessy Paradis Cognac
1 ounce fresh sour mix
1 splash Cinzano Rosso vermouth

Combine ingredients in mixing glass. Add ice, shake, and strain into glass.

FREDO'S FAVE

The choice of a bookish regular

1½ ounces Armagnac
1½ ounces Grand Marnier
Orange slice for garnish

Pour brandy and liqueur into ice-filled rocks glass. Stir and garnish.

GINICOT

Apricot brandy with gin

2 ounces apricot brandy
1 ounce gin
1 ounce fresh sour mix
Club soda

Combine brandy, gin, and sour mix in mixing glass. Add ice and shake. Pour with ice into glass and top with club soda to taste.

THE GREEN LANTERN

Serve with a power ring?

2 ounces X.O. Cognac
1 ounce Midori
1 ounce lemon juice

Combine ingredients in mixing glass. Add ice, shake, and strain into glass.

HARMONY

Armagnac in tune with our freshly-made sour mix

2 ounces Armagnac
1 ounce fresh sour mix
3 ounces club soda
Orange slice for garnish

Combine brandy and sour mix in mixing glass. Add ice, shake, and pour with ice into glass. Top with club soda and garnish.

HOERDEMANN HOWL

Sidecar variation said to make a quiet regular "howl with delight"

2 ounces Rémy Martin X.O. Cognac
1 ounce Cointreau
1 ounce lemon juice
½ ounce sweet vermouth
½ ounce peach schnapps
Lemon twist for garnish

Combine liquid ingredients in mixing glass. Add ice and shake. Strain into glass and garnish.

IRISH BEAUTY

With a French background

2 ounces Cognac
1 ounce Irish Mist

Pour Cognac and liqueur into snifter and swirl to mix.

KISSING COUSINS

KISSING COUSINS

They come from France.

2 ounces Cognac
1 ounce anisette

Combine brandy and liqueur in mixing glass. Add ice, shake, and strain into glass.

LEMON FROST

A tart treat

2 ounces brandy
1 ounce fresh sour mix
3 dashes Fee Brothers lemon bitters
Lemon peel spiral for garnish

Combine liquid ingredients in mixing glass. Add ice and shake. Strain into glass and garnish.

LIGHTNING FLASH

With bolts of vermouth
2 ounces brandy
½ ounce sweet vermouth
½ ounce dry vermouth
2 teaspoons Cointreau

Combine ingredients in mixing glass. Add ice, stir to chill, and strain into glass.

MINT LEAF

An eclectic mix
2 ounces brandy
½ ounce dry vermouth
½ ounce tawny port
1 splash white crème de menthe
1 ounce orange juice
1 teaspoon grenadine
Mint sprig for garnish

Combine liquid ingredients in mixing glass. Add ice and shake. Strain into glass and garnish.

MUSIC NOTE

Tinkle, tinkle, little cubes . . .
2 ounces brandy
1 ounce fresh sour mix
½ teaspoon grenadine
Orange slice for garnish
Maraschino cherry for garnish

Combine liquid ingredients in mixing glass. Add ice and shake. Pour with ice into rocks glass and garnish.

NATURE'S ESSENCE

With three fruit flavors
2 ounces brandy
1½ ounces maraschino liqueur
½ ounce peach schnapps
Lemon twist for garnish

Combine liquid ingredients in mixing glass. Add ice and shake. Strain into glass and garnish.

THE RUMSFELD

Love it or hate it.
2 ounces brandy
1 ounce light rum
1 ounce Cointreau
1 ounce fresh sour mix

Combine ingredients in mixing glass. Add ice, shake, and strain into glass.

SHADOW OF YOUR SMILE

Sing it out, Tony B.
Crushed ice
2 ounces brandy
1 ounce amaretto
1 ounce peach schnapps

Fill a rocks glass with crushed ice and pour in liquid ingredients. Stir.

SIDECAR

The classic from the Prohibition era
2 ounces Cognac
1 ounce fresh sour mix
1 splash Cointreau

Combine ingredients in mixing glass. Add ice, shake, and strain into glass.

SILVER STREAK

For those with a taste for gin
1½ ounces brandy
½ ounce gin
1 splash Rose's lime juice
Lime wedge for garnish

Pour brandy and gin into ice-filled rocks glass and add lime juice. Stir and garnish.

THE SIT-DOWN

The drink you can't refuse—and the priciest Cognac around
2 ounces Rémy Martin Louis XIII Cognac
1 fine cigar

Pour brandy into steamed snifter and light cigar. Sip, puff, and hope for the best.

SONNY'S LIMBO

A steel-drum dance of a drink
2 ounces peach brandy
2 ounces pineapple juice
Pineapple spear for garnish

Pour brandy and juice into ice-filled rocks glass. Stir and garnish.

SOUR CHERRY

Tart and refreshing
2 ounces cherry brandy
½ ounce lemon juice
4 ounces club soda
Lime wedge for garnish

Combine brandy and juice in mixing glass. Add ice, shake, and pour with ice into glass. Top with club soda and garnish.

SOUR GRAPES

Brandy with sour grape schnapps
1½ ounces brandy
½ ounce DeKuyper Grape Pucker
½ ounce fresh sour mix

Combine ingredients in mixing glass. Add ice, shake, and strain into glass.

SOUTHERN NAIL

Rémy meets Jack.
1½ ounces Rémy Martin V.S.O.P. Cognac
1 ounce Jack Daniels Tennessee whiskey

Pour Cognac and whiskey into ice-filled rocks glass and stir.

SUPREMO

The Spanish name speaks for itself.
2 ounces Cognac
1 ounce Fundador Brandy de Jerez

Pour brandies into ice-filled rocks glass and stir.

SWEET APPLE

Made with applejack brandy
2½ ounces applejack
1 ounce sweet vermouth
Apple slice for garnish

Combine brandy and vermouth in mixing glass. Add ice and stir to chill. Strain into glass and garnish.

SWEET IVORY

Fizzy and toothsome
2 ounces brandy
1 teaspoon superfine sugar
3 ounces club soda
Maraschino cherry for garnish

Combine brandy and sugar in mixing glass. Add ice, shake, and pour with ice into glass. Top with club soda and garnish.

SWEET SIDECAR

With sweet vermouth

2 ounces brandy

1 ounce sweet vermouth

1 ounce fresh sour mix

1 splash Cointreau

Maraschino cherry for garnish

Combine liquid ingredients in mixing glass. Add ice and shake. Strain into glass and garnish.

TERMINATOR COCKTAIL

Taken from a popular shot recipe

2 ounces Hiram Walker blackberry brandy

2 ounces dark rum

2 ounces cranberry juice

Lemon wedge for garnish

Pour liquid ingredients into ice-filled highball glass. Stir and garnish. Serve with a straw.

THEO'S CÁDIZ

A brandy variation on the liqueur-based Cádiz cocktail (page 161)

1 ounce blackberry brandy

½ ounce dry sherry

½ ounce triple sec

1 tablespoon light cream

Combine ingredients in mixing glass. Add ice, shake, and pour with ice into glass.

TREETOP

Lemon tree, very pretty . . .

2 ounces brandy

½ ounce Stolichnaya Limonnaya vodka

1 ounce fresh sour mix

Combine ingredients in mixing glass. Add ice, shake, and strain into glass.

THEO'S CÁDIZ

VANILLA DREAM

With a brandy-based liqueur that brings butterscotch to mind

2 ounces brandy

1 ounce Tuaca

1 ounce heavy cream

¼ teaspoon grated nutmeg, plus extra for sprinkling

Combine liquid ingredients and ¼ teaspoon nutmeg in mixing glass. Add ice and shake. Strain into glass and sprinkle with nutmeg.

WILLIAM TELL

Apple brandy shot through with lemon-lime

2 ounces apple brandy

4 ounces Sprite or 7UP

Lemon wedge for garnish

Pour brandy into ice-filled highball glass, top with soft drink, and garnish.

Nigronius Pontificus, by John Varriano; oil on linen (48" x 40") 2009

Paging Pablo Picasso

The Bronfman family, who built the Seagram Building and actively participated in the development of its huge new restaurant, sought in the late 1950s to display the work of some of the finest modern artists, including Pablo Picasso. When contacted, Picasso declined to create the wished-for large painting for the Pool Room, pleading too little time. Instead, he offered a canvas curtain painted for the Paris production of the ballet *The Three-Cornered Hat*—a prize that had been promised to New York's Museum of Modern Art, but was found to be too large for the museum walls.

The Bronfmans jumped at the chance and bought the curtain to hang in the Pool Room of The Four Seasons. Yet Restaurant Associates Vice President Joseph Baum had reservations about its placement. "It depicted a bullfight," he explained, "and I just didn't think that would go down well with customers dining on tournedos of beef." In the end, the Picasso curtain was hung in the spacious corridor between the restaurant's Pool Room and Grill Room, on a 20-foot-high travertine wall. To say the least, it was—and remains—a dramatic surprise for arriving diners and bargoers.

To this day, artworks are exhibited in the downstairs lobby on East 52nd Street. In times past, the most famous included Jackson Pollock's *Blue Poles* and Joan Miró's *Composition*. In fact, in the 1960s, The Four Seasons was the scene of a series of important exhibitions, some showcasing such emerging artists as Andy Warhol, Frank Stella, and Robert Rauschenberg.

LIQUEURS

By the end of the sixteenth century, the Italians, Germans, and Dutch were busily producing liqueurs. Today their successors follow the same two methods: **distillation**, with crushed plant matter distilled along with the alcohol (usually a neutral grain spirit); or **maceration**, which involves soaking the plant matter in a distilled neutral grain spirit to extract the flavors.

If making liqueurs is relatively simple, sorting them out from similar spirits is not. Blurry are the lines between liqueurs and aperitifs/digestives—which are, in fact, a subset of liqueurs. But why worry? We've packed a wealth of these spirits into two chapters (see Aperitifs and Digestives, page 175), and taste trumps categorization every time.

AMALFI COAST

The birthplace of Italy's lemony liqueur
2 ounces limoncello
1 ounce Cointreau
1 ounce lime juice
Lemon peel spiral for garnish

Combine liquid ingredients in mixing glass. Add ice and shake. Strain into glass and garnish.

AMARETTO SOUR

Almonds on the rocks
3 ounces amaretto
1 ounce fresh sour mix
Orange slice for garnish
Maraschino cherry for garnish

Combine amaretto and sour mix in mixing glass. Add ice and shake. Pour with ice into glass and garnish.

ANGEL'S DELIGHT

Pink and fluffy
½ ounce Bailey's Irish Cream
½ ounce white crème de cacao
½ ounce Godiva white chocolate liqueur
½ ounce Chambord
Whipped cream for garnish

Combine liqueurs in mixing glass. Add ice and shake. Strain into glass and top with whipped cream to taste.

APPLE BASKET

Three apple spirits in one
2 ounces Berentzen apple liqueur
½ ounce calvados
½ ounce applejack
Club soda
Thin apple slice for garnish

Pour liqueur and brandies into ice-filled white wine glass. Top with club soda to taste and garnish.

THE ARISTOCRAT

Class in a glass. Cognac-based Grand Marnier is the king of the orange liqueurs—rich but not excessively sweet.
2 ounces Grand Marnier Cuvée du Cinquantenaire
1 ounce Rémy Martin V.S.O.P. Cognac

Pour liqueur and Cognac into snifter and swirl to mix.

B & B STINGER

Mint nicely sets off a famed liqueur— B & B, a relatively dry mix of Bénédictine and brandy.
2 ounces B & B
1 ounce white crème de menthe

Combine liqueurs in mixing glass. Add ice, stir to chill, and strain into glass.

APPLE
BASKET

BANSHEE

Wail no more.

2 ounces crème de banane
1 ounce white crème de cacao
1 ounce light cream

Combine ingredients in mixing glass. Add ice, shake, and strain into glass.

BLUE CRUSH

A coconutty variation on the Blue Wave

1 ounce blue curaçao
1 ounce Cointreau
1 ounce Malibu rum
1 ounce vodka
Crushed ice
Orange twist for garnish

Combine liquid ingredients in mixing glass. Add ice and stir to chill. Strain into glass filled with crushed ice and garnish.

BLUE WAVE

Catch it, brudda!

1 ounce blue curaçao
1 ounce Cointreau
1 ounce white crème de cacao
½ ounce vodka

Combine ingredients in mixing glass. Add ice, stir to chill, and strain into glass.

BOCCE BALL

A classic, named for the Italian bowling game

3 ounces amaretto
4 ounces fresh orange juice

Pour liqueur and juice into ice-filled highball glass and stir.

BREAKFAST AT TIFFANY'S

Scenes for the 1960 movie were shot on the plaza of the Seagram Building, home of The Four Seasons.

1 ounce Southern Comfort
1 ounce orange juice
½ teaspoon grenadine
3 ounces Champagne

Combine liqueur, juice, and grenadine in mixing glass. Add ice and shake. Strain into glass and top with Champagne.

CÁDIZ

This vintage mix takes its name from the province in Andalusian Spain.

2 ounces Mr. Boston blackberry brandy
2 ounces amontillado sherry
½ ounce triple sec
1½ ounces heavy cream

Combine ingredients in mixing glass. Add ice, stir to chill, and pour with ice into glass.

THE CELIBATE

A potation almost light enough for abstainers

½ ounce Frangelico
3½ ounces club soda

Pour liqueur into ice-filled rocks glass. Top with club soda and stir.

CHATEAU KISS

Chambord is the Loire Valley château that gave the black raspberry liqueur its name.

2 ounces Baileys Irish Cream
1 ounce Chambord
½ ounce Grand Marnier

Pour ingredients into ice-filled rocks glass and stir.

CHATEAU MONK

Chambord and Fra Angelico's hazelnut liqueur say hello to a creamy Irish concoction.

2 ounces Baileys Irish Cream
1 ounce Frangelico
1 ounce Chambord

Pour ingredients into ice-filled rocks glass and stir.

CHERIE'S COINTREAU NOIR

After Rémy Cointreau's introduction of Cointreau Noir (70 percent Cointreau and 30 percent Cognac), our friend Cherie dreamed up this potent sipper.

1½ ounces Cointreau Noir
1½ ounces London dry gin
2 or 3 dashes Fee Brothers peach bitters
Orange blossom, calendula, or
**   nasturtium for garnish (see Flowers,**
**   page 29).**

Combine liquid ingredients in mixing glass. Add ice and shake. Strain into glass and garnish with the bloom of your choice.

CHERRY BONBON

With black cherry liqueur and chocolate

1 ounce Cherry Heering
1 ounce chocolate liqueur
1 ounce vodka
1 ounce heavy cream

Combine liqueurs and vodka in mixing glass. Add ice and shake. Strain into glass and add cream.

COINTREAU CLOSER

An after-dinner indulgence

2 ounces Cointreau
1 ounce white crème de cacao
1 ounce heavy cream

Combine ingredients in mixing glass. Add ice, shake, and strain into glass.

THE COMFORTER

Sip after supping on mac 'n' cheese?

1½ ounces white crème de menthe
1½ ounces port

Pour liqueur and port into liqueur glass and stir.

COOL KISS

Mucho minty

2 ounces peppermint schnapps
½ ounce blue curaçao
1 ounce lemon juice
4 ounces club soda

Combine schnapps, liqueur, and juice in mixing glass. Add ice and shake. Pour with ice into glass and top with club soda.

DE CHIRICO'S
DELIGHT

**COURT
JESTER**

*"Oh, that's rich!" Black cherry–flavored
Cherry Heering is also called Peter
Heering, after the Dane who created the
liqueur around 1835.*

1 ounce Cherry Heering
1 ounce white crème de cacao
1 ounce heavy cream
Maraschino cherry for garnish

Combine liquid ingredients in mixing
glass. Add ice and shake. Strain into
glass and garnish.

**THE DEAL
CLOSER**

Equal shares all around
1 ounce B & B
1 ounce white crème de cacao
1 ounce white crème de menthe

Pour ingredients into ice-filled rocks
glass and stir.

**DE CHIRICO'S
DELIGHT**

Green, like the artist's favorite color
2 ounces sambuca
1 ounce green Chartreuse
1 ounce Southern Comfort

Pour ingredients into ice-filled rocks
glass and stir.

**DOW
WOW**

*For when your fortunes suddenly take
a turn for the better*
2 ounces Drambuie
1 ounce Southern Comfort
1 ounce Scotch

Pour ingredients into liqueur glass
and stir.

**THE
EROICA**

Inspired by Beethoven's symphony
2 ounces Jägermeister
1 ounce Pernod
1 ounce orange juice
4 ounces club soda
Orange twist for garnish

Pour Jägermeister, Pernod, and juice
into ice-filled highball glass. Top with
club soda and garnish.

**FASCINATING
RHYTHM**

Get out your dancing shoes?
1 ounce Cointreau
1 ounce Potter's melon liqueur
1 ounce vodka
1 ounce peach juice
Crushed ice

Combine liquid ingredients in mixing
glass. Add ice, shake, and strain into
glass filled with crushed ice.

FRUIT BASKET

With three tree fruits
1 ounce peach schnapps
1 ounce sour apple schnapps
1 ounce apricot brandy

Combine ingredients in mixing glass. Add ice, stir to chill, and strain into glass.

FUZZY NAVEL

Think "navel orange" when sipping this elegantly simple cocktail, the creation of mixology guru and author Ray Foley.
1½ ounces peach schnapps
4 ounces orange juice

Pour schnapps and juice into ice-filled rocks glass and stir.

THE GOLD RUSH

With Goldschläger, the cinnamony Swiss liqueur flecked with gold leaf
1 ounce Goldschläger
½ ounce Jägermeister
½ ounce Absolut Peppar vodka
Club soda
Orange twist for garnish

Pour liqueurs and vodka into ice-filled rocks glass. Top with club soda to taste and garnish.

GRASSHOPPER

Mellow, rich, and classic
1 ounce white crème de menthe
1 ounce white crème de cacao
1 ounce light cream

Combine ingredients in mixing glass. Add ice, shake, and strain into glass.

GREEN GEISHA

Japanese honeydew liqueur flavored with ginger
2 ounces Midori
1 ounce grated fresh ginger

Combine ingredients in mixing glass. Add ice, shake, and strain into glass.

GREEN IRISH TWEED

Try it on for size.
Crushed ice
2 ounces Baileys Irish Cream
1 ounce green crème de menthe
1 ounce white crème de cacao

Fill a tulip glass with crushed ice and pour in liquid ingredients. Stir.

HARVEST CORDIAL

Apple and melon flavors punched up with lemon
1 ounce sour apple schnapps
1 ounce melon liqueur
1 ounce limoncello
1 ounce lemon juice

Combine ingredients in mixing glass. Add ice, shake, and strain into glass.

HEAT WAVE CORDIAL

In parts of the British Commonwealth, a cordial is a mix of liqueur and fruit juice.
1½ ounces Malibu rum
½ ounce peach schnapps
3 ounces orange juice
3 ounces pineapple juice

Pour ingredients into an ice-filled highball glass and stir.

The Green Fairy's Return

Absinthe, distilled in part from the herb wormwood, is greenish in color and licoracy in flavor. It is also the spirit associated with Parisian artists and writers and garden-variety bohemians of the late nineteenth century. Nicknamed "the green fairy," absinthe was first banned in 1906 because a ketone in wormwood oil—thujone—could cause hallucinations and even brain damage when the spirit was drunk over time and to excess.

A wealth of new absinthes with less thujone hit the market after the ban was lifted in 2007, but they too should be handled with care. Their 60-plus percent ABV (alcohol by volume) alone could have you seeing snakes on the ceiling.

ABSINTHE MARTINI

The iconic cocktail, with that storied "something extra"

2 ounces gin
½ ounce dry vermouth
½ ounce absinthe

Combine ingredients in mixing glass. Add ice, shake, and strain into glass.

BLUE MOOD

Chase it away.

2 ounces Cîroc vodka
1 ounce absinthe
1 ounce blue curaçao

Combine ingredients in mixing glass. Add ice, shake, and strain into glass.

THE MACABRE

Blood-red

2 ounces Absolut vodka
½ ounce absinthe
½ ounce Chambord
½ ounce grenadine

Combine ingredients in mixing glass. Add ice, shake, and strain into glass.

MOULIN ROUGE

Shades of Toulouse Lautrec

2 ounces peach schnapps
1 ounce absinthe
1 teaspoon grenadine
Club soda
Mint sprig for garnish

Combine schnapps, absinthe, and grenadine in mixing glass. Add ice, shake, and pour with ice into glass. Top with club soda to taste and garnish.

PAOLO AND FRANCESCA

Love in the inferno. Sambuca negra (black sambuca) is lightly flavored with coffee.

1 ounce absinthe
1 ounce sambuca negra
2 ounces hot espresso

Combine ingredients in mixing glass, shake, and pour into glass.

HELGA IN LOVE

She lusts for liqueurs.
1 ounce peach schnapps
1 ounce Southern Comfort
1 ounce apricot brandy
1 ounce limoncello

Combine ingredients in mixing glass. Add ice, stir to chill, and strain into glass.

THE HORSE'S MOUTH

Your straight shooter
1 ounce Southern Comfort
1 ounce Grand Marnier
1 ounce Cognac

Pour ingredients into liqueur glass and stir.

IRISH MONK

A blessed winter warmer
2 ounces Frangelico
2 ounces Jameson Irish whiskey

Pour liqueur and whiskey into ice-filled rocks glass and stir.

ITALIAN ROOT BEER

Close in taste to the old American favorite. For a fancier version, see Pretend Root Beer, page 170.
2 ounces Galliano, chilled
4 ounces Coca-Cola Classic, chilled

Pour liqueur and soft drink into white wine glass and stir.

JADE DREAM

Exotic and mesmerizing
1 ounce Potter's melon liqueur
1 ounce vodka
1 ounce apricot brandy
1 ounce light cream

Combine ingredients in mixing glass. Add ice, shake, and strain into glass.

KAREN'S CHOICE

A limoncello, cherry brandy, and lemon-lime combo
1 ounce limoncello
1 ounce cherry brandy
1 ounce lemon juice
1 ounce lime juice
Lime twist for garnish

Combine liquid ingredients in mixing glass. Add ice and shake. Strain into glass and garnish.

LA BOHÈME

To die for
2 ounces limoncello
1 ounce Pernod
1 ounce orange juice
4 ounces club soda

Pour liqueurs and juice into ice-filled highball glass. Top with club soda and stir.

LICORICE DELIGHT

The name says it all.
2 ounces sambuca
1 ounce white crème de cacao
1 ounce light cream

Combine ingredients in mixing glass. Add ice, shake, and strain into glass.

MANDOLIN

Inspired by the singing gondoliers of Venice
1 ounce Frangelico
1 ounce Grand Marnier
1 ounce Punt è Mes

Pour ingredients into liqueur glass and stir.

THE MARTHA LOU

A lively mix
2 ounces Southern Comfort
1 ounce amaretto
½ ounce sloe gin
½ ounce lemon juice
Club soda
Lemon twist for garnish

Combine liqueurs, sloe gin, and juice in mixing glass. Add ice, shake, and pour with ice into glass. Top with club soda to taste and garnish.

MELLOW ORANGE

With vanilla vodka
2 ounces Grand Marnier
1 ounce Stolichnaya Vanil
1 ounce orange juice

Combine ingredients in mixing glass. Add ice, shake, and pour with ice into glass.

MELON BALL CORDIAL

Honeydew, pineapple, and orange—spiked with vodka!
½ ounce DeKuyper's melon liqueur
2 ounces vodka
2 ounces pineapple juice
1 ounce orange juice

Pour ingredients into ice-filled rocks glass and stir.

MELON KISS

One smooth smooch
2 ounces Midori
1 ounce vodka
1 ounce light cream

Combine ingredients in mixing glass. Add ice, shake, and strain into glass.

NASDAQ JITTERS

Hits the spot when you need a stiff drink
1 ounce Drambuie
1 ounce B & B
1 ounce Scotch

Pour ingredients into ice-filled rocks glass and stir.

NEWTON'S APPLE

Bubbly inspiration
2 ounces Pimm's No. 1
1 ounce Bombay dry gin
1 ounce sour apple schnapps
3 ounces club soda

Pour Pimm's, gin, and schnapps into ice-filled highball glass. Top with club soda and stir.

NOISETTE ROSE

French for "pink nut"
2 ounces crème de noyaux
1 ounce white crème de cacao
1 ounce light cream

Combine ingredients in mixing glass. Add ice, shake, and strain into glass.

**ORANGE
CREAM**

Lip-licking good
2 ounces Grand Marnier
1 ounce white crème de cacao
1 ounce light cream

Combine ingredients in mixing glass.
Add ice, shake, and strain into glass.

**PEACHY
KEEN**

With a touch of coffee
1 ounce peach schnapps
½ ounce coffee liqueur
½ ounce bourbon
1 ounce vodka
1 ounce light cream

Combine ingredients in mixing glass.
Add ice, shake, and strain into glass.

**PEPPERMINT
PATTY**

Sweet as candy
1 ounce white crème de menthe
1 ounce dark crème de cacao
1 ounce chocolate liqueur
1 ounce vanilla-flavored vodka
Chocolate stick for garnish

Combine liquid ingredients in mixing
glass. Add ice and stir to chill. Strain
into glass and garnish.

**PEPPERMINT
SWIRL**

*Minty schnapps teams with coffee and
chocolate. The word schnapps ("mouthful")
is German, but most of these spirits, which
range from very dry to very sweet, are
produced in Denmark.*
1 ounce peppermint schnapps
1 ounce Kahlúa
½ ounce Godiva white chocolate liqueur
1 ounce light cream

Combine ingredients in mixing glass.
Add ice, shake, and strain into glass.

THE PIAZZA

Transports you to bella Italia
2 ounces Tuaca
1 ounce vodka
1 ounce fresh sour mix

Combine ingredients in mixing glass.
Add ice, shake, and strain into glass.

**PLANTATION
CORDIAL**

The crops? Melon and orange.
2 ounces Southern Comfort
2 ounces DeKuyper melon liqueur
4 ounces fresh orange juice

Pour ingredients into ice-filled
highball glass and stir.

Pousse-Cafés

Born in New Orleans during the Gilded Age, these elaborate, layered whimsies pushed the boundaries of the after-dinner drink. The colorful striations of spirits and liqueurs create a work of art of sorts, though one that offers only fleeting pleasure. (For layering directions, see page 24.)

Naturally, the ingredients in these recipes are listed in the order they're put in the glass. Pousse-café glasses—which usually hold 3 ounces—are available in some china and glassware stores but may be more easily ordered online. In fact, any clear 3-ounce glass will work for a pousse-café as long as it is somewhat slender.

CHERRY ALMOND MINT CREAM

A little bit of heaven?

½ ounce grenadine
½ ounce green crème de menthe
½ ounce amaretto
½ ounce kirsch
½ ounce brandy
Whipped cream for topping

Pour grenadine into a pousse-café glass and carefully layer remaining ingredients in the order listed. Top with whipped cream, taking care not to disturb the layers.

CHOCOLATE ORANGE DELIGHT

Rich and beautiful

½ ounce dark crème de cacao
½ ounce Cointreau
½ ounce Van Gogh chocolate liqueur
½ ounce vodka
½ ounce heavy cream

Pour crème de cacao into a pousse-café glass and carefully layer remaining ingredients in the order listed. Handle with utmost care when serving.

POUSSE-CAFÉ CLASSIQUE

A French Quarter specialty

½ ounce green Chartreuse
½ ounce maraschino
½ ounce cherry brandy
½ ounce kümmel
Whipped cream for topping

Pour Chartreuse into a pousse-café glass and carefully layer remaining ingredients in the order listed. Top with whipped cream, taking care not to disturb the layers.

POUSSE-CAFÉ STANDISH

A classic of its kind. One of the ingredients, kümmel, is a colorless liqueur with the scent of fennel, caraway, and cumin.

½ ounce grenadine
½ ounce white crème de menthe
½ ounce Galliano
½ ounce kümmel
½ ounce brandy

Pour grenadine into a pousse-café glass and carefully layer remaining ingredients in the order listed.

**PRETEND
ROOT BEER**

Made with Coke!
2 ounces Kahlúa
2 ounces Galliano
2 ounces Coca-Cola Classic
2 ounces club soda

Pour liqueurs into ice-filled highball glass. Top with cola and soda and stir.

**PURPLE
BLISS**

With black raspberry
1½ ounces Chambord
1 ounce apricot brandy
½ ounce pineapple juice

Combine ingredients in mixing glass. Add ice, shake, and strain into glass.

THE RELAXER

An almondy soother
2 ounces amaretto
1½ ounces dry vermouth

Combine liqueur and vermouth in mixing glass. Add ice, stir to chill, and strain into glass.

A WORD FROM THE BARTENDERS
When serving a liqueur neat, make sure it's at room temperature before pouring it into the glass. Remember, too, that liqueurs, with their complex flavors and aromas, are meant to be savored at a leisurely pace: Guzzling them is akin to drinking the last drops of a soup from the bowl when dining out.

**RIVERSIDE
DRIVE**

As estimable as the address
1 ounce limoncello
1 ounce Grand Marnier
1 ounce vodka
1 ounce cranberry juice
Orange twist for garnish

Combine liquid ingredients in mixing glass. Add ice and shake. Strain into glass and garnish.

**SHANNON'S
CORDIAL**

*The favorite of a liqueur lover
from Tennessee*
1 ounce Southern Comfort
1 ounce Cointreau
2 ounces orange juice

Pour ingredients into ice-filled white wine glass and stir.

**SIGNORE
O'BRIEN**

Irish with a touch of Italian
2 ounces Baileys Irish Cream
1 ounce Irish Mist
1 ounce amaretto

Pour ingredients into ice-filled rocks glass and stir.

**SKIP'S
COOLER**

A drink with a bubbly personality
2 ounces green crème de menthe
1 ounce Baileys Irish Cream
½ ounce triple sec
Club soda
Mint sprig for garnish

Combine liqueurs and triple sec in mixing glass. Add ice, shake, and pour with ice into glass. Top with club soda to taste and garnish.

SLOE AND EASY

A cocktail for a lazy afternoon

1 ounce sloe gin
½ ounce gin
½ ounce vodka
2 ounces orange juice
Orange slice for garnish

Pour liquid ingredients into ice-filled rocks glass. Stir and garnish.

SOUTHERN PLEASURE

Sip beneath a gnarled oak draped with Spanish moss.

1 ounce Southern Comfort
½ ounce peach schnapps
½ ounce apricot schnapps
1 ounce orange juice
1 ounce cranberry juice
Orange slice for garnish

Combine liquid ingredients in mixing glass. Add ice and shake. Pour with ice into glass and garnish. Serve with a straw, if desired.

THE SPARTAN

Spartan as in spare

1 ounce ouzo
7 ounces club soda

Pour ouzo into ice-filled highball glass. Top with club soda and stir.

STARRY SKIES

A flavorsome constellation

1 ounce amaretto
1 ounce Chambord
1 ounce Drambuie

Pour liqueurs into liqueur glass and stir.

SOUTHERN PLEASURE

STRAIGHT SAMBUCA

In Italian tradition, the three coffee beans represent health, wealth, and prosperity.

3 ounces sambuca
3 coffee beans

Pour sambuca into liqueur glass and drop in the coffee beans.

SWEET LASS

And a pretty colleen she is

1 ounce Baileys Irish Cream
1 ounce Jameson Irish whiskey
1 ounce Chambord
½ ounce grenadine

Combine ingredients in mixing glass. Add ice, shake, and strain into glass.

TEQUILA-CRANBERRY CORDIAL

With Agavero tequila liqueur

2 ounces Agavero
4 ounces cranberry juice
Orange slice for garnish

Pour liqueur and juice into ice-filled rocks glass. Stir and garnish.

TOASTED ALMOND

With coffee and cream

1½ ounces amaretto
1½ ounces Kahlúa
1 ounce heavy cream

Combine ingredients in mixing glass. Add ice, shake, and pour with ice into glass.

THE TREE HUGGER

A Four Seasons managing partner's tribute to his counterpart

1 ounce Jägermeister
1 ounce orange juice
½ teaspoon grenadine
3 ounces Champagne

Combine Jägermeister, juice, and grenadine in mixing glass. Add ice and shake. Strain into glass and top with Champagne.

TRUE LOVE

Warms your heart

1 ounce Chambord
1 ounce Grand Marnier
1 ounce B & B

Pour ingredients into liqueur glass and stir.

VELVET ALMOND

Not just any nut. Amaretto di Saronno, from Italy, is the best known of the almond-flavored liqueurs called amaretto.

1 ounce Amaretto di Saronno
1 ounce Grand Marnier
1 ounce heavy cream
Maraschino cherry for garnish

Combine liquid ingredients in mixing glass. Add ice and shake. Strain into glass and garnish.

VOLTAIRE'S SMILE

Bubbles to tickle your nose

1 ounce Pernod
1 ounce Chambord
2 ounces Champagne

Combine liqueurs in mixing glass. Add ice, shake, and strain into glass. Top with Champagne and stir.

WHITE CHOCOLATE KISS

Cheeky but smooth

2 ounces Godiva white chocolate liqueur
1 ounce white crème de cacao
1 ounce Grey Goose La Vanille vodka

Combine ingredients in mixing glass. Add ice, shake, and strain into glass.

APERITIFS & DIGESTIVES

Aperitifs and digestives (*digestifs* in French) are herb-based liqueurs traditionally drunk before or after a meal. Many are made from bitter plant materials that stimulate both the appetite and digestion—to name but a few, gentian root; Chinese rhubarb root; cinchona bark (the source of quinine); and the leaves of the artichoke plant. The end product is known as bitters.

Science has shown that alcohol itself stimulates the digestion. Yet it is the unusual flavors of aperitifs and digestives that make them a bartending staple. Cognac, Armagnac, apple-based calvados, and other brandies could also be called digestives because they're traditionally drunk after a meal; the same goes for the fortified wines port and Madeira. Depending on their sweetness, sherry and vermouth (two other fortified wines) can be enjoyed either before or after dinner.

Note: The digestives in this chapter are marked with an asterisk.

*AMARO AND TONIC

The digestive amaro (Italian for "bitter") is produced in distilleries all over Italy.
3 ounces Luxardo Amaro Abado
Tonic water
Lemon twist for garnish

Pour amaro into ice-filled rocks glass, top with tonic water to taste, and garnish.

THE AMBASSADOR

The nickname given to a diplomatic Grill Room regular from Europe
3 ounces Campari
2 ounces grapefruit juice
3 ounces club soda
Lime peel spiral for garnish

Pour Campari and juice into ice-filled highball glass. Top with club soda and garnish.

AMERICANO

Choose dry vermouth, if you like, when mixing this Campari classic.
2 ounces Campari
2 ounces sweet vermouth
4 ounces club soda
Lemon twist for garnish

Pour Campari and vermouth into ice-filled highball glass. Top with club soda and garnish.

ANGEL OF CORSICA

Beatific
1 ounce Dubonnet Blanc
1 ounce gin
1 ounce apricot brandy
1 ounce peach schnapps
Orange twist for garnish

Combine liquid ingredients in mixing glass. Add ice and shake. Strain into glass and garnish.

*AVERNA AND SODA

Averna is a fruity amaro from Sicily.
2 ounces Averna
Club soda
Orange twist for garnish

Pour amaro into ice-filled rocks glass, add club soda to taste, and garnish.

BELLA LIGURIA

Named for the beautiful Ligurian Sea off Italy's coast
2 ounces Campari
2 ounces Dubonnet Rouge
1 ounce orange juice
3 ounces club soda
Orange slice for garnish

Pour Campari, Dubonnet, and juice into ice-filled highball glass. Top with club soda and garnish.

*BON AMI

Your good French friend
1 ounce sweet vermouth
1 ounce dry vermouth
1 ounce Cognac
½ ounce Cointreau
Orange twist for garnish

Combine liquid ingredients in mixing glass. Add ice and stir to chill. Strain into glass and garnish.

CAMPARI BUON GIORNO

An Italian Mimosa (buon giorno is "good day"). Milan restaurateur Gaspare Campari formulated his mixture of bitters and fruit in 1860.

1 ounce Campari
1 ounce orange juice
3 ounces Champagne

Pour Campari and juice into ice-filled tulip glass. Top with Champagne and stir.

CAMPARI MADRAS

With orange and cranberry

3 ounces Campari
1 ounce vodka
2 ounces orange juice
1 ounce cranberry juice
Orange slice for garnish

Combine liquid ingredients in mixing glass. Add ice and shake. Strain into glass and garnish.

*CHARLIE'S BRISTOL CREAM COCKTAIL

A bubbly after-dinner soother concocted by bartender Charles

2 ounces Harvey's Bristol Cream sherry
Juice of 2 limes
1 ounce simple syrup (page 27)
Ginger ale
Mint sprig for garnish

Combine sherry, juice, and syrup in mixing glass. Add ice, shake, and pour with ice into glass. Top with ginger ale to taste and garnish.

CIAO BELLA

"Hello" to an Italian of the feminine persuasion. Punt è Mes is a pleasantly bittersweet, vermouth tasting of herbs and orange.

1 ounce Punt è Mes
1 ounce Cynar
1 ounce dry vermouth
Orange peel spiral for garnish

Combine liquid ingredients in mixing glass. Add ice and stir to chill. Strain into glass and garnish.

*CROWNING GLORY

Half Armagnac brandy, half pear eau-de-vie

1½ ounces Armagnac
1½ ounces Poire William

Combine Armagnac and eau-de-vie in mixing glass. Add ice, stir to chill, and strain into glass.

*CURTAIN CALL

DUBONNET FIZZ

Laced with cherry and lemon. "Kirsch" is short for the cherry eau-de-vie kirschwasser, from Germany.

2 ounces Dubonnet Rouge
1 ounce kirsch
1 ounce lemon juice
4 ounces club soda
Orange slice for garnish

Combine Dubonnet, kirsch, and juice in mixing glass. Add ice and shake. Strain into glass and add club soda. Stir and garnish.

EIFFEL TOWER

With the grape-flavored vodka from France

2 ounces dry vermouth
1 ounce gin
1 ounce Cîroc grape vodka
½ teaspoon Pernod

Combine ingredients in mixing glass. Add ice, stir to chill, and strain into glass.

EINE KLEINE NACHTMUSIK

"A Little Night Music," compliments of Mozart

2 ounces Jägermeister
2 ounces Punt è Mes
Orange twist for garnish

Combine liqueurs in mixing glass. Add ice and stir to chill. Strain into glass and garnish.

*CURTAIN CALL

Raspberry eau-de-vie with Champagne

2 ounces framboise
5 ounces Champagne
Raspberry for garnish

Pour framboise into flute, top with Champagne, and garnish.

Dry Sherry Meal Starters

Sherry, the storied fortified wine from the Andalusia region of Spain, is a traditional pre-dinner drink. Fino sherries—which include manzanilla, amontillado, and oloroso—are dry. Cream sherries (which are heavily sweetened olorosos), and Pedro Ximenez sherries, on the other hand, are typically drunk after dinner.

ALMOND DELUXE

Almond-flavored amaretto teams with manzanilla, a variety of fino sherry.
1½ ounces manzanilla sherry
½ ounce dry vermouth
1 ounce amaretto

Combine ingredients in mixing glass. Add ice, stir to chill, and strain into glass.

ANDALUSIA

A cocktail long venerated as an aperitif
2 ounces dry sherry of choice
½ ounce brandy
½ ounce light rum
Lemon twist for garnish

Combine ingredients in mixing glass. Add ice and stir to chill. Strain into glass and garnish.

CORONATION

With a touch of maraschino liqueur
½ ounce amontillado sherry
½ ounce dry vermouth
2 dashes orange bitters
1 dash maraschino

Combine ingredients in mixing glass. Add ice, stir to chill, and strain into glass.

GEORGIA ON MY MIND

With—what else?—peach
2 ounces dry sherry of choice
1 ounce peach schnapps
1 dash Fee Brothers peach bitters

Combine ingredients in mixing glass. Add ice, stir to chill, and strain into glass.

MACK 'N' MACK

The favorite a gentleman of a certain age and his son
1 ounce dry sherry of choice
½ ounce Scotch
2 dashes Cointreau
1 ounce orange juice
Orange twist for garnish

Combine liquid ingredients in mixing glass. Add ice and shake. Strain into glass and garnish.

TUSCAN SIPPER

For those fond of Tuaca, a butterscotchy liqueur
1 ounce dry sherry of choice
1 ounce Tuaca
Maraschino cherry for garnish

Combine sherry and liqueur in mixing glass. Add ice and shake. Strain into glass and garnish.

FOUR SEASONS BLUSHING ANGEL

A light and airy pre-dinner pleaser

2 ounces Dubonnet Rouge

1 ounce cranberry juice

4 ounces Champagne

Orange twist for garnish

Pour Dubonnet and juice into tulip glass. Top with Champagne, stir, and garnish.

FOUR SEASONS DUBONNET COSMO

An appetite-enhancing variation on the Cosmopolitan

1 ounce Dubonnet Rouge

1 ounce orange liqueur

1 ounce vodka

1 ounce cranberry juice

1 splash lime juice

Orange twist for garnish

Combine liquid ingredients in mixing glass. Add ice and shake. Strain into glass and garnish.

FRENCH COMFORT

One of these liqueurs originated in France, the other in New Orleans.

Crushed ice

3 ounces Lillet Blanc

1 ounce Southern Comfort

Orange twist for garnish

Fill a white wine glass with crushed ice and pour in liqueurs. Stir and garnish.

FOUR SEASONS BLUSHING ANGEL

*GRAPPA WITH LIME

Grappa is an Italian eau-de-vie distilled from pomace—the grape skins and seeds left over from winemaking.

2 ounces grappa

½ ounce gin

2 ounces lime juice

Lime slice for garnish

Combine liquid ingredients in mixing glass. Add ice and shake. Pour with ice into glass and garnish.

HAPPY HOUR

At a Paris bistro with an Italian clientele?

2 ounces Punt è Mes

½ ounce Cointreau

½ teaspoon Pernod

½ ounce Cognac

Orange twist for garnish

Combine liquid ingredients in mixing glass. Add ice and stir to chill. Strain into glass and garnish.

JUDITH'S CHOICE

A blend of sherry, Campari, and two fruits

2 ounces amontillado sherry

2 ounces Campari

Juice of half a lime

1 teaspoon raspberry syrup

Combine ingredients in mixing glass. Add ice, shake, and pour with ice into glass.

---

*KENTUCKY FINISHER

An after-dinner drink for country gentlemen of means

1½ ounces Hennessy X.O. Cognac

1 ounce Wild Turkey bourbon

Pour Cognac and bourbon into ice-filled rocks glass and stir.

KIND HEARTS AND CORONETS

Named for the film classic starring Alec Guinness as an Anglo-Italian. Pimm's No. 1 is an herby gin-based liqueur created by London restaurateur James Pimm in the 1880s.

2 ounces Pimm's No. 1

2 ounces Campari

4 ounces club soda

Orange twist for garnish

Pour Campari and Pimm's into ice-filled highball glass. Top with club soda and stir.

LA DOLCE VITA

Bittersweet, like the Fellini film

3 ounces Campari

1 ounce sambuca

Pour Campari and liqueur into ice-filled rocks glass and stir.

*LA MENTA

As minty as it gets. Branca Menta is mint-flavored Fernet-Branca, one of Italy's most widely exported amari.

2 sprigs mint

2 ounces Branca Menta

1 ounce fresh lemon juice

Club soda

Mint leaf for garnish

Muddle mint in bottom of mixing glass. Pour in amaro and juice. Add ice, shake, and strain into glass. Top with club soda to taste and garnish.

LILLET AUX AMANDES

The French aperitif Lillet, gin, and a touch of almond. Lillet—distilled from wine, brandy, and herbs—comes in blanc *(white) and* rouge *(red).*

1½ ounces Lillet Blanc

½ ounce gin

1 teaspoon amaretto

Combine ingredients in mixing glass. Add ice, shake, and strain into glass.

MEDITERRANEAN KISS

With the artichoke-based bitters Cynar (pronounced CHEE-nahr)

2 ounces Cynar

1 ounce peach schnapps

3 ounces club soda

Orange twist for garnish

Pour Cynar and schnapps into ice-filled highball glass. Top with club soda and garnish.

*MOONLIGHT SOOTHER

Especially nice after a heavy meal. Zwack Unicum, a bitters formulated in Hungary in the eighteenth century, is packed with forty-plus botanicals.

2 ounces light rum
½ ounce Unicum
Club soda
Lemon twist for garnish

Pour rum and bitters into ice-filled rocks glass. Top with club soda to taste and garnish.

OCTOPUS

Inky and intriguing

3 ounces Campari
1 ounce blue curaçao

Pour Campari and liqueur into ice-filled rocks glass and stir.

THE PARISIAN

With that elusive je ne sais quoi . . .

2 ounces dry vermouth
1 ounce Cointreau
1 ounce apricot brandy
½ teaspoon Pernod

Pour ingredients into ice-filled rocks glass and stir.

PÊCHE PLAISANTE

Starring a very pleasant white peach aperitif from Provence

2 ounces Henri Bardouin RinQuinQuin
Club soda

Pour aperitif into ice-filled rocks glass, top with club soda to taste, and stir.

PHANTOM OF DELIGHT

Named for Wordsworth's "lovely apparition"

2 ounces Jägermeister
1 ounce Chambord
Orange twist for garnish

Combine liqueurs in mixing glass. Add ice, stir to chill, strain into glass, and garnish.

PINK ANGEL

Campari provides the color.

3 ounces Campari
1 ounce white crème de cacao
4 ounces club soda
Orange twist for garnish

Pour Campari and liqueur into ice-filled highball glass. Top with club soda and garnish.

*PINK GIN

The bitters turns the drink a light pink.

1 teaspoon Angostura bitters
2½ ounces gin, chilled
Ice water chaser (optional)

Chill glass. Pour bitters into liqueur glass, then swirl glass to coat the interior. Discard bitters and pour in gin. Serve with glass of ice water, if desired.

*POSTSCRIPT

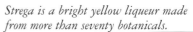

Strega is a bright yellow liqueur made from more than seventy botanicals.

1 ounce grappa
1 ounce Strega
1 ounce orange juice

Combine ingredients in mixing glass. Add ice, shake, and strain into glass.

*RUMARO

Sip after a big meal.
2 ounces Fernet-Branca
2 ounces dark rum
Lemon twist for garnish

Pour amaro and rum into ice-filled rocks glass. Stir and garnish.

ST. TROPEZ

A taste of the French Riviera
4 ounces Dubonnet Rouge
4 ounces orange juice
Orange slice for garnish

Combine Dubonnet and juice in mixing glass. Add ice and shake. Pour with ice into glass and garnish.

*SOFT SPLENDOR

Inspired by a line from the poet Shelley
2 ounces sweet vermouth
1 ounce apricot brandy
1 ounce Chambord
Rose petal for garnish

Combine liquid ingredients in mixing glass. Add ice and stir to chill. Strain into glass and garnish.

SUNSET COCKTAIL

A rosy prelude to dinner
2 ounces Dubonnet Blanc
1 ounce Cherry Heering
2 ounces orange juice
3 ounces club soda
Orange slice for garnish
Maraschino cherry for garnish

Pour Dubonnet, brandy, and juice into ice-filled highball glass. Top with club soda and garnish.

TE AMO

"I love you" in Italy
1 ounce Punt è Mes
1 ounce peach schnapps
1 ounce dry vermouth
Orange peel spiral for garnish

Combine liquid ingredients in mixing glass. Add ice and stir to chill. Strain into glass and garnish.

TESTA ROSSA

Named after the Ferrari "redhead" auto
1 ounce dry vermouth
1 ounce Dubonnet Rouge
1 ounce amaretto
Lemon twist for garnish

Combine liquid ingredients in mixing glass. Add ice and stir to chill. Strain into glass and garnish.

*VELVET HAMMER

A classic digestive
2 ounces vodka
1 ounce white crème de cacao
1 ounce light cream

Combine ingredients in mixing glass. Add ice, shake, and strain into glass.

*VELVET HAMMER

VERMOUTH AND CASSIS

A traditional pre-dinner pairing

Crushed ice
2 ounces dry vermouth
2 ounces crème de cassis
Lemon twist for garnish

Fill a white wine glass with crushed ice and add vermouth and liqueur. Stir and garnish.

VERMOUTH COCKTAIL

Two vermouths plus fizz

2 ounces sweet vermouth
2 ounces dry vermouth
2 dashes Peychaud's bitters
4 ounces club soda
Orange twist for garnish

Pour vermouths and bitters into ice-filled white wine glass. Top with club soda, stir, and garnish.

*YOURS TRULY

Sincerely good

1 ounce apricot brandy
1 ounce Punt è Mes
½ ounce Cointreau
1 ounce dry vermouth
Orange twist for garnish

Combine liquid ingredients in mixing glass. Add ice and stir to chill. Strain into glass and garnish.

Bubbly Afternoon, by John Varriano; oil on linen (40" x 30") 2009

CHAMPAGNE & WINE

Champagne is frequently embellished with a few drops of this or that, but **red** and **white still wines** also lend themselves to the mixologist's art. So do **fortified wines** like sherry, vermouth, and port.

You'll also do well to remember that Champagne isn't the first and last word in sparkling white wine. **Cava** (from Spain) and **Prosecco** (from Italy) are less bubbly than Champagne, but that's actually a plus for some wine drinkers. Scout around and you'll even find a bubbly red: sparkling **Shiraz**.

A note of interest: If this book had been published forty years ago, it probably wouldn't include a chapter devoted to wine-based cocktails. Before 1970, Americans much preferred whiskey and beer over the fruit of the vine, and wine lovers often had to take along their own bottles of wine when dining out.

**ACADIAN
COOLER**

A hearty hello to our French-Canadian neighbors
½ ounce sweet vermouth
5 ounces Champagne
Orange twist for garnish

Pour liqueur and vermouth into tulip glass. Top with Champagne and garnish.

ADONIS

Not just for the handsome
2 ounces dry sherry
½ ounce sweet vermouth
1 dash orange bitters

Combine ingredients in mixing glass. Add ice, stir to chill, and strain into glass.

**THE
ANGLOPHILE**

Beefed-up bubbly
3 drops Beefeater gin
6 ounces Champagne

Pour gin into flute and top with Champagne.

**ATLANTA
COOLER**

Red wine laced with the ATL's best-known product: Coke. Try this with one of the inexpensive dry reds from Chile.
5 ounces dry red wine
1 ounce Coca-Cola Classic
Orange slice for garnish
Lemon slice for garnish

Pour wine into ice-filled rocks glass. Top with soft drink, stir, and garnish.

AUBRIETTA

Named for the pretty purple plant. For the wine, try Riesling, whose Kabinett, Spätlese, and Auslese styles go from semisweet to sweet to sweetest.
7 ounces sweet white wine
½ ounce framboise
½ ounce DeKuyper Pucker grape liqueur

Combine ingredients in mixing glass. Add ice, stir to chill, and strain into glass.

**BELLE OF
THE BALL**

Red wine waltzes with OJ.
3 ounces dry red wine
2 ounces orange juice
1 ounce fresh sour mix
Orange peel spiral for garnish

Combine liquid ingredients in mixing glass. Add ice and shake. Pour with ice into glass and garnish.

**BERRY
COOLER**

The berries: black currant, black raspberry
Crushed ice
6 ounces sweet white wine
2 ounces Absolut Kurant vodka
½ ounce Chambord

Fill a tulip glass with crushed ice and pour in liquid ingredients. Stir.

BIG RED

Tart and ruby-colored.
6 ounces dry red wine
3 ounces cranberry juice
2 splashes red vermouth
Crushed ice

Combine liquid ingredients in mixing glass. Shake and strain into glass filled with crushed ice.

BORDEAUX EXPRESS

Whisks you away

6 ounces Bordeaux wine of choice
½ ounce Cointreau
½ ounce crème de cassis
½ ounce dry vermouth

Combine ingredients in mixing glass. Add ice, stir to chill, and strain into glass.

BRANDIED PORT

An elegant pairing

4 ounces port
½ ounce brandy

Pour port into liqueur glass and top with brandy.

BROOKLYN HEIGHTS

Top drawer

1 ounce apricot brandy
5 ounces Champagne

Pour brandy into flute and top with Champagne.

CHAMPAGNE AND SCHNAPPS

Flavor a glass of bubbly as you please.

2 to 4 drops schnapps of choice
6 ounces Champagne

Drop schnapps into flute and top with Champagne.

CHAMPAGNE BLEU

Tinted with Beaujolais and blueberry

½ ounce Beaujolais red wine
½ ounce blueberry syrup
4 ounces Champagne

Pour wine and syrup into flute, swirl to mix, and top with Champagne.

CHAMPAGNE BOHÈME

A taste of absinthe for the bohemian

1 sugar cube
½ ounce absinthe
5½ ounces Champagne
Orange twist for garnish

Place sugar cube in bottom of flute and pour in absinthe. Once cube is soaked, pour in Champagne and garnish.

CHAMPAGNE COCKTAIL

One of the classics

1 sugar cube
2 or 3 dashes Angostura bitters
1 ounce Cognac
5 ounces Champagne
Orange slice for garnish
Maraschino cherry for garnish

Place sugar cube in bottom of tulip glass and soak with bitters. Add Cognac and top with Champagne. Stir and garnish.

CHAMPAGNE LIMON

Flavored with limoncello

½ ounce limoncello
½ ounce club soda
5 ounces Champagne

Pour liqueur and club soda into flute and top with Champagne.

DANISH RUBY

With the black cherry–flavored Danish liqueur

½ ounce Cherry Heering
5½ ounces Champagne

Pour liqueur into flute and top with Champagne.

EUROPEAN SWINGER

À votre santé, babe! Sauternes is a sweetish white wine from the Bordeaux wine-growing region of France.

4 ounces Sauternes
1 ounce dry vermouth
½ ounce Chambord
3 ounces club soda
3 blueberries for garnish

Combine wine, vermouth, and liqueur in mixing glass. Add ice, stir to chill, and strain into glass. Top with club soda and garnish.

FOUR SEASONS BELLINI

The original Bellini, which was invented at Harry's Bar in Venice, used white peach puree.

4 drops peach schnapps
6 ounces Champagne

Drop schnapps into flute and top with Champagne.

FRENCH ORGASM

Ouiiii! Go with a Sauvignon Blanc or a dry Pinot Grigio.

6 ounces dry white wine
½ ounce Cointreau
½ ounce Rose's lime juice
Club soda

Pour wine, liqueur, and juice into ice-filled white wine glass. Top with club soda to taste and stir.

A WORD FROM THE BARTENDERS

When it comes to wine, the definitions of "dry" and, especially, "sweet"—aren't exactly cut-and-dried. Still, some wines definitely fall into one category or the other (think "dessert wines"). Below are a few notes we hope will help guide you through the maze.

Reds. Assume that a red wine is dry unless the label (or your wine merchant) indicates otherwise. Also be aware that "fruity" better describes most sweetish reds, and Beaujolais is one of the fruitiest. Truly sweet reds include those made from the Lambrusco grape in the *amabile* and *dolce* styles; the fortified wine port; and late-harvest Zinfandels and Cabernet Sauvignons, made from grapes picked when the sugars are at their most concentrated.

Whites. Sauvignon Blanc, Pinot Grigio, and the sec (dry) style of Chenin Blanc are among the driest whites. Sweet whites include Vouvrays in the *moelleux* and *doux* styles; Rieslings in the Kabinett, Spätlese, and Auslese styles (the last often considered a dessert wine); ice wines; Sauternes; Gewürztraminer; and cream and Pedro Ximenez sherries.

GRAND CHAMPAGNE

Two French favorites join hands. Grand Marnier's exquisite flavor comes from bitter orange peel, vanilla bean, and spices.

3 drops Grand Marnier
6 ounces Champagne
Orange twist for garnish

Drop liqueur into tulip glass, top with Champagne, and garnish.

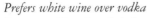

HILARY WALLBANGER

Prefers white wine over vodka

3 ounces white wine of choice
3 ounces orange juice
1 ounce Galliano

Pour wine and juice into ice-filled white wine glass and stir. Float liqueur on top.

THE JACKIE LEE

An amusing play on tradition

½ ounce gin
½ ounce absinthe
4 ounces Champagne
1 ounce club soda

Pour gin and absinthe into tulip glass and stir. Top with Champagne and club soda and stir.

KINGSTON KOOLER

Percolates like a reggae song. If you can't find sparkling Shiraz in a wine store, search it out online.

3 drops Jamaican rum
6 ounces sparkling Shiraz
Lemon twist for garnish

Drop rum into tulip glass, top with Champagne, and garnish.

KIR

Created by Canon Félix Kir, mayor of Dijon, in the 1850s. A dry Chenin Blanc is a good wine choice.

8 ounces dry white wine
¼ ounce crème de cassis
Lemon twist for garnish

Pour wine and cassis into white wine glass, swirl, and garnish.

KIR ROYALE

The Kir gone bubbly

2 drops crème de cassis
6 ounces Champagne
Lemon twist for garnish

Drop cassis into flute, top with Champagne, and garnish.

LAHAINA PALM

Champagne à la Maui

1 ounce coconut water
4 ounces Champagne

Pour coconut water into flute and top with Champagne.

LIMONBERRY

Icy white wine with black raspberry and lemon

Crushed ice
6 ounces white wine of choice
½ ounce Chambord
3 drops limoncello
½ ounce club soda
Lemon peel spiral for garnish

Fill a tulip glass with crushed ice and pour in wine and liqueurs. Top with club soda and garnish.

THE MATADOR

Sherry gets red—and hot.

4 ounces Tio Pepe dry sherry
2 ounces Punt è Mes
2 ounces tomato juice
3 dashes Tabasco
Lime wedge for garnish

Combine liquid ingredients in mixing glass. Add ice and stir to chill. Pour with ice into glass and garnish.

MIMOSA

The drink that launched a thousand brunches.

2 ounces orange juice
4 ounces Champagne

Pour orange juice into flute and top with Champagne.

MISS LINDA'S PLEASURE

The favorite of a first lady of fashion

½ ounce vodka
½ ounce Chambord
3 drops lemon juice
5 ounces Champagne

Pour vodka, liqueur, and juice into flute and top with Champagne.

MOTHER OF PEARL

Flavored with pineapple and honeydew

1 ounce Midori
1 ounce pineapple juice
4 ounces Champagne

Pour liqueur and juice into flute and top with Champagne.

PASSION FIZZ

NOUMÉA COOLER

Named after the seductive colonial French capital in the South Pacific

4 ounces cranberry juice
½ ounce passion fruit puree
6 ounces Champagne
Orange peel spiral for garnish

Combine juice and puree in mixing glass. Add ice and shake. Pour with ice into glass and top with Champagne. Stir and garnish.

PASSION FIZZ

As in Passiflora edulis, *or passion fruit. Try Cava or Prosecco as the bubbly.*

4 ounces sparkling white wine
2 ounces passion fruit puree
1 splash dry vermouth
Lemon twist for garnish

Combine liquid ingredients in mixing glass. Add ice and shake. Strain into glass and garnish.

PORT PLEASANT

A creamy winter delight

2 ounces port
1 ounce Cognac
½ ounce light cream
2 dashes dark crème de cacao
Nutmeg for sprinkling

Combine liquid ingredients in mixing glass. Add ice and shake. Strain into glass and sprinkle with nutmeg.

PORTUGUESE DAISY

Gussied-up ruby port

2 ounces ruby port
1 ounce brandy
1 ounce fresh sour mix
½ teaspoon grenadine
Lemon peel spiral for garnish

Combine liquid ingredients in mixing glass. Add ice and shake. Strain into glass and garnish.

RED WINE REFRESHER

Bubbling with lemon-lime and ginger sodas. Look to Argentina or Chile for your dry red.

4 ounces dry red wine
2 ounces Sprite or 7UP
2 ounces ginger ale
Lemon twist for garnish

Pour wine into ice-filled highball glass. Top with soft drinks, stir, and garnish.

RICK'S WHITEWATER

Rapids you'll be happy to shoot. To balance the sweet triple sec, choose dry Sauvignon Blanc or Pinot Grigio.

Crushed ice
4 ounces white wine of choice.
½ ounce triple sec
Sprite or 7UP

Fill a highball glass with crushed ice and pour in wine and liqueur. Top with soft drink to taste and stir.

SANIBEL COOLER

For the thirsty beachcomber?

3 drops blue curaçao
1 drop Southern Comfort
6 ounces Champagne
Orange twist for garnish

Pour liqueurs into tulip glass. Top with Champagne and garnish.

SEÑORA VALDEZ

Coffee meets Champagne.

3 drops Kahlúa
6 ounces Champagne

Drop Kahlúa into flute and top with Champagne.

STRAWBERRY CHAMPAGNE

With fruit puree

1 ounce strawberry puree
5 ounces Champagne
Quarter of fresh strawberry for garnish

Pour puree into flute, top with Champagne, and drop garnish into glass.

Spritzers

A spritzer is technically a drink made with half wine and half club soda, but we're leaving the amount of club soda (and the choice of a highball or red wine glass) up to you. And though these recipes call for ice, remember that a straight-up spritzer is still a spritzer—and a less watery one at that.

GEWÜRZ SPRITZER

Sweet or dry Gewürz? Your call. The Gewürztraminer grape is grown in vineyards worldwide, but your best bets are Gewürzes from Germany (the grape's birthplace) and Alsace.

4 ounces Gewürztraminer wine
2 ounces dry vermouth
Club soda

Pour wine and vermouth into ice-filled glass. Add club soda to taste and stir.

MADEIRA SPRITZER

A different take on the spritzer
Crushed ice
4 ounces Madeira
2 ounces black cherry schnapps
Club soda

Fill a glass with crushed ice and pour in Madeira and schnapps. Top with club soda to taste and stir.

MARSALA SPRITZER

Made with the Sicilian fortified wine
Crushed ice
4 ounces Marsala
2 ounces lime juice
Club soda
Lime twist for garnish

Fill a glass with crushed ice and pour in wine and juice. Add club soda to taste and garnish.

RED WINE SPRITZER

This drink has two types of soda. Try one of the two sweet reds made from the Lambrusco grape: amabile *or the sweeter* dolce.

Crushed ice
6 ounces sweet red wine
Club soda
Sprite or 7UP
Lemon slice for garnish

Fill a glass with crushed ice and pour in wine. Add club soda to taste and garnish.

WHITE WINE SPRITZER

The spritzer at its most basic
Crushed ice
8 ounces white wine of choice
Club soda
Lemon twist for garnish

Fill a glass with crushed ice and pour in wine. Add club soda to taste and garnish.

ZINFANDEL SPRITZER

With Zinfandel red wine
Crushed ice
4 ounces Zinfandel
Club soda
Orange wedge for garnish

Fill a glass with crushed ice and pour in wine. Add soda to taste and garnish.

SWEETHEART

With honey, grapes, and Prosecco, the Italian sparkling wine

4 seedless white grapes
1½ teaspoons honey
1 ounce vodka
5 ounces Prosecco, chilled
Lemon twist for garnish

Muddle grapes and honey in bottom of mixing glass and add vodka. Add ice and shake. Strain into glass and top with Prosecco. Stir and garnish.

TEAR DROP

Nothing to cry about. Here's your chance to try one of the two sweeter Vouvray wines from France—moelleux or doux.

4 ounces sweet white wine
1 ounce peach schnapps
½ ounce fresh sour mix
Club soda
Lemon wedge for garnish

Combine wine, schnapps, and sour mix in mixing glass. Add ice and shake. Pour with ice into glass, top with club soda to taste, and garnish.

VANILLA SKIES

Not a cloud in sight

½ ounce Tuaca
½ ounce blue curaçao
6 ounces Champagne

Pour liqueurs into flute and top with Champagne.

WHITE WINE COOLER

A lemon-lime soda version of the spritzer (see facing page)

4 ounces white wine of choice
2 ounces Sprite or 7UP
Lemon slice for garnish

Pour wine into ice-filled tulip glass. Top with soft drink and garnish.

ZOE'S CABERNET COBBLER

Cobbler is an old name for wine-based cocktails.

6 ounces Cabernet Sauvignon
1 teaspoon superfine sugar
Crushed ice
3 ounces club soda
Orange slice for garnish
Maraschino cherry for garnish

Combine wine and sugar in mixing glass. Add ice, shake, and pour into glass filled with crushed ice. Top with club soda and garnish. Serve with a straw.

ZOE'S CABERNET COBBLER

The Four Seasons Wine Dinners

Wine is to an establishment like The Four Seasons as Beluga caviar is to the fussiest gourmet—only the best quality will do. The wine list presented to diners is a fantastic array of nearly four hundred selections from France, Italy, California, New York State, and a few other parts of the world.

Wine has also been the centerpiece of the restaurant's private wine dinners, which feature tastings of selected vintages. The dinners got their start at a storied affair held on January 18, 1973. The purpose was for the famous chef Paul Bocuse to introduce Americans to a selection of Georges Duboeuf wines. When word got out that Bocuse himself would cook, more than four thousand callers set the Four Seasons switchboard alight seeking a ticket.

As related by John Mariani and Alex von Bidder in *The Four Seasons—A History of America's Premier Restaurant*, "Bocuse brought his own [ingredients] from France, arriving at JFK Airport with foie gras, truffles, cream, [and] butter." He got them through customs only by choosing a line with "the stoutest customs inspector, believing such a man would appreciate good food and pass him through. After telling the inspector the truffles were only after-dinner chocolates, Bocuse sailed through." The dinner was a resounding success.

Bar patrons at The Four Seasons benefit indirectly from the wine dinners whenever one of the selections is well received and finds its way to the bar. The bar wines tilt toward the continental, but that doesn't mean customers can't enjoy a cocktail made with, say, California Chenin Blanc, Long Island Merlot, Argentine Malbec, or Australian Cabernet-Shiraz.

PUNCHES

If you think punch isn't punch unless it's served in a great big bowl, think again. The earliest punches were single drinks, like the ones you'll find here. Punch bowl–size recipes are on pages 204–05, where you'll find Four Seasons specials good for ladling up in—you guessed it—spring, summer, fall, and winter.

The origin of punch remains in doubt, but all signs point to India. In *Travels in India in the Seventeenth Century*, John Fryer wrote, ". . . the English on the Coast [almost surely from the East India Company] make that enervating Liquor called Punch (which is Indostan for Five) from Five Ingredients." Some food-and-drink historians have ascertained that the five components were wine or spirits; water or milk; lemon or lime; sugar; and spice(s)—all found in one drink or another in the pages that follow.

BRANDY PUNCH

BLUE BLAST

Blue as in blueberry
1 ounce light cream
1 ounce DeKuyper blueberry liqueur
1 ounce blue curaçao
1 ounce orange juice
1 ounce fresh sour mix
1 teaspoon superfine sugar
3 or 4 blueberries for garnish

Combine liquid ingredients and sugar in mixing glass. Add ice and shake. Pour with ice into glass and garnish.

ASHLEY'S SPECIAL

Raises your spirits
1 ounce Southern Comfort
1 ounce vodka
½ ounce amaretto
½ ounce orange juice
1½ ounces pineapple juice
2 dashes grenadine
1 dash Rose's lime juice
Maraschino cherry for garnish
Lime slice for garnish

Combine liquid ingredients in mixing glass. Add ice and shake. Pour with ice into glass and garnish.

BOURBON PUNCH

With five fruit juices, no less
1½ ounces bourbon
½ ounce orange juice
½ ounce grapefruit juice
½ ounce lemon juice
½ ounce lime juice
½ ounce pineapple juice
Orange peel spiral for garnish

Combine liquid ingredients in mixing glass. Add ice and shake. Pour with ice into glass and garnish.

BLOOD ORANGE PUNCH

With juice of the orange of a different color
2 ounces vodka
1 ounce Grand Marnier
1 ounce grenadine
2 ounces blood orange juice
½ ounce fresh sour mix
1 teaspoon superfine sugar
Blood orange slice for garnish

Combine liquid ingredients and sugar in mixing glass. Add ice and shake. Pour with ice into glass and garnish.

BRANDY PUNCH

With the bonus of bubbles
1 ounce brandy
½ ounce Cointreau
1 ounce orange juice
1 ounce lemon juice
1 dash grenadine
¼ teaspoon superfine sugar
Club soda
Orange slice for garnish
Lemon slice for garnish

Combine brandy, liqueur, juices, grenadine, and sugar in mixing glass. Add ice and shake. Strain into glass, add club soda to taste, and garnish.

CAPTAIN MORGAN PUNCH

Think pirates of the Caribbean

2 ounces Captain Morgan rum
1 ounce Stolichnaya Ohranj vodka
1½ ounces pineapple juice
1½ ounces orange juice
1 splash grenadine
Lemon wedge for garnish

Combine liquid ingredients in mixing glass. Add ice and shake. Pour with ice into glass and garnish.

CHOCOLATE PUNCH

No fruit, but who cares?

1 ounce chocolate liqueur
1 ounce dark crème de cacao
1 ounce white crème de cacao
2 ounces light cream
1 teaspoon superfine sugar
2 ounces club soda
Chocolate stick for garnish

Combine liqueurs, cream, and sugar in mixing glass. Add ice and shake. Strain into glass, top with club soda, and garnish.

COSMOPOLITAN PUNCH

An icy twist on the Cosmo

2 ounces vodka
1 ounce Cointreau
1 ounce orange juice
1 ounce cranberry juice
½ ounce fresh sour mix
Lemon wedge for garnish

Combine liquid ingredients in mixing glass. Add ice and shake. Pour with ice into glass and garnish.

CRANBERRY PUNCH

With a little apple and pineapple thrown in

1½ ounces vodka
2 ounces cranberry juice
1 ounce apple juice
1 ounce pineapple juice
Sprite or 7UP
Orange slice for garnish

Combine juices in mixing glass. Add ice, shake, and strain into glass. Top with soft drink to taste and garnish.

82ND AIRBORNE PUNCH

A heady salute to the troops

½ ounce vodka
½ ounce dark rum
½ ounce tequila
½ ounce Cointreau
½ ounce orange juice
½ ounce cranberry juice
½ ounce grapefruit juice
½ ounce fresh sour mix
1 teaspoon superfine sugar
Lime slice for garnish

Combine liquid ingredients and sugar in mixing glass. Add ice and shake. Pour with ice into glass and garnish.

A WORD FROM THE BARTENDERS

When you want to make a splash at a party, just multiply the ingredients in the recipes in this chapter to punch bowl size and float the garnishes on top. If there are exceptions to the rule, it's the punches that include any carbonated beverages, whose bubbles will die a quick death in the punch bowl.

ENGLISH PUNCH

Pimm's and gin entertain a tart Italian.

2 ounces Pimm's No. 1
1 ounce gin
2 ounces limoncello
2 ounces cranberry juice
½ ounce fresh sour mix
Lemon wedge for garnish

Combine liquid ingredients in mixing glass. Add ice and shake. Pour with ice into glass and garnish.

FRENCH PUNCH

Boasting a fine Cognac

2 ounces Rémy Martin V.S.O.P.
1 ounce cranberry juice
1 ounce mandarin orange juice
Club soda
Lemon wedge for garnish

Combine Cognac and juices in mixing glass. Add ice, shake, and pour with ice into glass. Add club soda to taste and garnish.

GAYNELLE'S BURGUNDY PUNCH

Pinot noir is the dominant grape in Burgundy wine, so any Pinot Noir wine will serve the purpose.

2 ounces red Burgundy
½ ounce brandy
½ ounce triple sec
½ ounce pomegranate juice
1 ounce sour mix
Club soda
Lemon peel spiral for garnish

Combine wine, brandy, liqueur, juice, and sour mix in mixing glass. Add ice, shake, and pour with ice into glass. Add club soda to taste and garnish.

GINGER PUNCH

Well-spiked ginger ale

1 ounce vodka
1 ounce sambuca
1 ounce fresh sour mix
1 teaspoon superfine sugar
Ginger ale
Lemon slice for garnish
Lime slice for garnish

Combine vodka, liqueur, sour mix, and sugar in mixing glass. Add ice, shake, and pour with ice into glass. Add ginger ale to taste and garnish.

GREG'S MILK PUNCH

Enriched by the velvety texture and toffee notes of Baileys Irish Cream

2 ounces Baileys Irish Cream
1 ounce white crème de cacao
1 ounce heavy cream
Club soda
Nutmeg for sprinkling

Combine liqueurs and cream in mixing glass. Add ice and shake. Strain into glass, top with club soda to taste, and sprinkle with nutmeg.

HUDSON VALLEY PUNCH

Scotch, crème de cacao, and three fruit juices

1 ounce Scotch
1 ounce dark crème de cacao
1 ounce orange juice
1 ounce grapefruit juice
1 ounce cranberry juice
½ teaspoon superfine sugar
Orange slice for garnish

Combine liquid ingredients and sugar in mixing glass. Add ice and shake. Pour with ice into glass and garnish.

IRENE'S LAST CALL PUNCH

Not just for nightcaps

1 ounce vodka
1 ounce sambuca
½ ounce Cointreau
½ ounce pineapple juice
½ ounce tangerine juice
½ ounce grapefruit juice
½ ounce fresh sour mix
½ teaspoon superfine sugar
Lemon wedge for garnish

Combine liquid ingredients and sugar in mixing glass. Add ice and shake. Pour with ice into glass and garnish.

IRISH PUNCH

For something different on March 17

2 ounces Irish whiskey
½ ounce green crème de menthe
1½ ounces fresh sour mix
1½ ounces pineapple juice
1 teaspoon superfine sugar
Pineapple spear for garnish

Combine liquid ingredients and sugar in mixing glass. Add ice and shake. Pour with ice into glass and garnish.

ITALIAN PUNCH

With Prosecco, the Italian sparkling wine

½ ounce Campari
½ ounce sambuca
6 ounces Prosecco
Orange slice for garnish
Lemon slice for garnish

Combine Campari and liqueur in ice-filled highball glass. Top with Prosecco and garnish.

MERRY MELON PUNCH

KENTUCKY PUNCH

Galloping fruit flavor

2 ounces Maker's Mark bourbon
1 ounce limoncello
½ ounce orange juice
½ ounce cranberry juice
½ ounce grapefruit juice
½ ounce pineapple juice
½ ounce fresh sour mix
1 splash grenadine
1 teaspoon superfine sugar
Orange slice for garnish

Combine liquid ingredients and sugar in mixing glass. Add ice and shake. Pour with ice into glass and garnish.

MERRY MELON PUNCH

With the flavor of honeydew

2 ounces DeKuyper melon liqueur
1 ounce vodka
½ ounce orange juice
½ ounce pineapple juice
1 ounce fresh sour mix
1 teaspoon superfine sugar
Maraschino cherry for garnish

Combine liquid ingredients and sugar in mixing glass. Add ice and shake. Pour with ice into glass and garnish.

Party Punches

Some of these party punches are mixed with sorbet to add a velvety texture—so you might want to add sorbet whenever you prepare single-glass punches in larger quantities. Don't be afraid to experiment, since one of the beauties of punch is its flexibility. Note: The approximate number of cups the recipes yield is given at the end of each.

Fruit-juice ice cubes Ice made from fruit juice won't water down punch, and in fact adds a little more flavor. Make cubes by filling an ice tray with juice, then freezing. When using plain ice in party punch, blocks are preferable to cubes because they slow dilution. For blocks of ice, pour liquid into pint-size milk cartons and freeze, then peel the carton off ice blocks. Make at least four trays and two blocks so you can keep the punch cold as the party progresses.

SPRING PUNCH

With the taste of fresh raspberries

- 4 cups vodka
- 4 cups Stolichnaya Vanil vodka
- 2 cups Cointreau
- 2 pints raspberry sorbet
- 2 cups raspberry puree
- 1 cup grenadine
- 1 cup superfine sugar
- Cranberry juice ice cubes
- 4 cups fresh raspberries for garnish

Combine liquid ingredients and sugar in punch bowl, stirring until sugar dissolves. Add ice and garnish. Makes about 20 cups.

SUMMER PUNCH

With a bit of a Latino beat

- 4 cups rum
- 4 cups silver tequila
- 1 pint orange sorbet
- 2 cups strawberry puree
- 1 cup grenadine
- 1 cup superfine sugar
- Pineapple juice ice cubes
- 4 cups cubed fresh pineapple for garnish
- 4 oranges, sliced, for garnish

Combine liquid ingredients and sugar in punch bowl, stirring until sugar dissolves. Add ice and garnish. Makes about 20 cups.

AUTUMN PUNCH

Red apples and cranberry
4 cups vodka
4 cups apple brandy
2 cups Berentzen apple liqueur
2 cups cranberry juice
2 cups apple puree
1 cup superfine sugar
Cranberry juice ice cubes
4 apples, cored and sliced, for garnish

Combine liquid ingredients and sugar in punch bowl, stirring until sugar dissolves. Add ice and garnish. Makes about 18 cups.

WINTER PUNCH

Cognac and Grand Marnier meet the mango.
4 cups Rémy Martin V.S.O.P. Cognac
4 cups Grand Marnier
1 pint mango sorbet
2 cups mango puree
Orange juice ice cubes
4 cups sliced mangoes for garnish

Combine liquid ingredients in punch bowl. Stir, add ice, and garnish. Makes about 20 cups.

HOLIDAY PUNCH

Eggnog as rich as you'll find
4 cups Baileys Irish Cream
2 cups white crème de cacao
2 cups Harvey's Bristol Cream sherry
4 cups store-bought eggnog
1 cup superfine sugar
1 or 2 blocks ice
½ cup nutmeg for sprinkling

Combine liquid ingredients and sugar in punch bowl, stirring until sugar dissolves. Add ice and garnish. Makes about 15 cups.

PRESIDENT'S DAY PUNCH

With the fruit of the cherry tree
2½ cups light rum
4 ounces cherry brandy
2 pints cherry vanilla sorbet
2 cups cherry puree
1 cup grenadine
2 cups superfine sugar
Cranberry juice ice cubes
4 cups fresh cherries, pitted, for garnish

Combine liquid ingredients and sugar in punch bowl, stirring until sugar dissolves. Add ice and garnish. Makes about 20 cups.

MEXICAN PUNCH

¡Ay, caramba!

2 ounces silver tequila
1 ounce fresh sour mix
1 ounce pineapple juice
1½ ounces mango juice
1½ ounces cranberry juice
½ teaspoon superfine sugar
Pineapple spear for garnish

Combine liquid ingredients and sugar in mixing glass. Add ice and shake. Pour with ice into glass and garnish.

OSCAR'S MADEIRA PUNCH

Created by a Portuguese chef. The fortified wine Madeira is named for its birthplace, an island group off the coast of Portugal.

2½ ounces Madeira
1 ounce Cognac
1 ounce orange juice
1 ounce lemon juice
1 teaspoon superfine sugar
4 ounces chilled Champagne
Lemon slice for garnish

Combine Madeira, Cognac, juices, and sugar in mixing glass. Add ice, shake, and strain into glass. Top with Champagne and garnish.

PAM'S PEAR PUNCH

Perfect for people who prize pears

1 ounce pear-flavored vodka
1 ounce Poire William
½ ounce pineapple juice
½ ounce orange juice
½ ounce fresh sour mix
Club soda
Pear slice for garnish

Combine vodka, brandy, juices, and sour mix in mixing glass. Add ice, shake, and pour with ice into glass. Top with club soda to taste and garnish.

RASPBERRY PUNCH

Raspberries, in the form of framboise and Chambord, share the highball glass with orange and cranberry.

1½ ounces framboise
½ ounce Chambord
½ ounce vodka
1½ ounces orange juice
1½ ounces cranberry juice
½ teaspoon superfine sugar
3 raspberries for garnish

Combine liquid ingredients and sugar in mixing glass. Add ice and shake. Pour with ice into glass and garnish.

RHINE DREAM

Made with medium-sweet riesling

2 ounces Riesling Spätlese
½ ounce kirsch
1 ounce orange juice
1 or 2 dashes Angostura bitters
Club soda

Combine wine, brandy, juice, and bitters in mixing glass. Add ice, shake, and pour with ice into glass. Top with club soda to taste and stir.

SOUR APPLE APPLE PUNCH

Tart but delish

1 ounce vodka
1 ounce sour apple schnapps
1 ounce fresh sour mix
3 ounces apple juice
1 teaspoon superfine sugar
Apple slice for garnish

Combine liquid ingredients and sugar in mixing glass. Add ice and shake. Pour with ice into glass and garnish.

VANILLA PUNCH

Rich, creamy, spicy

2 ounces Absolut Vanilia vodka
1½ ounces Captain Morgan rum
1½ ounces pineapple juice
1½ ounces heavy cream
1 teaspoon superfine sugar
Nutmeg for sprinkling

Combine liquid ingredients and sugar in mixing glass. Add ice and shake. Strain into glass and sprinkle with nutmeg.

YANKEE PUNCH

A cheer for the indomitable Bronx Bombers

1 ounce vodka
1 ounce Malibu rum
½ ounce peach schnapps
½ ounce fresh sour mix
1 ounce tangerine juice
1 ounce cranberry juice
½ teaspoon superfine sugar
Lemon wedge for garnish

Combine liquid ingredients and sugar in mixing glass. Add ice and shake. Pour with ice into glass and garnish.

FROZEN
DRINKS

Frozen margaritas (pages 136–37) and frozen daiquiris (pages 114–15) are hardly the only icy palate pleasers in the bartender's catalog of drinks. The freezes on these pages range far and wide, calling on spirits and mixes and garnishes from across the spectrum. Cases in point: the tequila cream liqueur in Tequila Frost (page 215); the grated ginger in Oona's Ginger and Lemon (page 214); and the licorice stick garnish in Roman Desire (page 215).

Before you get started, read about pre-crushing ice for the blender in—drum roll, please—About Ice, on page 25. It's also a good idea to turn to page 28 and read up on the use of sorbet, advice that applies to ice cream as well.

ALPINE FROST

With pleasantly bitter Jägermeister
1 ounce vodka
1 ounce Jägermeister
1 ounce peach schnapps
1 ounce heavy cream
¾ cup crushed ice

Combine ingredients in blender, blend until smooth, and pour into glass.

BANANA CREAM

A cool way to get your potassium
1 ounce light cream
1 ounce crème de banane
1 ounce heavy cream
Half a medium-size banana
¾ cup crushed ice

Combine ingredients in blender, blend until smooth, and pour into glass.

BANANAS FROSTER

For cooling off in a Caribbean cabana
½ ounce Captain Morgan rum
½ ounce crème de banane
1 medium banana
2 scoops vanilla ice cream
Cinnamon for sprinkling

Combine rum, liqueur, banana, and ice cream in blender. Blend until smooth, pour into glass, and sprinkle with cinnamon.

BLOODY POM

THE BLIZZARD

Wallops of flavor
1 ounce brandy
1 ounce light rum
1 ounce Baileys Irish Cream
1 ounce Tia Maria
1 splash light cream
2 scoops vanilla ice cream
Nutmeg for sprinkling

Combine liquid ingredients and ice cream in blender. Blend until smooth, pour into glass, and sprinkle with nutmeg.

BLOODY POM

A favorite in Australia
2 ounces vodka
2 ounces pomegranate juice
½ cup crushed ice

Combine vodka, juice, and ice in blender. Blend until smooth, pour into glass.

BLUEBERRY CHILL

A no-nonsense blueberry freeze

2 ounces Smirnoff Blueberry vodka
1 cup fresh blueberries
½ cup crushed ice

Combine ingredients in blender, blend until smooth, and pour into glass.

BLUE VELVET

With black raspberry and melon liqueurs

1 ounce Chambord
1 ounce Potter's melon liqueur
½ cup vanilla ice cream
Whipped cream for topping
3 or 4 drops blue curaçao for drizzling

Combine liqueurs and ice cream in blender. Blend until smooth and pour into glass. Top with whipped cream and drizzle with blue curaçao.

CARIBBEAN COOLER

A short trip to Barbados by way of Japan and Germany

1 ounce Malibu rum
1 ounce Midori
1 ounce peach schnapps
1 ounce lime juice
¾ cup crushed ice
Thin slice honeydew melon for garnish

Combine liquid ingredients and ice in blender. Blend until smooth, pour into glass, and garnish.

CHARLOTTE'S MUDSLIDE

The secret is in the vanilla bean ice cream.

2 ounces Baileys Irish Cream
2 ounces Kahlúa
2 ounces vanilla-flavored vodka
2 scoops vanilla bean ice cream

Combine ingredients in blender, blend until smooth, and pour into glass.

DARK CHERRY DREAM

For Cherry Heering lovers

2 ounces vodka
1 ounce Cherry Heering
2 scoops vanilla ice cream
¼ cup crushed ice

Combine ingredients in blender, blend until smooth, and pour into glass.

FROSTED APRICOT STINGER

With apricot brandy and crème de menthe

1 ounce apricot brandy
1 ounce white crème de menthe
1 ounce white crème de cacao
1 ounce orange juice
¾ cup crushed ice

Combine ingredients in blender, blend until smooth, and pour into glass.

FROSTY BLUE UMBRELLA

The answer when a summer storm keeps you indoors?

1 ounce vodka
1 ounce white crème de cacao
½ ounce blue curaçao
1 scoop vanilla ice cream
¼ cup crushed ice

Combine ingredients in blender, blend until smooth, and pour into glass.

Chocolate Freezes

Satisfy that never-ending craving for chocolate with one of these frozen drinks, two of which are flavored with white chocolate. Lovers of white chocolate should also note three other recipes in the chapter: Frosty Blue Umbrella (page 211), Frozen Monk (facing page), and Peppermint Frost (page 214).

CHOCOLATE ALMOND FREEZE

Hits the spot
1 ounce amaretto
1 ounce white crème de cacao
2 scoops chocolate ice cream
Shaved chocolate for garnish

Combine liqueurs and ice cream in blender. Blend until smooth, pour into glass, and garnish.

FROZEN MOCHA

Can you spell luxurious?
1 ounce vodka
1 ounce dark crème de cacao
1 ounce Kahlúa
1 ounce heavy cream
¾ cup crushed ice

Combine ingredients in blender, blend until smooth, and pour into glass.

FROSTY THE SNOWMAN

With chocolate chip eyes and a bright red nose
1 ounce vodka
1 ounce Godiva white chocolate liqueur
1 ounce heavy cream
½ cup ice
Whipped cream for topping
2 chocolate chips for garnish
1 Maraschino cherry for garnish

Combine vodka, liqueur, cream, and ice in blender. Blend until smooth and pour into glass. Top with whipped cream, two chocolate chips as eyes, and a cherry "nose."

POLAR BEAR

A vicarious roll in the snow
2 ounces Absolut Vanilla vodka
1 ounce white crème de cacao
1 ounce Godiva white chocolate liqueur
¾ cup crushed ice

Combine ingredients in blender, blend until smooth, and pour into glass.

FROSTY NOGGIN

A dandy holiday eggnog
1½ ounces light rum
¼ ounce white crème de menthe
3 ounces prepared eggnog
2 scoops vanilla ice cream
Whipped cream for topping
3 or 4 drops cherry syrup

Combine rum, liqueur, eggnog, and ice cream in blender. Blend until smooth and pour into glass. Top with whipped cream and drizzle with cherry syrup.

FROZEN LEMON DROP

An icy palate cleanser
2 ounces Absolut Citron vodka
1 ounce Cointreau
1 ounce lemon juice
1 teaspoon superfine sugar
½ cup crushed ice

Combine ingredients in blender, blend until smooth, and pour into glass.

FROZEN MONK

Chills out in Italy
1 ounce vodka
1 ounce Frangelico
1 ounce white crème de cacao
½ ounce amaretto
1 ounce heavy cream
¾ cup crushed ice

Combine ingredients in blender, blend until smooth, and pour into glass.

GREEN TEA-RASPBERRY DREAM

GREEN TEA-RASPBERRY DREAM

An after-dinner drink and dessert twofer
1 ounce Stolichnaya Razberi vodka
½ cup fresh raspberries
¾ pint green tea ice cream
¼ cup crushed ice
1 to 3 raspberries for garnish

Combine vodka, fruit, ice cream, and ice in blender. Blend until smooth, pour into glass, and garnish.

LATIN CONNECTION

Italian liqueur, St. Croixan rum
2 ounces Tuaca
1 ounce Cruzan light rum
½ ounce Cointreau
½ cup crushed ice
Club soda

Combine liqueurs, rum, and ice in blender. Blend until smooth, pour into glass, and top with club soda to taste.

MATTY'S FREEZE

With a touch of passion fruit
2 ounces light rum
¾ ounce brandy
2 teaspoons passion fruit juice
1 teaspoon lime juice
½ cup crushed ice
Lime slice for garnish

Combine liquid ingredients and ice in blender. Blend until smooth, pour into glass, and garnish.

MAUI BREEZE

A Euro-tropical freeze
½ ounce amaretto
½ ounce Cointreau
½ ounce brandy
2 ounces guava juice
2 ounces mango juice
1 ounce fresh sour mix
¾ cup crushed ice

Combine ingredients in blender, blend until smooth, and pour into glass.

NORMANDY WINTER

Two cold monks and a Scot
1 ounce Frangelico
1 ounce Bénédictine
1 ounce Drambuie
1 ounce heavy cream
½ cup crushed ice

Combine ingredients in blender, blend until smooth, and pour into glass.

NORWEGIAN FREEZE

With a lingonberry liqueur
2 ounces Skyy Vanilla vodka
½ ounce Lillehammer
2 scoops vanilla ice cream
¼ cup crushed ice
Berry of choice for garnish

Combine vodka, liqueur, ice cream, and ice in blender. Blend until smooth, pour into glass, and garnish.

OONA'S GINGER AND LEMON

A playful blend
2 ounces Absolut Limon
1 ounce fresh lemon juice
1 ounce simple syrup (page 27)
1 tablespoon grated ginger
¾ cup crushed ice
Lemon twist for garnish
Mint sprig for garnish

Combine liquid ingredients, ginger, and ice in blender. Blend until smooth, pour into glass, and garnish.

PEPPERMINT FROST

Serving up holiday joy
1 ounce vodka
1 ounce green crème de menthe
1 ounce white crème de cacao
1 ounce heavy cream
¾ cup crushed ice
Candy cane for garnish

Combine liquid ingredients and ice in blender. Blend until smooth, pour into glass, and garnish.

ROMAN DESIRE

Hard to resist

1 ounce Smirnoff Vanilla vodka
1 ounce sambuca
1 ounce white crème de cacao
1 ounce heavy cream
¾ cup crushed ice
Black licorice stick for garnish

Combine liquid ingredients and ice in blender. Blend until smooth, pour into glass, and garnish.

SIBERIAN WINTER

Bundle up tight.

2 ounces vodka
1 ounce Frangelico
1 ounce heavy cream
½ cup crushed ice

Combine ingredients in blender, blend until smooth, and pour into glass.

THE SNOW QUEEN

Deigns to amuse

2 ounces vodka
½ ounce sambuca
½ ounce white crème de cacao
1 ounce heavy cream
¾ cup crushed ice

Combine ingredients in blender, blend until smooth, and pour into glass.

STRAWBERRY BLAST

With fresh fruit

2 ounces Stolichnaya Vanil vodka
1 ounce Chambord
3 strawberries, halved
1 ounce heavy cream
¾ cup crushed ice
Strawberry for garnish

Combine vodka, liqueur, fruit, cream, and ice in blender. Blend until smooth, pour into glass, and garnish.

SWEDISH BLIZZARD

Sweden's famous vodka gets even colder.

2 ounces Absolut vodka
1 ounce Grand Marnier
1 ounce white crème de cacao
1 ounce heavy cream
¾ cup crushed ice

Combine ingredients in blender, blend until smooth, and pour into glass.

TEQUILA FROST

Who knew tequila could taste so rich and creamy?

1 ounce 1926 Tequila Cream liqueur
1 ounce grapefruit juice
1 tablespoon honey
1 scoop vanilla ice cream
1 ounce heavy cream
¼ cup crushed ice

Combine ingredients in blender, blend until smooth, and pour into glass.

TSUNAMI

Carries you away
1 ounce light rum
1 ounce melon liqueur
1 ounce orange juice
1 ounce pineapple juice
½ ounce Goya cream of coconut
¾ cup crushed ice
Lime slice for garnish
Maraschino cherry for garnish

Combine liquid ingredients and ice in blender. Blend until smooth, pour into glass, and garnish.

VAL D'AOSTA

A coffee-flavored freeze named for the region in the snowy Italian Alps
2 ounces sweet vermouth
1 scoop coffee ice cream
1 ounce pasteurized egg white
½ cup crushed ice

Combine ingredients in blender, blend until smooth, and pour into glass.

WINTRY NIGHT

Turn up the thermostat and enjoy.
2 ounces whiskey of choice
1 ounce coffee liqueur
1 scoop coffee ice cream
¼ cup crushed ice

Combine ingredients in blender, blend until smooth, and pour into glass.

HOT DRINKS

Toasty-warm drinks come into their own in cold weather, but they can make appealing after-dinner drinks any time of the year. And they hardly have to be based on coffee only. Tea, apple cider, and any number of spirits fill the bill when they share the glass with the right mixers. Take, for example the Tipsy Earl (page 225), which is Earl Grey tea flavored with cream sherry. Or Café Fernet (page 220), Italy's traditional combo of coffee and Fernet-Branca.

Glassware is an important consideration when serving hot drinks, of course, since you don't want a glass to crack when you pour in just-boiled water. In other words, don't even think of serving any of these drinks in Grandmother's crystal stemware unless you've brought the temperature down to warm. The vessels of choice are an Irish coffee glass or teacup, either of which you might want to steam beforehand (see page 25).

AGAVERO DREAM

Damiana flower gives the liqueur Agavero its lovely vanilla scent.

4 ounces hot coffee, sweetened to taste
2 ounces Agavero
2 ounces light cream

Pour coffee into Irish coffee glass, add liqueur and cream, and stir.

ANNIE'S CHERRY PIE

Dessert by the hearth?

3 ounces cherry brandy
3 ounces heavy cream
2 ounces cherry puree
Cinnamon for sprinkling

Heat liquid ingredients but do not boil. Pour into steamed snifter and sprinkle with cinnamon.

BARBADOS TEA

Rich and spicy

4 ounces hot black tea, sweetened to taste
1 ounce Mount Gay rum
1 ounce heavy cream
Nutmeg for sprinkling

Pour tea into cup and add rum and cream. Stir and sprinkle with nutmeg.

CAFÉ CARIBE

Flavored with rum and orange liqueur.

6 ounces hot coffee
1 ounce light rum
1 ounce triple sec

Pour coffee into mug, add rum and triple sec, and stir.

CAFÉ FERNET

With the Italian digestive Fernet-Branca

4 ounces hot coffee, sweetened to taste
1 ounce Fernet-Branca
Whipped cream for topping

Pour coffee into tulip glass and add Fernet-Branca. Stir and top with whipped cream.

CAFÉ MEXICANO

Time to open the Kahlúa bottle

4 ounces hot coffee, sweetened to taste
2 ounces Kahlúa
Whipped cream for topping
Cinnamon for sprinkling

Pour coffee into Irish coffee glass and add liqueur. Stir, top with whipped cream, and sprinkle with cinnamon.

CAFÉ ROYALE

Rhapsody in a snifter. The coffee can be sweetened or unsweetened.

4 ounces hot coffee
2 ounces brandy
2 ounces heavy cream

Pour coffee into snifter, add brandy and cream, and stir.

CINNAMON ROLL

Not suitable for breakfast!

6 ounces hard apple cider
2 ounces cinnamon schnapps
Cinnamon stick for garnish

Heat cider and pour into mug. Add schnapps, stir, and garnish.

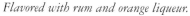

CURRANT EVENT

Black currant takes the spotlight. This fruit is acidic, so substituting whole milk or cream for the skim milk will leave you with a slightly curdled drink.

4 ounces hot black currant tea, unsweetened

2 ounces skim milk (creamy style)

1 ounce crème de cassis, plus extra for drizzling

Whipped cream for topping

Pour tea into Irish coffee glass and add milk and liqueur. Stir, top with whipped cream, and drizzle with more liqueur.

DR. CORPION'S COLD CHASER

Bartender Charles's teapot diaphoretic (sweat inducer) will perk you up when you have a cold. You'll need a 3-cup teapot, a saucer, and a handheld strainer.

1 cup grated ginger

2 lemons, quartered

1 ounce Barcardi 151

3 teaspoons honey, divided

Boiling water

1 teaspoon honey to coat rim of glass

Spoon grated ginger into teapot. Squeeze quartered lemons over pot and drop in rinds. Add rum and 2 teaspoons honey. Fill teapot with just-boiled water, cover, and let steep for 2 to 3 minutes. Spread 1 teaspoon honey on a saucer; coat rim of a glass by pressing it into honey. Strain mixture in teapot into glass and garnish. Makes 1 cup.

HAZELNUT DREAM

Adrift on a Frangelico cloud

6 ounces hot coffee, sweetened to taste

2 ounces Frangelico

Whipped cream for topping

Chopped hazelnuts for garnish

Pour coffee into Irish coffee glass and add liqueur. Stir, top with whipped cream, and sprinkle with chopped nuts.

HOT APPLE PIE

Almost as good as mom's

2 ounces boiling water

2 ounces light rum

2 ounces calvados, plus extra for drizzling

½ teaspoon cinnamon

Whipped cream for topping

Pour boiling water into Irish coffee glass and add rum, calvados, and cinnamon. Stir, top with whipped cream, and drizzle cream with calvados.

HOT BUTTERED BOURBON

Beloved by Southerners of a certain age

2½ ounces Wild Turkey bourbon

3 ounces apple cider

1 cinnamon stick

1 tablespoon unsalted butter

Nutmeg for garnish

Combine bourbon, cider, and cinnamon stick in small saucepan. Heat to a simmer, add butter, and stir until butter is melted. Discard cinnamon stick, pour bourbon mixture into steamed glass, and sprinkle with nutmeg.

Holiday Party Warmers

The fireplace is crackling away and the scent of evergreens and cinnamon wafts through the air. There's no mistaking it: The holidays are here. The recipes for these hot holiday punches yield about 8 cups each.

HARD HOT CHOCOLATE

Use premium chocolate milk (be it cow's milk or soy) for this party pleaser.

6½ cups chocolate milk
1½ cups bourbon
3 cinnamon sticks
Chocolate shavings for garnish

Combine milk, bourbon, and cinnamon sticks in a large saucepan. Heat over medium heat, stirring often, until the milk begins to steam. Pour into a large heat-proof bowl and top each serving with chocolate shavings.

HOT APPLE CIDER

What could be more traditional?

8 cups hard apple cider
¼ cup Vermont maple syrup
2 cinnamon sticks
1½ teaspoons whole cloves
1½ teaspoons whole allspice berries
1 lemon peel cut into strips
1 orange peel cut into strips

Combine cider and syrup in large saucepan. Place all spices in cheesecloth bag, tie tightly, and add to pan. Heat over medium heat until hot. Discard spice bag. Pour cider into serving bowl and garnish.

MULLED WINE

Use a full-bodied red wine.

1 orange, sliced
Whole cloves
½ cup sugar
2 cups citrus-flavored herb tea
1 tablespoon lemon zest
1 bottle red wine
2 cinnamon sticks

Use orange slices and cloves to make citrus wheels (page 31); set wheels aside. Combine sugar, tea, and zest in a large enameled or stainless steel pot. Bring to a boil over medium heat, reduce heat to low, and simmer for 15 minutes. Remove from heat and let cool slightly. Add wine, cinnamon, and citrus wheels. Reheat before serving, but do not boil.

SPICED CRANBERRY CIDER

Cranberry juice and cider

4 cups cranberry juice
4 cups hard apple cider
¼ cup brown sugar, packed
3 cinnamon sticks
1½ teaspoons whole cloves
1 lemon, thinly sliced, plus extra lemon slices for garnish

Combine juice, cider, sugar, spices, and thinly sliced lemon in a large saucepan. Bring to a boil, reduce heat, and simmer for 15 to 20 minutes. Let cool slightly, then strain into large heatproof bowl. Serve warm, topping each serving with a lemon slice.

HOT BUTTERED RUM

The old-fashioned favorite

4 ounces boiling water
1 teaspoon brown sugar
3 ounces dark rum
1 tablespoon unsalted butter
Nutmeg for sprinkling
Citrus wheel for garnish (optional)

Pour boiling water into Irish coffee glass, add sugar, and stir. Add rum and butter and stir until butter is melted. Sprinkle with nutmeg and garnish with citrus wheel, if desired (page 31).

HOT BUTTERED WINE

A variation on a theme

4 ounces boiling water
4 ounces muscatel wine
1 tablespoon unsalted butter
2 teaspoons Vermont maple syrup
Nutmeg for sprinkling

Pour boiling water into Irish coffee glass and add muscatel. Add butter and syrup, stir until butter is melted, and sprinkle with nutmeg.

HOT CHERRY BLOSSOM

Japan meets Denmark.

4 ounces hot green tea, sweetened
**   to taste**
2 ounces Cherry Heering

Pour hot tea into cup, add liqueur, and stir.

HOT TEA TODDY

Not just for Aunt Bertha

4 ounces hot black tea
1 teaspoon honey
2 ounces gold rum
1 pinch cinnamon
Ginger ale, at room temperature

Pour hot tea into steamed Irish coffee glass, add honey, and stir. Add rum and cinnamon and stir again. Top with ginger ale to taste and stir.

INDIAN SUMMER

Apples all the way

5 ounces hard apple cider
2 ounces sour apple schnapps
Cinnamon stick for garnish

Heat cider and pour into mug. Add schnapps, stir, and garnish.

IRISH COFFEE

On St. Patrick's Day, try drizzling green crème de menthe on the topping.

4 ounces hot coffee, sweetened to taste
2 ounces Irish whiskey
Whipped cream for topping
Green crème de menthe (optional)

Pour coffee into Irish coffee glass and add whiskey. Stir, top with whipped cream, and drizzle with crème de menthe, if desired.

JAMAICAN COFFEE

With a layer of cream

4 ounces hot coffee, sweetened to taste
2 ounces Appleton Estate rum
2 ounces heavy cream

Pour hot coffee into Irish coffee glass. Add rum, stir, and float cream on top.

LE GRAND CAFÉ

A creamy indulgence

6 ounces hot coffee, sweetened to taste
1 ounce Grand Marnier
1 ounce Frangelico
2 drops dark crème de cacao
⅛ teaspoon nutmeg
Nutmeg for sprinkling

Pour coffee into steamed snifter, then add remaining liquid ingredients and ⅛ teaspoon nutmeg. Stir and sprinkle with nutmeg.

LEMONY LICK

Ideal for a frigid night

5 ounces hot lemon herb tea, sweetened to taste
1 ounce limoncello
Lemon wedge for garnish

Pour hot tea into cup and add liqueur. Stir and garnish.

LUIGI'S ALMOND TRUFFLE

Borders on dessert

4 ounces hot chocolate
2 ounces amaretto
2 ounces almond herb tea
Whipped cream for topping

Pour hot chocolate into Irish coffee glass. Add liqueur and tea, stir, and top with whipped cream.

MINTY APPLE

Cider with mint and cream

6 ounces hard apple cider
1 ounce peppermint schnapps
Whipped cream for topping

Heat apple cider and pour into Irish coffee glass. Add schnapps, stir, and top with whipped cream.

PEACH COBBLER

Cider goes peachy.

6 ounces hard apple cider
2 ounces peach schnapps
Peach slice for garnish

Heat cider and pour into mug. Stir in schnapps and garnish.

PÊCHE DE PROVENCE

Peach tea spiked with RinQuinQuin, a white peach aperitif from the south of France

4 ounces hot peach herb tea, sweetened to taste
3 ounces heavy cream, warmed
1 ounce Henri Bardouin RinQuinQuin
Allspice or mace for garnish

Pour tea into Irish coffee glass. Stir in cream and aperitif and sprinkle with spice of choice.

PEPPERMINT PLEASER

A double whammy for mint lovers
**5 ounces hot peppermint herb tea,
   sweetened to taste**
2 ounces peppermint schnapps

Pour hot tea into mug and stir in schnapps.

SPIKED HOT CHOCOLATE

As you like it
7 ounces hot chocolate
**1 ounce rum, whiskey, peppermint
   schnapps, or Chambord**
Whipped cream for topping
Cinnamon for sprinkling

Pour hot chocolate into Irish coffee glass and stir in spirit or liqueur of choice. Top with whipped cream and sprinkle with cinnamon.

TENNESSEE TRAVELER

With Tennessee whiskey
6 ounces hot coffee
2 ounces Jack Daniels Tennessee whiskey
Whipped cream for topping

Pour hot coffee into Irish coffee glass. Stir in whiskey and top with whipped cream.

TIPSY EARL

Earl Grey gets his groove on.
1 ounce Harvey's Bristol Cream sherry
**6 ounces hot Earl Grey tea, sweetened to
   taste**

Pour sherry into tulip glass and top with tea.

TOASTED MONK

Likes marshmallows
4 ounces hot coffee, sweetened to taste
2 ounces B & B
2 ounces heavy cream
Toasted marshmallow for garnish

Pour hot coffee into steamed snifter and stir in liqueur. Float cream on top and garnish.

TRADITIONAL HOT TODDY

*Hot toddies were once considered
medicinal. Hmmm . . .*
½ teaspoon superfine sugar
6 ounces boiling water
2 ounces whiskey or gin
Lemon slice for garnish
Nutmeg for sprinkling

Place sugar in bottom of mug, add boiling water, and stir. Add spirit and stir. Add garnish and sprinkle with nutmeg.

VELVET ITALIAN

Bella!
4 ounces hot coffee
1½ ounces amaretto
½ ounce brandy
2 ounces heavy cream

Pour coffee into steamed Irish coffee glass and stir in liqueur, brandy, and cream.

YO-HO-HO

Cider with spiced rum
6 ounces hard apple cider
2 ounces Captain Morgan rum

Heat apple cider, pour into mug, and stir in rum.

NO-
ALCOHOL
DRINKS

The alcohol-free cocktails, smoothies, and bubblers on these pages are tailor made for youngsters, nondrinkers, and designated drivers. All of the fruit-based drinks—which in a few cases come close to passing for the real thing—not only taste good but will also give you a healthful shot in the arm. What's more, there is no shortage of variety. The nectar-based Angelic Peach (page 228) is light as a cloud compared to the soy milk– and peanut butter–based Muscle Shirt Smoothie (page 231).

All of the recipes are the sort you might want to triple or quadruple so that you can keep them in the fridge for the family. But you'll be wise to make short work of any drinks that include carbonated beverages, which sometimes lose their sparkle even before you can toast "To Your Health!"

BLUE HEAVEN

A.J.'S SURPRISE

To indulge your inner child
8 ounces whole milk
2 tablespoons chocolate syrup
1 teaspoon maraschino cherry juice
Whipped cream for topping
Maraschino cherry for garnish

Pour milk, syrup, and maraschino juice into tulip glass. Stir, then add a dollop of whipped cream and top with a cherry.

ANGELIC PEACH

Lifts your spirits
2 ounces peach nectar
4 ounces Sprite or 7UP
Peach slice for garnish

Pour nectar and soft drink into ice-filled rocks glass. Stir and garnish.

BANANA-GINGER SMOOTHIE

Makes you wanna say wow
1 medium banana, sliced
2 scoops ginger ice cream
2 tablespoons vanilla yogurt

Combine ingredients in blender, blend until smooth, and pour into glass.

BLUE HEAVEN

The blueberry hits the heights.
4 ounces blueberry juice
2 ounces skim milk (creamy style)
1½ teaspoons raspberry syrup
Fresh blueberries for garnish

Combine liquid ingredients in mixing glass. Add ice and shake. Strain into glass and garnish.

CAMERON'S COOLER

Iced tea goes uptown.
3 ounces black or green tea, sweetened to taste and chilled
1½ ounces tangerine juice
1½ ounces pineapple juice
Orange peel spiral for garnish

Pour chilled tea and juices into ice-filled highball glass. Stir and garnish. Serve with a straw, if desired.

THE CARRIE NATION

A temperate pick-me-up
12 ounces ginger ale
1 splash grenadine
1 splash lemon juice
Lemon slice for garnish

Pour liquid ingredients into ice-filled highball glass. Stir and garnish.

CHOCOLATE-CINNAMON SHAKE

Chocolate milk dressed to the nines

8 ounces whole milk

1 tablespoon chocolate syrup

⅛ teaspoon cinnamon, plus extra for sprinkling

Whipped cream for topping

Combine milk, syrup, and ⅛ teaspoon cinnamon in mixing glass. Add ice, shake, and pour into glass. Top with whipped cream and sprinkle with cinnamon.

C.J.'S FIZZER

Simple 'n' sweet

6 ounces apple juice

6 ounces Sprite or 7UP

Apple slice for garnish

Pour juice and soft drink into ice-filled highball glass. Stir and garnish.

CRANBERRY DELIGHT

With some tangerine thrown in for good measure

2 ounces cranberry juice

2 ounces tangerine juice

4 ounces club soda

Orange slice for garnish

Pour juices into ice-filled highball glass. Top with club soda and garnish.

ELIZABETH THE GREAT

Created by bartender Greg for his eldest child

3 ounces orange juice

3 ounces cranberry juice

1 dash lemon juice

6 ounces club soda

Combine juices in mixing glass. Add ice, shake, and pour with ice into glass. Top with club soda and stir.

EVAN'S EFFERVESCENCE

Sparkling with color and flavor

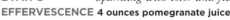
4 ounces pomegranate juice

4 ounces blueberry juice

4 ounces Sprite or 7UP

Pour juices into ice-filled highball glass and top with soft drink. Serve with a straw, if desired.

GINGER-LYCHEE SMOOTHIE

Exotic and tempting

2 scoops ginger ice cream

½ cup diced lychees

¼ cup crushed ice

Ground ginger for sprinkling

Combine ice cream, fruit, and ice in blender. Blend until smooth, pour into glass, and sprinkle with ginger.

I SAY AÇAÍ

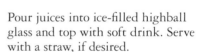

Like this: ah-sigh-EE

2 ounces açaí juice

3 ounces passion fruit nectar

Club soda

Combine juices in ice-filled highball glass, stir, and top with club soda to taste.

Fruit Smoothies

The small wonder known as the blender transforms fruit into a drink fit for the gods—the smoothie. In these four recipes, experiment with different fruit juices and add milk or yogurt, if you like.

COCOBERRY

Coconut and strawberry team up with pineapple.

2½ ounces frozen strawberries
1 ounce cream of coconut
2 ounces pineapple juice
1 ounce fresh sour mix
Strawberry for garnish

Process frozen strawberries in blender, then add juice, cream of coconut, and sour mix. Blend until smooth, pour into glass, and garnish.

PURPLE FLASH

Fresh blueberries with a bit of pomegranate syrup

½ cup plain yogurt
½ cup blueberries
1 teaspoon pomegranate syrup
½ cup crushed ice

Combine ingredients in blender, blend until smooth, and pour into glass.

SANDY'S SMOOTHIE

As effervescent as you please

½ cup frozen strawberries
½ cup frozen peaches
1 cup orange juice
½ cup crushed ice
Club soda
Fresh strawberry for garnish

Process frozen fruit in blender. Add juice and ice, blend until smooth, and pour into glass. Add club soda to taste and garnish.

TROPICAL TWISTER

A swirl with fruit

½ cup pineapple chunks
½ cup chopped strawberries
4 ounces orange juice
½ cup crushed ice
Orange slice for garnish
Strawberry for garnish

Process pineapple in blender, then add strawberries, juice, and ice. Blend until smooth, pour into glass, and garnish.

LATIN BEAT

OJ flavored with açaí, the palm berry from the rain forests of Latin America

3 ounces orange juice
1 ounce açaí juice
Sprite or 7UP

Pour juices into ice-filled highball glass, stir, and top with soft drink to taste.

MANGO FIZZ

A tropical turn-on

4 ounces mango juice
1 teaspoon lime juice
Club soda
Lime wedge for garnish

Pour juices into ice-filled highball glass. Top with club soda to taste and garnish.

MARY ROSE'S COCONUT ICED TEA

Extra refreshing

3 ounces black or green tea, sweetened to taste and cooled
3 ounces coconut water
Mint sprig for garnish

Pour chilled tea and coconut water into ice-filled highball glass, stir, and garnish. Serve with a straw, if desired.

MIKE'S DELIGHT

Ginger ale gets fancy.

1½ ounces orange juice
1 ounce lemon juice
1 splash grenadine
Ginger ale

Combine juices and grenadine in mixing glass. Add ice, shake, and pour with ice into glass. Top with ginger ale to taste.

THE MOVIE STAR

Sip while wearing shades.

3 ounces tangerine juice
3 ounces cranberry juice
1 dash lemon juice
6 ounces ginger ale
Orange peel spiral for garnish

Pour juices into ice-filled highball glass. Top with ginger ale and garnish.

MUSCLE SHIRT SMOOTHIE

For a thicker high-protein drink, freeze the banana first.

1 cup cold soy milk (vanilla or chocolate)
1 medium banana, sliced if frozen
2 tablespoons creamy peanut butter

Combine ingredients in blender, blend until smooth, and pour into glass.

NICK'S FAVORITE

With plenty of fruit

3 ounces pineapple juice
3 ounces orange juice
½ ounce fresh sour mix
½ teaspoon passion fruit syrup
2 ounces club soda
Orange slice for garnish
Maraschino cherry for garnish

Combine juices, sour mix, and syrup in mixing glass. Add ice, shake, and pour with ice into glass. Top with club soda and garnish.

RYAN'S COCOPAYA

RED RAPTURE

With three tasty juices
2 ounces pomegranate juice
2 ounces cranberry juice
2 ounces apple juice
Orange slice for garnish

Combine liquid ingredients in mixing glass. Add ice and stir to chill. Strain into glass and garnish.

ROOT BEER SWEETIE

Not just for kids
3 ounces orange juice
¼ teaspoon superfine sugar
9 ounces root beer
Maraschino cherry for garnish

Combine juice and sugar in highball glass. Stir to dissolve sugar, then add ice. Top with root beer, stir, and garnish.

PAPAYA POP

Papaya and lime make beautiful music together.
6 ounces papaya nectar
1 tablespoon lime juice
6 ounces Sprite or 7UP
Lime twist for garnish

Pour nectar and juice into ice-filled highball glass. Top with soft drink, stir, and garnish.

RYAN'S COCOPAYA

A coconut and papaya blend
3 ounces papaya puree
3 ounces coconut water
Superfine sugar to taste
2 or 3 dashes allspice or nutmeg

Combine ingredients in mixing glass. Add ice, shake, and pour with ice into glass. Serve with a straw, if desired.

PEACH DREAM

Visions of peach and citrus
3½ ounces peach nectar
2 ounces orange juice
1 splash lemon juice
1 splash grenadine
Club soda
Orange slice for garnish

Combine nectar, juices, and grenadine in mixing glass. Add ice, shake, and pour with ice into glass. Add club soda to taste and garnish.

SAMMY'S GALLOPING PUNCH

A young equestrienne's favorite
1 ounce cranberry juice
1 ounce grapefruit juice
1 ounce pineapple juice
Sprite or 7UP

Pour juices into ice-filled highball glass, stir, and top with soft drink to taste.

SPARKLING GRAPE

Lime gives this white grape cooler an edge.

8 ounces white grape juice

1 tablespoon lime juice

4 ounces sparkling water

Pour juices into ice-filled highball glass. Top with water and stir.

SPICY NIGHT

A variation on the best-known nonalcoholic drink: the Virgin Mary

8 ounces tomato juice

2 drops lemon juice

2 drops Tabasco

Tonic water

Lime slice for garnish

Combine juices and Tabasco in ice-filled glass. Top with tonic water to taste, stir, and garnish.

SPRITELY APRICOT

Sprite makes friends with the small orange fruit.

8 ounces apricot nectar

4 ounces Sprite

Lime wedge for garnish

Pour nectar into ice-filled highball glass. Top with soft drink, stir, and garnish.

TRIPLE TREAT

Garnished with three fruits

4 ounces grapefruit juice

1 dash lemon juice

8 ounces ginger ale

Lemon slice for garnish

Orange slice for garnish

Maraschino cherry for garnish

Pour grapefruit juice into ice-filled highball glass, then add lemon juice. Top with ginger ale and garnish.

A WORD FROM THE BARTENDERS

We're no health experts, but that doesn't mean we can't relay the nutritional benefits of some of the fruit juices found in this chapter. After all, when you're enjoying something nonalcoholic, why not get a dose of nature's medicine to boot?

Açaí berry Bursting with antioxidants, plus vitamins A, B, C, and E

Apricot Provides the antioxidant beta carotene, plus potassium and iron

Blueberry Packed with brain-friendly antioxidants

Cranberry Provides lots of vitamin C and hippuric acid (good for the urinary tract)

Orange Great source of vitamin C; also provides beta carotene, folate, thiamine, and potassium

Peach Serves up a good deal of vitamin A and some vitamin C and potassium

Pineapple Rich in vitamin C, plus vitamin B_6, folate, thiamine, iron, and magnesium

Pomegranate Rich in heart-friendly antioxidants, plus vitamin C and potassium

Tomato Good source of the antioxidant lycopene, vitamins A and C, folate, and potassium

TROPICAL SPLASH

Comes into its own at the beach

6 ounces mango juice

6 ounces orange juice

1 dash Angostura bitters

Orange peel spiral for garnish

Combine juices and bitters in mixing glass. Add ice and shake. Pour with ice into glass and garnish.

**VIRGIN
COLADA**

The chaste Piña Colada
4 ounces pineapple juice
1½ ounces cream of coconut
1 teaspoon lime juice
½ cup crushed ice
Pineapple spear for garnish
Maraschino cherry for garnish

Combine juices, cream of coconut, and ice in blender. Blend until smooth, pour into glass, and garnish.

**VIRGIN
MARY**

This vodka-free version of the Bloody Mary is said to have been conceived in a Nantucket bar at the height of the Roaring Twenties.
4 ounces tomato juice
1 splash lemon juice
½ teaspoon Worcestershire sauce
Tabasco to taste
Salt and pepper to taste
Lime wedge for garnish

Pour liquid ingredients into ice-filled rocks glass and add salt and pepper. Stir and garnish.

**WALT'S
SOUR
RUBY**

With Ruby Red grapefruit
2 ounces Ruby Red grapefruit juice
1 teaspoon fresh sour mix
4 ounces club soda

Combine juice and sour mix in mixing glass. Add ice, shake, and strain into glass. Top with club soda and stir.

**WILD
RAIN**

Let it pour.
2 ounces guava juice
2 ounces orange juice
2 ounces cranberry juice
Club soda
Orange slice for garnish

Combine juices in mixing glass. Add ice, shake, and pour with ice into glass. Top with club soda and garnish.

BAR
BITES

The *Four Seasons Book of Cocktails* wouldn't be complete without some nibbles to serve at dinner parties and larger affairs, so the Four Seasons kitchen has come up with a few recipes suited to spring, summer, fall, and winter. All of the recipes that follow serve six or twelve, so augment or downsize them as you wish.

SPRING

ENDIVE WITH GORGONZOLA

Endive spears are tailor-made for holding something delicious—in this case, two cheeses. If you like, substitute other crumbly strong cheeses, like Stilton and Maytag, for the gorgonzola. You can also garnish the endive spears with your choice of sprouts—mustard, bean, or whatever strikes your fancy.

> **4 ounces cream cheese**
> **¼ pound gorgonzola cheese**
> **2 or 3 heads Belgian endive**
> **¼ cup port wine**
> **Sprouts of choice for garnish**

1. Bring the cream cheese and half the Gorgonzola to room temperature. Cut remaining half of latter into small, thin pieces.

2. Cut a small portion off the bottom of each endive head, then separate twelve leaves and place them on a platter.

3. Combine the port, softened cream cheese, and gorgonzola in a food processor or blender or mix by hand in a large bowl.

4. Spoon the mixture into a pastry bag with a flat or zigzag tip. Pipe an equal amount of cheese onto each endive spear.

5. Top each filled spear with a little of the reserved gorgonzola, then garnish with sprouts. Makes 12.

SKEWERED HAMACHI, MINTED PEA SHOTS

How's this for a treat? A morsel of flavorful sushi with a chilled shot of minty green pea soup as a chaser. The sushi is hamachi, the Japanese name for young yellowtail—a species of the tunalike fish known as amberjack, named (and valued) for its golden flesh. If your fish market doesn't stock hamachi, use fresh sushi-grade tuna as a substitute.

4 tablespoons extra virgin olive oil, divided
1 small shallot, finely diced
1 cup vegetable stock
1 cup fresh English peas
12 mint leaves, divided
3- to 3½-ounce hamachi fillet, cut into six cubes
Salt and freshly ground black pepper
Juice of half a lemon

1. Put six shot glasses in the freezer to chill.

2. Heat 2 tablespoons olive oil in a medium saucepan over low heat. Add the shallot and sauté until soft and translucent.

3. Add the stock and simmer for about 5 minutes, stirring occasionally. Add the peas and simmer for 1 minute longer. Set the mixture aside to cool for about 10 minutes.

4. Transfer the pea mixture to a food processor or blender, add 4 mint leaves, and blend to a fine cream. Immediately pour the mixture into a bowl set in a larger bowl of ice water, then place in the freezer for about 30 minutes.

5. Meanwhile, chop the remaining mint leaves. Season the hamachi cubes with salt and pepper to taste. Beat the lemon juice into the remaining oil and toss the hamachi and mint in the mixture.

6. Thread each hamachi cube onto a small skewer and chill in the refrigerator for about 5 minutes. To serve, fill the frosted shot glasses with the pea soup and place a hamachi skewer atop each. Makes 6.

WHITE ASPARAGUS CROSTINI

Crostini (Italian for "little toasts") are typically topped with something delicious—in this recipe, ricotta and white asparagus. Sweet-tasting white asparagus is simply green asparagus grown with soil mounded around the stalks, shielding them from the sun. The result? Asparagus with little or no green-producing chlorophyll.

1 baguette or similar long, thin bread loaf
12 spears white asparagus
2 tablespoons extra virgin olive oil
Salt and freshly ground pepper
6 tablespoons sheep's milk ricotta

1. Preheat the oven to 350°F. Slice the baguette on the diagonal into ½-inch slices. Snap off the woody parts of the asparagus spears.

2. Toast the bread in the oven for about 10 minutes, taking care not to let it grow too dark. In the meantime, fill a skillet or saucepan with 2 inches water and bring it to a boil.

3. Add the asparagus to the boiling water, reduce heat, and simmer for 2 or 3 minutes until tender. Remove the spears from the pan and place them on paper towels to drain.

4. Cut off the asparagus tips (reserve the stems for another use). Drizzle the tips with olive oil, and season with salt and pepper to taste.

5. Arrange the toasts on a platter. Top each toast with a tablespoon of ricotta and two asparagus tips, and serve. Makes 6.

SUMMER

CHERRY TOMATOES WITH PEEKYTOE CRABMEAT

The meat of the peekytoe crab (a.k.a. Maine rock crab or sand crab) is prized for its fresh, sweet taste. The leg has a sharp point that turns inward—hence the name "pick-ed toe" ("pick-ed" being Down East slang for "pointed"), which morphed into "peekytoe." In this recipe, peeled cherry tomatoes hold the succulent crabmeat.

6 cherry tomatoes (each about 1½ inches in diameter)
1 cup peekytoe crabmeat
3 tablespoons mayonnaise
2 tablespoons grated fresh ginger
2 tablespoons chopped chives
2 tablespoons extra virgin olive oil
Salt and freshly ground black pepper

1. Put several ice cubes in a large bowl of cold water and set aside. Bring a medium saucepan of water to a boil.

2. Cut a shallow "x" in the non-stem end of each cherry tomato. Drop the tomatoes into the boiling water for about 15 seconds. Scoop them out and plunge them into the ice water. When they are cool to the touch, peel them by gently squeezing them and slipping them out of their skin.

3. With a very sharp knife, slice the top off each tomato. Use a small melon baller to scoop out the seeds and pulp, then place the tomatoes upside down on paper towels to drain.

4. In a medium bowl, mix the crabmeat with the mayonnaise, ginger, chives, and oil. Season to taste with salt and pepper.

5. Fill each tomato with the crab mixture and serve immediately. Makes 6.

CRISP SQUASH BLOSSOMS

No edible flower is more in demand than zucchini blossoms, which appear at farmer's markets and gourmet food stores (and untold numbers of home vegetable gardens) in summer. Choose brightly colored, unwilted blossoms and store them for no longer than a day. The batter that will coat the flowers calls for 00 Italian flour, the very fine type used for pizza dough—but all-purpose flour will do in a pinch.

> 12 zucchini blossoms
> 1¼ cups 00 Italian flour or all-purpose flour
> 1½ teaspoons baking powder
> 3 large eggs
> 1¼ cups sparkling water
> Kosher salt and freshly ground black pepper
> 3 quarts (12 cups) sunflower or peanut oil
> 1 lemon, cut into 6 wedges

1. Remove the stems from the zucchini blossoms by cutting just below the bulb. Discard the stems and slice the flowers in half lengthwise, starting at the bulb end. Gently open the blossoms to expose more surface area.

2. Sift the flour and baking powder into a small bowl and set aside.

3. Crack the eggs into a large bowl and whisk until well blended. Whisk the flour mixture into the eggs in a slow, steady stream until the flour is fully incorporated. Whisk in the sparkling water until the batter has a smooth, creamy texture. Season with salt and pepper to taste.

4. Pour the oil into a deep fryer and heat it to 350°F. Line a plate with paper towels.

5. Dip the squash blossoms into the batter and dab them along the rim of the bowl to remove any excess. Carefully drop the blossoms into the hot oil, cooking only a few at a time. When the blossoms are crisp and golden (3 to 4 minutes), remove them from the oil with a slotted spoon and place them on paper towels to drain.

6. Immediately season the crisp blossoms with salt and pepper to taste and serve with lemon wedges on the side. Makes 12.

WATERMELON BALSAMICO

Watermelon flavored with balsamic vinegar and a superior sea salt: What's not to like? The original balsamic vinegar is also the best—aceto balsamico tradizionale, from the Italian province of Modena. Less costly is the condimento grade of Modena balsamic vinegar. The other seasoning in the recipe is soft, white, flaky Maldon salt, harvested by hand in the marshlands of Essex, England.

12 1-inch squares seedless watermelon
3 tablespoons extra virgin olive oil
2 teaspoons Maldon salt
3 tablespoons balsamic vinegar

1. Using a small melon baller, carve a half-circle from one side of each melon cube.

2. Place the cubes on a plate and drizzle with the olive oil. Sprinkle with the sea salt.

3. Using tongs, transfer the watermelon to a serving platter, cavity up. Divide the balsamic vinegar between the cavities and serve. Makes 12.

AUTUMN

Clarifying Butter

Clarified butter = butter minus its water and milk solids. Its primary virtue is a higher smoke point, which reduces the cook's risk of burning sautéed foods. Clarified butter will also keep much longer than regular butter.

To clarify butter, melt it slowly in a small skillet over low heat. As the components separate, skim the foam off the top with a spoon and discard it. Once the white milk solids have settled on the bottom of the pan, gently pour the clear butter into a small bowl, taking care to leave the solids behind. One stick (8 tablespoons) of butter yields about 6 tablespoons of clarified butter.

POTATO-WRAPPED LANGOUSTINE WITH CAVIAR

Attention serious cooks: If you don't already own a mandoline (or mandolin) slicer, this recipe alone is reason to buy one. This chef's tool, available in kitchen stores and online, will slice, julienne, or ripple-cut any firm food with precision and finesse. In this recipe, ultra-thin potato slices are wrapped around langoustine tails. The langoustine, also known as Norway lobster, is a small, prawnlike crustacean with sweet flesh.

> **6 langoustine tails (18 to 20 ounces total), shelled**
> **Salt and freshly ground black pepper**
> **1 large Yukon Gold potato, peeled**
> **3 tablespoons clarified butter (see box)**
> **3 tablespoons Osetra caviar**
> **1 teaspoon chopped chives**

1. Wash the langoustine tails, pat them dry, and season them with salt and pepper to taste.

2. Using a mandoline, make one paper-thin potato slice for each langoustine and trim the slices to about 2 inches long and 1½ inches wide. Place a langoustine tail in the center of each slice lengthwise, then quickly fold the slice over and press the ends together. (The potato's natural starch will create a tight seal.)

3. Transfer the wrapped tails to the refrigerator and chill for about 10 minutes.

4. Place a sauté pan over low heat and add the clarified butter. Increase the heat slightly and add the wrapped tails. Cook for about a minute, turning the tails frequently until the meat is lightly golden.

5. Transfer the tails to paper towels and pat them dry. Arrange the tails on a platter, top each one with caviar and chives, and serve immediately. Makes 6.

NEW POTATO SKINS WITH CRÈME FRAICHE AND PESTO

Crème fraiche is thinner than sour cream but firm enough to spoon into the hollowed-out skins of new potatoes. Two buying tips: Choose the roundest new potatoes you can find. And, if using prepared pesto, buy the best!

6 new potatoes
1 tablespoon extra virgin olive oil
Salt and freshly ground black pepper
½ cup crème fraiche
4 tablespoons pesto

1. Preheat oven to 275°F. Meanwhile, rinse the potatoes well and place on a lightly greased baking tray. Bake for 35 minutes, then remove from the oven and let potatoes cool.

2. Preheat oven to 375°F. Cut potatoes in half and remove the flesh with a melon ball scoop (save it to use in another recipe). Brush the inside and outside of each skin with oil and sprinkle with salt and pepper to taste.

3. Place skins on a baking sheet, cut side down, and bake for 5 to 10 minutes or until golden brown. Let cool.

4. Once the skins have cooled, fill each with a dollop of crème fraiche, then top with a teaspoon of pesto. Transfer to a platter and serve. Makes 12.

CHOCOLATE GRAPES

Be they red or green, grapes love a coating of chocolate. These bonbons fall into the "can't eat just one" category, so you'll be wise to allow several grapes for each party guest. As any chocoholic knows, the percentage listed on the label of a given chocolate indicates its proportion of cocoa solids—a higher percentage means a darker, more intense chocolate.

7 ounces chocolate (65% cocoa)
¼ cup cocoa powder
12 seedless grapes

1. Melt the chocolate in a double boiler or in a microwave oven. Spread the cocoa powder on a plate.

2. One at a time, gently ease the grapes onto the tines of a fork and dip them into the melted chocolate. As the chocolate begins to set (which happens almost immediately), remove each grape from the fork, roll it in the cocoa, and place it on a baking sheet lined with wax paper.

3. Place the pan of grapes in the refrigerator to further set the chocolate.

4. Before serving, remove the grapes from the refrigerator and let them sit at room temperature for at least 10 minutes. Transfer them to a serving bowl or small platter to serve. Makes 12.

WINTER

OYSTERS YUZU

Three helpful FYIs: 1) Kumamoto oysters, a Japanese import cultivated on the West Coast, are hailed for their buttery and slightly fruity taste; 2) Yuzu juice, now easier to find thanks to the Internet, comes from a Japanese citrus fruit whose pulp tastes like a blend of lime, lemon, and grapefruit; 3) Osetra caviar is from sturgeon in the Caspian Sea and has a pleasantly nutty quality.

6 Kumamoto oysters
1 tablespoon chopped tarragon
1 teaspoon yuzu juice
2 tablespoons extra virgin olive oil
2 tablespoons Osetra caviar

1. Shuck the oysters and reserve 6 half-shells.

2. Combine tarragon, yuzu juice, and oil in a large bowl. Add the oysters and toss to combine.

3. Slip each oyster back into a shell with a spoon. Top each with a teaspoon of caviar and serve immediately. Makes 6.

SMOKED SALMON ROULADE

These salmon rolls, wrapped much like small pieces of candy and then halved, are topped with caviar. The recipe calls for strongly flavored Sevruga caviar, but any type you choose will do. To keep the chive "ribbons" from breaking, blanch by plunging them into boiling water for 6 seconds; then flush with cold water and pat dry.

6 slices smoked salmon
½ tablespoon sour cream
½ tablespoon wasabi mustard
12 chives, blanched
4 tablespoons Sevruga caviar

1. One at a time, lay the salmon slices between sheets of parchment or wax paper and pound them thin.

2. In a small mixing bowl, combine the sour cream and wasabi mustard and stir until mixed.

3. Spoon equal amounts of the mixture onto the center of each salmon slice. Roll up the slices and tie off each end with a chive.

4. Cut the rolls in half and top each with a teaspoon of caviar. Makes 12.

TOASTED BRIOCHE WITH QUINCE AND FOIS GRAS

Luxury comes in small bites when these canapés are set out for guests. The "secret ingredient" is the Spanish delicacy known as membrillo—quince paste, in English. You won't find it at the corner store, but it's readily available at gourmet markets or online. Fois gras tops the membrillo, and if you want to go all out when you season it, use Maldon sea salt. (See Watermelon Balsamico, page 241.)

2 or 3 brioche rolls
3½ tablespoons membrillo (quince paste)
2 teaspoons sherry vinegar
Sea salt and freshly ground black pepper
6 slices foie gras (each about ¼ inch thick and 2 inches in diameter)

1. Preheat oven to 400°F. Slice enough brioche to make six slices, each about ½ inch thick and 2 inches in diameter. Toast the slices until golden brown (8 to 10 minutes) and keep them warm.

2. Combine the membrillo, vinegar, and a pinch each of salt and pepper in a food processor or blender and blend until smooth. Spread the mixture on the toasts.

3. In a small nonstick sauté pan over medium-high heat, add the foie gras. Cook for one minute on each side. Remove it from the pan and pat it dry with a clean kitchen towel.

4. To serve, place a slice of foie gras on each prepared toast, sprinkle with salt to taste, and serve immediately. Makes 6.

INDEX

AJ.'s Surprise, 228
Abilene Lariat, 130
Abra Cadabra, 84
absinthe, 165
Absinthe Martini, 165
ABV. *see* alcohol by volume (ABV)
The Academic, 68
Act Two, 56
Adonis, 188
After the Rain, 130
Agavero Dream, 220
The Alamo, 130
The Alchemist, 84
alcohol by volume (ABV)
    absinthe, 165
    proof gauges and, 19
alcohol-free drinks, 227–234.
    *see also individually named
    drinks*
Algonquin, 56
Almond Deluxe, 179
Almond Joy, 108
Aloha, 130
Alpine Frost, 210
Amalfi Coast, 160
Amaretto Sour, 160
Amaro and Tonic, 176
The Ambassador, 176
Ambrosia, 84
Americano, 176
Anchors Aweigh, 46
Andalusia, 179
Andromeda, 68
Angel of Corsica, 176
Angela's Choice, 108
Angelic Peach, 228
Angel's Breast, 68
Angel's Delight, 160
The Anglophile, 188
Anna Karenina, 84
Annie's Cherry Pie, 220
The Ansonia, 68
aperitifs, 175
    cocktails prepared with, 176–

184. *see also individually named
    drinks*
Apollo, 68
Apple Basket, 160
Apple Brandy Rickey, 146
Apple Fizz, 108
apple juice, 25
Apple Martini, 84
Apple Pie, 108
Apple Triptych, 149
Applesauce, 108
Apricot Fizz, 146
Apricot-Guava Daiquiri, 114
Apricot Kiss, 146
Apricot Margarita, 130
Apricot Sour, 146
Arcadian Cooler, 188
Archbishop, 68
Argyll, 36
The Aristocrat, 160
Armagnac, 145
Armagnac with Mint, 146
The Arthur, 68
Artichoke High, 130
Ascot, 68
Ashley's Special, 200
Astor Place, 69
Astoria Special, 69
Athena, 69
Atlanta Cooler, 188
Aubrietta, 188
The Auld Resting Chair, 36
Autumn Leaf, 36
Autumn Punch, 205
Avenue B, 69
Averna and Soda, 176
Azteca, 130

•

B & B Stinger, 160
Babylon Sour, 46
Banana Cream, 210
Banana Cream Pie, 108
Banana Daiquiri, 114
Banana-Ginger Smoothie, 228

Banana Spilt, 84
Bananarama, 84
Bananas Froster, 210
Banshee, 161
bar bites (recipes)
    for Autumn, 242–244
    for Spring, 236–238
    for Summer, 239–241
    for Winter, 245–247
bar equipment
    additional, 14–15
    essential, 11–14
Barbados Tea, 220
Barcelona Baby, 146
barspoon, 12
Basic Scotch and Soda, 40
Bastard Child, 108
Bee Line, 69
Beekman Place, 46
Bella Liguria, 176
Belle of the Ball, 188
Benson Express, 36
Berry Cooler, 188
Bette's Choice, 69
Big Hit, 109
Big Red, 188
Bilbo B., 69
Birth of Venus, 85
bitters, 26
Black Cherry Martini, 95
Black Rock, 56
Black Russian, 85
Blackberry Blast, 147
Blackjack, 147
Blackstone, 56
Bleecker Street, 69
blended Scotch, 35
blender, 14
blending technique, 23
Blissful Banana, 147
Blissful Brother, 109
The Blizzard, 210
Blood Orange Punch, 200
Blood Pom, 210

Bloody Brit, 70
Bloody Bullshot, 85
Bloody Maria, 131
Bloody Mary, 85
Blue Banana, 85
Blue Blast, 200
Blue Crush, 161
Blue Hawaii, 109
Blue Heaven, 228
Blue Inca, 86
Blue Margarita, 131
Blue Mood, 165
The Blue Period, 86
Blue Sky, 70
Blue Velvet, 211
Blue Wave, 161
Blueberry Chill, 211
Blueberry Tart, 85
Bluebird, 86
Blushing Scot, 36
Bobby Burns Martini, 36
Bocce Ball, 161
Boilermaker, 56
Bon Ami, 176
Bordeaux Express, 189
Border Crossing, 131
bottle opener, 14
Bourbon and Soda, 46
Bourbon and Sprite, 46
bourbon-based cocktails, 45–53.
    *see also individually named
    drinks*
Bourbon Breeze, 46
Bourbon Cream Float, 46
Bourbon Fruit Fizz, 46
Bourbon Godfather, 47
Bourbon John Collins, 47
Bourbon Kiss 1, 47
Bourbon Kiss 2, 47
Bourbon Lime Rickey, 47
Bourbon Manhattan, 47
Bourbon Milk Punch, 47
Bourbon Mist, 47
Bourbon Old-Fashioned, 48

Bourbon Pie, 48
Bourbon Punch, 200
Bourbon Sour, 48
brandewijn, 145
Brandied Port, 189
brandy
    age definitions, 147
    cocktails prepared with, 145–
        154. *see also individually named*
        drinks
Brandy à l'Ananas, 147
Brandy Alexander, 147
Brandy and Soda, 147
Brandy Candy Cane, 147
Brandy Punch, 200
Brave Bull, 131
Braveheart, 70
Breakfast at Tiffany's, 161
Bright Star, 86
Bronfman family, 157
Bronx Tale, 70
Bronze Bullet, 148
Brooklyn Bridge, 109
Brooklyn Heights, 189
Brooklyn Nite, 70
Bullshot, 86
Burnt Cherry, 148
butter, clarifying, 242
Butterfly Wing, 86

C.J.'s Fizzer, 229
Cactus, 131
Cádiz, 161
Caesar, 48
Café Caribe, 220
Café Fernet, 220
Café Mexicano, 220
Café Mystique, 148
Café Royale, 220
California Sky, 131
calvados, 145
    cocktails made with, 149
Calvados au Citron, 149
Calvados Cooler, 149
Cameron's Cooler, 228
Campari Buon Giorno, 177
Campari Madras, 177
can opener, 14
Candy Apple, 109
Candy Cane, 87

Cape Cod, 87
Capri, 87
Captain Morgan Punch, 201
Caressing Breeze, 110
Caribbean Cocktail, 110
Caribbean Cooler, 211
Caribbean Twilight, 110
Carlito's Way, 110
Carousel, 70
The Carrie Nation, 228
Carthusian Monk, 110
Catapult, 70
Catch-22, 56
Catherine the Great, 87
Catskill Cocktail, 56
Cava, 187
The Celibate, 161
Cello's Dream, 87
Centrifuge, 148
Century, 70
Champagne, 187
    cocktails prepared with, 188–
        195. *see also individually named*
        drinks
Champagne and Schnapps, 189
Champagne Bleu, 189
Champagne Bohême, 189
Champagne Cocktail, 189
Champagne Limon, 190
Chandelier, 71
The Chapultepec, 131
Charles's Ward Eight, 57
Charlie's Bristol Cream Cocktail,
    177
Charlotte's Mudslide, 211
Charmed, 148
Chateau Kiss, 162
Chateau Martini, 75
Chateau Monk, 162
Chelsea, 88
Cheri's Cointreau Noir, 162
cherries, as garnish, 29
Cherry Almond Mint Cream, 169
Cherry Bonbon, 162
Cherry Pie, 88
CHERRY TOMATOES WITH
    PEEKYTOE CRABMEAT, 239
chilling glasses, 24
Chinatown, 88
chocolate, as garnish, 29

Chocolate Almond Freeze, 212
Chocolate-Cinnamon Shake, 229
Chocolate-Covered Cherry, 148
Chocolate-Covered Orange, 110
chocolate freezes, 212
CHOCOLATE GRAPES, 244
Chocolate Mint Cocktail, 111
Chocolate Orange Delight, 169
Chocolate Punch, 201
chocolate shavings and sticks, 29
Chocolate Tequila Martini, 132
Chocolate Twister, 111
Chocorita, 136
Ciao Bella, 177
Cinnamon Apple Margarita, 136
Cinnamon Roll, 220
Cîroc Rock, 88
citrus fruits
    juice amounts from, 31
    making citrus wheel garnish
        from, 31
citrus juicers, 13
citrus juices, 26
    fresh *vs.* bottled/canned, 99
citrus stripper, 14
City Stormer, 57
clarifying butter, 242
Classic Mint Julep, 51
Classic Stinger, 148
The Cloisters, 71
The Club Bouncer, 148
club soda. *see* soda
coasters, 14
Cock O' The Beaver, 36
cocktail onions, as garnish, 30–31
cocktail shakers, 11–12
Cocoberry, 230
coconut, cream of, 26
Coconut Cream, 132
coconut water, 26
Coffee Margarita, 136
Cognac, 145
Cognac Japonais, 150
Cointreau Closer, 162
The Coliseum, 111
The Comforter, 162
Commedia dell'Arte, 71
Commodore, 57
Connolly, 57
Cool Kiss, 162

Cooper Union, 88
Coral Gables Scotch and Soda, 40
corkscrew, 14
Coronation, 179
Cosmopolitan, 88
Cosmopolitan Punch, 201
Costa Mesa, 132
Court Jester, 163
Cranberry Delight, 229
Cranberry Punch, 201
The Crater, 71
cream
    light and heavy, 26
    whipped, as garnish, 31
cream of coconut, 26
cream sherry, 179
Creamsicle, 88
Creamy Dream, 88
Creamy Nut, 150
Crema Frîa, 132
Crescent Moon, 132
CRISP SQUASH BLOSSOMS, 240
Crowning Glory, 177
Crusader, 71
crushed ice, 14, 25
Crystal Palace, 132
Cuba Libre, 111
Currant Event, 221
Curtain Call, 178
Custer's Last Stand, 48
cutting board, 14

D. L. Cocktail, 48
Daiquiri/daiquiris, 111. *see also*
    specifically named daiquiris
    frozen, 114–115
Damsel, 71
Danish Ruby, 190
Dan's Desert Inn, 111
Dark Cherry Dream, 211
De Chirico's Delight, 163
De Guayaba Margarita, 135
The Deal Closer, 163
Dear Vere, 72
Dee Dee's Manhattan, 57
Delancey, 72
Delilah, 89
Delmonico, 72
Diamond in the Rough, 132
digestives, 175

cocktails prepared with, 176–
    184. *see also individually named
    drinks*
Dirty Gin Martini, 75
Dirty Mary, 89
Ditzy Blonde, 89
Dixie Julep, 51
Doña Diego, 111
Donkey Express, 111
Dow Wow, 163
Dr. Corpion's Cold Chaser, 221
Dreamy, 72
Driving, 132
Dry Manhattan, 61
dry sherry, 179
Dry Sherry Martini, 89
Dubonnet Fizz, 178
Dubonnet Manhattan, 49
    •
East End Avenue, 72
East River Cocktails, 57
Eastern Express, 112
eau-de-vie, 177
Edgar's British Peppermint, 72
Edie's Choice, 49
Eiffel Tower, 178
The 1812, 112
82nd Airborne Punch, 201
Eine Kleine Nachtmusik, 178
Elixir of Love, 150
Elizabeth the Great, 229
ENDIVE WITH GORGONZOLA, 236
English Punch, 202
Equalizer, 49
Equestrian, 73
The Eroica, 163
European Swinger, 190
Evan's Effervescence, 229
The Explorer, 133
Extreme Sour Apple, 112
    •
Fairy Tale, 73
Fancy Scotch, 36
Fascinating Rhythm, 163
Faust, 73
The Fidel, 112
Fifth Avenue, 150
52nd Street Cocktail, 58
The 59th Street Bridge, 58
Fighting Irish, 150

flavorings
    for cocktails, 19
    in spirits, 32–33
    vodka, 89
Flight of the Bumblebee, 89
Flirtini, 89
floating technique, 24
Florentine, 73
flowers, as garnish, 29
food (bar bites) recipes, 236–247
Foreign Legion, 112
Four Seasons Bellini, 190
Four Seasons Blue Monday, 58
Four Seasons Blushing Angel, 180
Four Seasons Dubonnet Cosmo,
    180
Four Seasons Hurricane, 112
Four Seasons Margarita, 133
Four Seasons Mint Julep, 51
Four Seasons Paradise Cocktail,
    113
Four Seasons Restaurant
    about, 9–10
    architectural design, 43
    artwork in, 157
    bartender cocktail creations, 64
    "magic curtains" at, 105
    naming of, 81
    wine dinners at, 196
Four Seasons Rob Roy, 37
Four Seasons Shamrock, 58
Four Seasons Sidecar, 150
Four Seasons Summer Blossom, 37
Four Seasons Whiskey Sour, 58
Four-Seasons–style twist, 31
Foxy Squirrel, 113
Frangelico Rum Fizz, 113
Fredo's Fave, 150
French Comfort, 180
French Connection, 49
French Island, 113
French Martini, 90
French Orgasm, 190
French Punch, 202
Fringe Benefits, 73
Frosted Apricot Stinger, 211
Frosted Rose, 133
frosting, glasses and rims, 25
    for margaritas with salt, 133
Frosty Blue Umbrella, 211

Frosty Noggin, 213
Frosty the Snowman, 212
Frosty Witch, 133
froth, tip on making, 37
Frothy Lime, 113
frozen daiquiris, 114–115
frozen drinks, 209–216. *see also
    individually named drinks*
    blending tip, 23
    chocolate, 212
    daiquiris, 114–115
    margaritas, 136–137
Frozen Lemon Drop, 213
frozen margaritas, 136–137
Frozen Mocha, 212
Frozen Monk, 213
fruit
    as garnish, 30, 56
    muddled, for martinis, 95
Fruit Basket, 164
fruit brandies, 145
fruit juices. *see also* citrus juices
    ice cubes made from, 204–205
    nutritional benefits of, 233
fruit nectars/purees, 27
Fruit Salad, 90
fruit smoothies, 230
    blending tip, 23
    with ginger ice-cream, 228, 229
    high-protein, 231
fruit syrups, 26
Fruity Mist, 116
Fuzzy navel, 164
    •
garnishes, 29–31
Gaynelle's Burgundy Punch, 202
The General Lee, 49
The Genie, 90
Gentle Juan, 133
Gentle Pink, 73
Georgia on My Mind, 179
Georgia Spritzer, 116
Gewürtz Spritzer, 194
Gin and Bitters (Pink Gin), 182
Gin and Tonic, 73
gin-based cocktails, 67–80. *see also
    individually named drinks*
Gin Daisy, 73
Gin Fizzer, 74
Gin Gibson, 74

Gin Gimlet, 74
Gin Madras, 74
Gin Martini, 75
gin martinis, 75
Gin Presbyterian, 74
Gin Sour, 74
Ginger-Lychee Smoothie, 229
Ginger Margarita, 136
Ginger Punch, 202
Gingerly, 74
Ginicot, 150
The Giselle, 116
glasses/glassware
    chilling, 24
    frosting, 25
    for hot drinks, 219
    pousse-café, 169
    serving options and, 91
    steaming, 25
    types of, 16–17
Godchild, 90
Godfather, 37
Godmother, 90
Gold Leaf, 133
The Gold Rush, 164
Golden Drop, 74
Golden Gondola, 90
Golden Isle, 116
Grand Champagne, 191
Grand Tour, 76
The Grape-Sta, 116
Grappa Tequila, 134
Grappa with Lime, 180
Grasshopper, 164
Green Devil, 76
"green fairy" (absinthe), 165
Green Geisha, 164
Green Iguana, 134
Green Irish Tweed, 164
The Green Lantern, 151
Green River, 76
Green Tea-Raspberry Dream, 213
The Greenie, 76
Greg's Chocolate Martini, 90
Greg's Milk Punch, 202
Greyhound, 91
The Guadalupe, 134
Guinevere's Smile, 37
Gulf of Mexico, 134
    •

half and half, using as cream
  substitute, 26
Happy Hour, 180
Hard Hot Chocolate, 222
Harlem Nights, 76
Harmony, 151
Harvest Cordial, 164
Harvey Wallbanger, 91
Haunted Bride, 76
Hawaiian Sour, 116
Hazelnut Cooler, 116
Hazelnut Dream, 221
Headless Horseman, 91
Headless Jockey, 49
Heat Wave Cordial, 164
Helga in Love, 166
Herby Peach, 58
High Note, 91
Hilary Wallbanger, 191
Hoerdemann Howl, 151
Hole in One, 37
Holiday Punch, 205
holiday punches, hot, 222
  serving tips, 224
home bar
  equipment for, 11–15
  glassware for, 16–17
  stocking the, 19
Homer's Choice, 77
Honeydew, 134
Honeypie, 116
The Horse's Mouth, 166
Hot Apple Cider, 222
Hot Apple Pie, 221
hot buttered drinks
  with bourbon, 221
  with rum, 223
  with wine, 223
Hot Cherry Blossom, 223
hot drinks, 219–225. see also hot
  buttered drinks; individually
  named drinks
  glasses for, 219
  handling and reheating, 224
  holiday punches, 222
Hot Sour, 134
Hot Tea Toddy, 223
hot toddies, 223, 225
Hudson Valley Punch, 202
Hudson View Cocktail, 58

•

I Say Açaí, 229
Ice Age, 91
ice bucket, 13
ice crusher, 14
ice cubes
  freezing and using, tips on, 25
  from fruit juice, for punches,
    204–205
Ice Pick, 134
ice scoop, 12–13
ice tongs, 13
Iced Hazelnut Cream, 117
Icicle, 134
Icy Dog, 91
The Impresario, 92
Indian Summer, 223
ingredients
  in common spirits and brands,
    32–33
  flavorings, 19, 32–33
  mixers, 19, 25–29
  quality of, 127
Inverness Shores, 38
Irene's Last Call Punch, 203
Irish, 59
Irish Beauty, 151
Irish Coffee, 223
Irish Cooler, 58
Irish Echo, 135
Irish Monk, 166
Irish Punch, 203
Irish Rusty Nail, 38
Isla De Vieques, 117
Island Delight, 92
Italian Cooler, 117
Italian Lemonade, 92
Italian Punch, 203
Italian Root Beer, 166

•

The Jackie Lee, 191
Jacques Rose, 149
Jade Dream, 166
Jamaican Coffee, 223
Jamaican Thrill, 117
jiggers, 13
John Collins, 38
Jolly Green Gigante, 117
Jubilee, 92
Jubilee Cooler, 117

Judith's Choice, 181
juicers, 13
juleps, mint, 51

•

Karamazov, 92
Karen's Choice, 166
Kate's Fave, 77
Kathy's Kick, 77
Kentucky Finisher, 181
Kentucky Hombre, 135
Kentucky Kiss, 49
Kentucky Punch, 203
Kind Hearts and Coronets, 181
Kingston Cooler, 191
Kir, 191
Kir Royale, 191
Kissing Cousins, 151
Kiwi Surprise Daiquiri, 114
knife, 14

•

La Bamba, 135
La Bohême, 166
La Dolce Vita, 181
La Gioconda, 92
La Granada, 135
La Menta, 181
Lahaina Palm, 191
L'Anisette, 59
Laser Beam Fizz, 50
Latin Beat, 231
Latin Connection, 213
Latin Twist, 77
The Latino, 93
layering technique, 24
Le Barbancourt, 117
Le Grand Café, 224
Lemon Fizz, 117
Lemon Frost, 151
lemon-lime soft drinks, 27
Lemony Lick, 224
Liberty Fizz, 118
Licorice Delight, 166
Lightning Flash, 152
Lillet aux Amandes, 181
Lime in the Sun, 118
The Limey, 93
Limonberry, 191
Lincoln Center, 93
liqueurs
  cocktails prepared with, 159–

172. see also individually named
  drinks
herb-based. see aperitifs;
  digestives
production methods, 159
serving tips, 170
Louisville Slugger, 50
Luigi's Almond Truffle, 224
Lulu's Fizz, 50
Lychee Martini, 95
Lynchburg Lemonade, 59

•

The Macabre, 165
Mack 'n' Mack, 179
Madeira Spritzer, 194
Mai Tai, 118
Mandolin, 167
Mango Daiquiri, 114
Mango Fizz, 231
Mango Margarita, 136
Mango Martini, 95
Manhattan Cowboy, 50
maraschino cherries, 29
margaritas. see also individually named
  margaritas
  frozen, 136–137
  salt-rimmed glass for, tips on
    preparing, 133
Marsala Spritzer, 194
The Martha Lou, 167
martinis. see also individually named
  martinis
  gin, 75
  with muddled fruit, 95
The Mary Lou, 114
Mary Rose's Coconut Iced Tea,
  231
The Matador, 192
The Matilda, 118
Matty's Freeze, 214
Maui Breeze, 214
The McCarver, 38
measuring spoons, 13
Mediterranean Kiss, 181
Mellow Orange, 167
Melon Ball, 93
Melon Ball Cordial, 167
Melon Berry Punch, 203
Melon Kiss, 167
Melon Margarita Martini, 135

Merry Berry, 93
Metropolitan, 93
Mexican Bandit, 137
Mexican Doctor, 137
Mexican Egg Cream, 137
Mexican Highball, 138
Mexican Holiday, 138
Mexican Punch, 206
Mexican Stinger, 138
Mexicana, 137
mezcal, tequila vs., 143
Mezcal Martini, 138
Miami Beach Cocktail, 38
Miami Cocktail, 118
The Midtown, 50
Mike's Delight, 231
milk, 26
Mimosa, 192
Mind Eraser, 138
mint juleps, 51
Mint Leaf, 152
Minticello, 59
Minty Apple, 224
Miró, Jean, 157
Miss Linda's Pleasure, 192
Mission Impossible, 50
mixers, 19, 25–29
mixing glass, 12
mixing techniques, 21–25
Mock Mint Julep, 51
Moho Martini, 75
Mojito, 118
The Monk, 77
Monterey Sunset, 138
Moonlight Jig, 59
Moonlight Soother, 182
Moscow Mule, 93
Mother of Pearl, 192
Moulin Rouge, 165
Mount Etna, 94
Mounted Cop, 60
The Movie Star, 231
muddler, 13
muddling technique, 23
    fruit-based martinis and, 95
Mudslide, 94
Mulled Wine, 222
Muscle Shirt Smoothie, 231
Music Note, 152
Music Tree, 138

•

napkins, 14
Napoleon, 77
NASDAQ Jitters, 167
Nature Girl, 77
Nature's Essence, 152
Negroni, 77
Negrumi, 119
Neon Light, 94
NEW POTATO SKINS WITH CRÈME
    FRAICHE AND PESTO, 243
New York Skyline, 139
Newton's Apple, 167
Nick's Favorite, 231
no-alcohol drinks, 227–234. see also
    individually named drinks
No-Frills Vodka Martini, 94
Noisette Rose, 167
Normandy Winter, 214
Norwegian Freeze, 214
Nouméa Cooler, 192
Nut Twofer, 119
Nuts 'n' Berries, 94
Nuts to You Margarita, 136
Nutty Islander, 119

•

Octopus, 182
Old-Fashioned, 61
Old San Juan, 119
olives, as garnish, 30
onions, as garnish, 30–31
Oona's Ginger and Lemon, 214
Opening Night Cocktail, 60
Ophelia, 94
Orange Blossom, 78
Orange Bubbler, 119
Orange Cream, 168
Orange Delight, 96
OYSTERS YUZU, 245

•

Pago Pago, 119
Pam's Pear Punch, 206
Paolo and Francesca, 165
Papaya Pop, 232
Paris Opera, 78
The Parisian, 182
Park Avenue Sour, 60
Parking Meter, 60
party punches, 204–205
    tips on preparing, 201

Passion Fizz, 192
Passion Fruit Margarita, 137
Passionate Peach, 96
Paul's Fire Island Punch, 96
Peach Cobbler, 224
Peach Dream, 232
Peach Fixer, 119
Peach Margarita, 139
Peachy Keen, 168
Pêche de Provence, 224
Pêche Plaisante, 182
Peppermint Frost, 214
Peppermint Patty, 168
Peppermint Patty Sour, 120
Peppermint Pleaser, 225
Peppermint Swirl, 168
Percolator, 96
Peter T.'s Martini, 75
The Petitioner, 120
Phantom of Delight, 182
The Piazza, 168
The Picadilly, 78
Picasso, Pablo, 157
Piña Colada, 120
Pineapple Express, 120
Pineapple Fizz, 120
pineapple juice, 25
Pineapple Martini, 95
Pink Angel, 182
Pink Gin, 182
Pink Lady, 78
Pink Panther, 78
Pink Pussycat, 78
Pink Rose, 78
Pink Squirrel, 79
pitcher, 14
Plantation Cordial, 168
Plymouth Rock, 52
Polar Bear, 212
The Politician, 96
Pollock, Jackson, 157
Polly's Choice, 120
Pomegranate Martini, 96
Pomme Rouge, 149
The Poolside, 79
Port Pleasant, 193
Portia's Choice, 52
Portuguese Daisy, 193
Postscript, 182
POTATO-WRAPPED LANGOUSTINE

WITH CAVIAR, 242
The Potion, 97
pouring technique, 23
Pousse-Café Classique, 169
Pousse-Café Standish, 169
pousse-cafés, 169
President's Day Punch, 205
Pretend Root Beer, 170
Prohibition Express, 52
proof gauges, 19
Prosecco, 187
punches, 200–207. see also
    individually named punches
    fruit juice ice cubes for,
        204–205
    hot, 222
    origins of, 196
    preparing in quantity, 201,
        204–205
Purple Bliss, 170
Purple Flash, 230
Purple Heather Highball, 38
Purple Passion, 97

•

Queen Mum, 79

•

Raindrop, 139
Rasmopolitan, 97
Raspberry Margarita, 139
The Rasputin, 97
Ravel's Bolero, 120
Ravishing Hazel, 120
The Real Man, 97
reamers, 13
Red Apple, 139
Red Raptures, 232
Red Wine Refresher, 193
Red Wine Spritzer, 194
red wines, 190
The Relaxer, 170
Rendezvous, 97
Rhine Dream, 207
Rick's Whitewater, 193
Riverside Drive, 170
Rob Roy, 39
Roman Desire, 215
Root Beer Highball, 79
Root Beer Sweetie, 232
Rosita, 139
Rosy Glow, 97

Rowan's Red Rose, 121
Royal Rush, 98
Royal Sour, 121
Raspberry Punch, 206
Ruby Royale, 79
rum
    cocktails prepared with, 107–
        127. *see also individually named
        drinks*
    soft drinks with, 125
    types of, differences between,
        112
Rum and Cel-Ray, 125
Rum and Cream Soda, 125
Rum and Dr. Pepper, 125
Rum and Ginger, 125
Rum and Lime, 125
Rum and RC, 125
Rum and Root Beer, 125
Rum Jubilee, 121
Rum Lemon Drop, 121
Rum Lover's Fruit Cup, 121
Rum Mudslide, 122
Rum Nutshaker, 122
Rum Old-Fashioned, 122
Rum Presbyterian, 122
Rum Rico, 122
Rum Sangria, 122
Rum Screwdriver, 123
Rum Shaker, 123
Rum Stinger, 123
Rum Twister, 123
Rumaro, 183
Rummy Meditation, 121
Rummy Mint Fizz, 122
Rums Aweigh, 122
The Rumsfeld, 152
Russian Alexander, 98
Russicano, 98
Rusty Nail, 39
Rusty Screw, 60
Rusty Spike, 52
Rusty Stake, 139
Ryan's Cocopaya, 232
Rye Fizz, 60
rye whiskey cocktails, 61

salt-rimmed margarita, tips on
    preparing, 133
Salty Dog, 98

Sammy's Galloping Punch, 232
San Juan Daiquiri, 115
Sandy's Smoothie, 230
Sanibel Cooler, 193
Sazerac, 61
Scitalina, 39
Scotch Ale, 39
Scotch Alexander, 39
Scotch-based cocktails, 35–42. *see
    also individually named
    drinks*
    with soda, 40
Scotch Blossom, 39
Scotch by the Pool, 39
Scotch Cablegram, 41
Scotch Cider, 41
Scotch Cooler, 40
Scotch Gimlet, 41
Scotch Highball, 40
Scotch Milk Punch, 41
Scotch Mist, 41
Scotch Old-Fashioned, 41
Scotch on the Grill, 41
Scotch on the Rocks, 41
Scotch Radke, 42
Scotch Rickey, 40
Scotch Sour, 42
Scotch Stinger, 42
Scotch Street, 42
Scottish Maiden, 42
Screwdriver, 98
Sea Breeze, 98
Seaside, 60
Selection Eight, 99
seltzer water, 28–29
Señor Zeus, 115
Señora Caesar, 123
Señora Mariposa, 123
Señora McGillicuddy, 123
Señora Valdez, 193
Seraphim, 79
7 and 7, 62
Sex in the Mountains, 52
Sex in the Pool, 99
Sex in the Valley, 52
Sex on the Beach, 99
Sexy Maiden, 79
Shadow of Your Smile, 152
shaken cocktails, 12
    technique, 22

tips on, 49
Shannon's Cordial, 170
Sharma Daiquiri, 115
shavings, chocolate, 29
sherry, dry and cream, 179
Shipwreck, 124
Siberian Winter, 215
Sidecar, 152
Signore O'Brien, 170
Silver Lining Martini, 99
Silver Streak, 153
simple syrup (recipe), 27
Singapore Sling, 80
single malt Scotch, 35
The Sit-Down, 153
SKEWERED HAMACHI, MINTED PEA
    SHOTS, 237
Skip's Cooler, 170
Sloe and Easy, 171
Sloe Tequila, 140
Slow Comfortable Screw, 99
small-batch bourbons, 45
Smithtown, 62
SMOKED SALMON ROULADE, 246
smoothies. *see fruit smoothies*
The Snow Queen, 215
Snow Storm, 99
soda, 28
    Scotch and, 40
    wine spritzers with, 194
soft drinks, 27
    with rum, 125
Soft Splendor, 183
Soho Martini, 75
Sonny's Limbo, 153
sorbet, 28
Sour Apple Apple Punch, 207
Sour Apple Cocktail, 124
Sour Cherry, 153
Sour Emperor, 124
Sour Grapes, 153
sour mix, fresh (recipe), 28
Sour Raspberry, 115
Sour Thorn, 124
South of the Border, 140
The Southern Belle, 124
Southern Breeze, 52
Southern Cream Pie, 53
Southern Nail, 153
Southern Pleasure, 171

Southern Settler, 53
Southern Skies, 100
Southside Cocktail, 80
Spanish Impressionist, 140
Sparkling Grape, 233
sparkling water, 28–29
sparkling white wines, 187
    cocktails with, 188–195
The Spartan, 171
Spiced Cranberry Cider, 222
Spiced Hot Chocolate, 225
spices, 28
Spicy Mary, 100
Spicy Night, 233
spirits
    checking proof of, 19
    main ingredients/flavorings of,
        32–33
    in well-stocked home bar, 19
Spring Break, 140
Spring Punch, 204
Spritely Apricot, 233
spritzers, 194
Squirrel's Nest, 124
St. Barts, 123
St. Tropez, 183
Starburst, 124
Starry Skies, 171
Statue of Liberty, 53
steaming glasses, 25, 224
Stiff Pear, 140
still water, bottled *vs.* tap, 29
stirred cocktails, 12
    stirring in glass, 23
    technique, 22
    tips on, 49
stopper, Champagne bottle, 14
Straight Sambuca, 171
strainer, 12
straining technique, 23
Strawberry Blast, 215
Strawberry Champagne, 193
Strawberry Daiquiri, 115
Strawberry Margarita, 140
Strawberry Whip, 140
straws, 14
Suburban, 100
Subway Car, 62
Succulent Melon, 124
sugars, 28

Summer Cooler, 100
Summer Punch, 204
Summer Scotch Cocktail, 42
Summer Snap, 100
Sunset Cocktail, 183
Supremo, 153
Swedish Blizzard, 215
Sweet Apple, 153
Sweet Bourbon Manhattan, 53
Sweet Ivory, 153
Sweet Lass, 171
Sweet Manhattan, 61
Sweet Sidecar, 154
Sweetheart, 195
Swiss Alps, 100
swizzle sticks, 14
syrups, 27
•
Tannhauser, 101
Taxi Cab, 62
Te Amo, 183
Tear Drop, 195
Ten High, 140
Tennessee Lightin' Fizz, 62
Tennessee Traveler, 225
Tequila and Pimm's, 140
Tequila and Tonic, 141
Tequila Angel, 141
Tequila Apricot Cooler, 141
Tequila Azul, 141
tequila-based cocktails, 129–143. see
    also individually named
    drinks
Tequila Canyon, 141
Tequila Collins, 142
Tequila Coulds, 141
Tequila-Cranberry Cordial, 172
Tequila Frost, 215
Tequila Gimlet, 142
Tequila Greyhound, 142
Tequila Manhattan, 142
Tequila Mockingbird, 142
Tequila Old-Fashioned, 142
Tequila Pres, 142
Tequila Screwdriver, 142
Tequila Sour, 143
Tequila Sunrise, 143
Tequila Sunset, 143
Tequila Verde, 143
Terminator Cocktail, 154

Testa Rossa, 183
Theo's Cádiz, 154
Three-Pear Highball, 101
Thundercloud, 101
Tijuana Express, 126
Tim Tam, 53
Tipperary Scotch Cocktail, 42
Tipsy Earl, 225
TNT, 53
Toasted Almond, 172
TOASTED BRIOCHE WITH QUINCE
    AND FOIE GRAS, 247
Toasted Monk, 225
Tom Collins, 80
tomato juice, 25
toothpicks, cocktail, 14
Top Banana, 101
Topaz, 101
Tower of Babel, 126
Traditional Hot Toddy, 225
The Tree Hugger, 172
Treetop, 154
Triple Treat, 233
Triton, 80
Trixie's Tropical Dream, 101
Tropical Breeze 1, 126
Tropical Breeze 2, 126
Tropical Splash, 233
Tropical Twister, 230
True Love, 172
Truffle, 102
Tsunami, 216
Tuscan Sipper, 179
twists, as garnish, 31
Two-For-One, 126
•
Val d'Aosta, 216
Vanilla Dream, 154
Vanilla Punch, 207
Vanilla Skies, 195
Vanillarita, 137
vegetable peeler, 14
vegetables, as garnish, 30
Velvet Almond, 172
Velvet Hammer, 183
Velvet Italian, 225
Vera Cruz, 143
Vermouth and Cassis, 184
Vermouth Cocktail, 184
Very Berry Berry, 126

Vick's Pick, 62
Vika's Vodka Cocktail, 102
Virgin Colada, 234
Virgin Mary, 234
Virgin Skies, 126
Viva Europa, 102
vodka
    cocktails prepared with,
        83–104. see also
        individually named drinks
    new flavorings for, 89
    for Vodka Gibson, tips on, 102
Vodka and Tonic, 102
Vodka Collins, 102
Vodka Gibson, 102
Vodka Gimlet, 102
Vodka Gingerly, 103
Vodka Grasshopper, 103
Vodka Madras, 103
Vodka Negroni, 103
Vodka Orange Blossom, 103
Vodka Sour, 103
Vodka Stinger, 104
Vodkameister, 103
Voltaire's Smile, 172
V.S., defined, 147
V.S.O.P., defined, 147
•
Walt's Sour Ruby, 234
Ward Eight, 61
The Warsaw, 104
"water-of-life," 177
WATERMELON BALSAMICO, 241
Watermelon Daiquiri, 115
waters, 28–29
whipped cream, as garnish, 31
whiskey-based cocktails, 55–63. see
    also individually named
    drinks
rye whiskey, 61
Whiskey Driver, 62
Whiskey Fizzer, 63
Whiskey Godfather, 63
Whiskey Mint Cooler, 63
Whiskey Orchard, 63
Whiskey Pres, 63
Whiskey Stinger, 63
WHITE ASPARAGUS CROSTINI, 238
White Chocolate Kiss, 172
White Fruit Margarita, 137

White Island, 127
White Russian, 104
White Wine Cooler, 195
White Wine Spritzer, 194
white wines, 190
Wicked Monk, 104
Wild Rain, 234
William Tell, 154
Will's Peppermint Stick, 63
The Windsurfer, 127
wine
    cocktails prepared with,
        188–195.
        see also individually
        named drinks
    red, tips on selecting, 190
    sparkling white, 187
white, tips on selecting, 190
wine dinners, at The Four Seasons
    Restaurant, 196
Winter Punch, 205
Wintry Night, 216
Wonky Donkey, 143
Woo Woo, 104
•
The Xenia, 104
X.O., defined, 147
Xylophone, 104
•
The Y'all Come, 53
Yankee Punch, 207
Yo-Ho-Ho, 225
Yours Truly, 184
•
Zinfandel Spritzer, 194
Zoe's Cabernet Cobbler, 195
Zombie, 127

ABOUT THE AUTHOR

FRED DuBOSE is a writer, editor, and book developer who lived and worked in Brussels, Sydney, Atlanta, and the Pacific island nation of Tonga before moving to Manhattan in the mid-1980s. He served as executive editor of the Publishing Projects division of Reader's Digest Australia and as editorial director of the Illustrated Reference Books division of Reader's Digest US. He has also conceived and written an eclectic collection of books of his own, including *The Total Tomato; Four Great Southern Cooks; The Ultimate Bartender's Guide* (on which *The Four Seasons Book of Cocktails* is based); *The Ultimate Wine Lover's Guide* (with Evan Spingarn); *CollegeQuest: The Right Place Guide to Colleges & Universities;* and *Oh, Say Did You Know?* (with Martha Hailey).

A native Texan, DuBose is a graduate of the University of Texas–Austin and received an MA in Journalism from the University of Missouri–Columbia.

ACKNOWLEDGMENTS

The author, restaurant, and publisher gratefully acknowledge the help offered by the following people and businesses.

Marc Balter	Diane Mitchell	67 Wine & Spirits
Richard Berenson	Barbara Morgan	Acker Merrall & Condit
Ray Foley	Derek Pickett	Astor Wines & Spirits
Gina Graham	Emily Seese	Balter Sales Company
Justin Hertzbach	Gammon Sharpley	Beacon Wines & Spirits
Denise Kolditz	Evan Spingarn	Harlem Vintage
Regina McMenamin	Angela Traver	Nancy's Wine for Foods
Nancy Maniscalco	Len Vigliarolo	Schumer's Wine & Liquors

ABOUT THE FOUR SEASONS

The Four Seasons Restaurant is considered the ultimate in fine dining, architecture, and style. Both the Philip Johnson-designed interiors and the famous Seagram Building in which the restaurant stands were designated as landmarks by the New York City's Landmarks Preservation Commission in 1989. For more than half a century, the establishment *Town & Country* called "the favorite restaurant in the world" has stood for excellence in every respect.

"Picasso Alley"—named for the Pablo Picasso–painted stage curtain hung on one of the travertine walls—links two magnificent dining rooms. The Grill Room boasts soaring French walnut walls and, above the bar, a shimmering brass sculpture crafted by Richard Lippold. The Pool Room is centered with a bubbling marble fountain flanked by trees that change with the seasons. In both rooms, "power lunchers" and diners from far and wide savor award-winning seasonal specialties, all prepared with the freshest of local ingredients.

The managing partners of The Four Seasons Restaurant are Alex von Bidder (left, in a portrait by John Varriano) and Julian Niccolini (not pictured).